Recreating Motherhood

OTHER BOOKS BY BARBARA KATZ ROTHMAN

In Labor: Women and Power in the Birthplace
(*Also published* as Giving Birth)

The Tentative Pregnancy:
How Amniocentesis is Changing
the Experience of Motherhood

Centuries of Solace:
Expressions of Maternal Grief in Popular Literature
(with Wendy Simonds)

The Encyclopedia of Childbearing:
Critical Perspectives
(Editor)

Genetic Maps and Human Imaginations:
The Limits of Science in Understanding Who We Are

Recreating Motherhood

BARBARA KATZ ROTHMAN

RUTGERS UNIVERSITY PRESS
New Brunswick, New Jersey, and London

First published in 1989 by W. W. Norton & Company,
New York, New York
Reprinted in 2000 by Rutgers University Press,
New Brunswick, New Jersey

Library of Congress Cataloging-in-Publication Data

Rothman, Barbara Katz.
Recreating Motherhood / Barbara Katz Rothman.
p. cm.
Originally published: New York : Norton, 1989.
Includes bibliographical references and index.
ISBN 0-8135-2874-7 (pbk. : alk. paper)
1. Motherhood. 2. Patriarchy. 3. Feminism. 4. Technology—Social aspects. I. Title.
HQ759.R68 2000
306.874′3—dc21 00-032349

British Cataloging-in-Publication Data for this book is available from the British Library

Manufactured in the United States of America

To the memory of
Daniel H. Katz
and
Irwin "Red" Berken

Contents

Preface and Acknowledgments to the 2000 Edition

Books age oddly. Some things remain as fresh as the day they were written; some are outdated before the bound galleys are ready.

After more than a decade, most of this book was still current; some things needed updating. The major change has been in the "framing" of the problem. I was inspired to write this book originally because of what was known as the "Baby M" case. Probably a third of my students at the City University of New York weren't even in the country yet when that case was in the news; and my own college-age daughter said to me, "Baby who?"

Specific cases come and go. Babies M, Jessica, Faye, Doe, and Louise are babies no longer, but motherhood remains a troubling topic in America and I remain fascinated by it. Soccer moms and welfare moms, lesbian mothers and infertile would-be mothers, adoptive mothers, birth mothers, and mothers of septuplets all make their way into the news. This book remains my attempt to make sense of it all.

While paragraphs and pages have been inserted throughout and dozens of new references added, there are four main pieces of new writing. A new section has been added to the introduction called "Mothering in America." This section was written with my own Sociology of the Family students in mind, explaining why we need to talk about "mothering" when we study "family." The section on "surrogacy" has been expanded, with information about the current status of that industry. There is a very full new chapter, "Reflections on a Decade," which explores the way that new reproductive technologies combine with new marketing and new genetics to pose very troubling social questions. A related discussion of the new reproductive technologies is added to the final chapter on social policy.

I remain grateful to all of the people I thanked for the first edition of this book and add here my youngest daughter, Victoria, to the members of my family—Hesch, Daniel, Leah, and my mother—all of whom continually make sure I understand just how complicated, and rewarding, mothering is.

My study group has also added some new members, and I thank Carolle Charles and Susan Farrell for their ongoing help in my work. Ariel Ducey served as research assistant on a recent project for the Ford Foundation, and I drew on the work she did for that in updating this book. Ann Pappert and Janet Gallagher were also especially helpful and giving of time. Heather Dalmage has had considerable influence on my thinking in matters of family and the social order. Wendy Simonds remains a dearest friend and colleague, who helped in those roles in this edition as well as the last. My daughter Leah Colb Rothman grew into the role of research assistant vacated by Wendy, which completes yet another circle.

Acknowledgments to the First Edition

Like babies, books come into the world in a web of social relationships. And like mothers, authors need to be nurtured themselves if they are to be able to nurture and create. My thanks to all those who have nurtured me through this project, and through my life, most especially my parents, Marcia Katz Berken and Irwin Berken; my children Daniel and Leah Colb Rothman; and my husband, Herschel Rothman. His commitment to fathering has made my experience of mothering what it has been, and for that and all else, I am eternally grateful.

My editor, Mary Cunnane, has been a good midwife for this project—and she knows that is the highest praise I can offer. She has guided, led, pushed, pulled, encouraged, and—what midwives do best—taught.

This book owes a particular debt to Wendy Simonds, who seemingly effortlessly slips from the role of research assistant extraordinaire (able to come up with anything from old copies of *Vogue* to current obstetrical literature) to the role of colleague, to (with maybe more effort) biking companion as we struggle uphill in Prospect Park, huffing, puffing, and discussing. My appreciation to both the Department of Sociology of the Graduate Center of the City University of New York and the PSC-CUNY awards which provided funding for her assistance, and to Baruch College, which has provided a more than congenial and supportive work environment.

A number of people have read all or selected chapters of this book, and offered helpful comments, including Susan Farrell, Janet Glass, Helen Jacobson, William Pearce, Caroline Whitbeck, Mary White, and my agent, Carol Mann. My thanks to all of them. In addition, I have had enormously helpful conversations with people over the past several years, and particularly want to thank Lori Andrews, Susan Maizel Chambre, Wendy Chavkin, Janet Gallagher, Kit Gates, Lois Gould, Ruth Hubbard, Rayna Rapp, Irving Kenneth Zola (who asked precisely the right question and nodded at precisely the right moment), the group organized by Nadine Taub, and the students in my course "Motherhood" at the CUNY Graduate Center.

Everything I write is shaped by the influence of my teacher, mentor, and friend Judith Lorber, and by my study group, however scattered we may be: they ask the hard questions, over and over again, until I have to answer them. My love and gratitude to Maren Lockwood Carden, Betty Leyerle, Eileen Moran, and Rosalyn Weinman.

Part I

Introduction[1]

On Family

When I first sat down to write this book, I had recently had the interesting experience of trying to put together a very short family photo album for a celebration of the Bar Mitzvah of my son, Dan. A colleague had just done one for his daughter, and it seemed to be a lovely idea to copy.

My colleague began his with a family tree. I started but it got complicated, messy: we had divorces, deaths, remarriages, too many convoluted branches somehow. And besides, those flat generational lines in no way represented family to me: I have first cousins I haven't seen in twenty-five years, but great-aunts, second cousins twice removed, and close friends that feel very much like part of my family. So I scratched the tree idea, and went straight to the photos.

Here, too, I looked at what my colleague had done, going back to great-great-grandparents. He had wedding photos, formal portraits. I went to my albums, and found myself passing over these formal pictures, but I was captivated by a picture of my great-grandfather holding infant me on his lap, one of my grandmother sitting with an arm around my shoulders as I, aged nine, squinted without my glasses into the Kodak Brownie. I put together a page like that of "my side" of the family, and another page of my husband's side, and then began on the pictures of my son. I wasn't thinking about it, just leafing through photo albums, boxes, pictures stuck in as bookmarks, photos framed on my wall or curling on my bookshelf, and taking out what struck me. And here's what I got: Dan's uncle holding him on his lap in the kitchen; his father holding him while *his* father looked on; the very elderly, now deceased rabbi Dan loved, carrying him into the temple social hall after his naming; aunts holding him, great-aunts and great-uncles holding him; playing with a balloon with his aunt on his grandparents' living room floor; his uncle and grandfather transferring four-day-old Dan without "dropping his head," their cats' cradle of arms suspending him as both men laughed into the camera. They were nurturing pictures, one after another. It wasn't by lineage that I saw Dan's first thirteen years, but by nurturance: people holding, greeting, caring, tending, teaching.

For me, the idea of nurturance as mattering more than genetics, loving more than lineage, care more than kinship, is not just an intellectual fancy. It's really there, in my heart. The writing of this book, the attempt to carve out a new definition of motherhood, of relationships, of parents and of children, was not just an intellectual exercise. This was how, halfway through my life and halfway through what I thought were the active years of mothering, I chose to live my life.

My family has grown in the years since the first edition of this book was published. We adopted a third child, an African American baby girl, and so became an interracial family. Because of the very values and understandings on which this book is based, we have made it an open adoption, keeping in touch with my daughter's birth family. So my family includes all kinds of relationships for which a standard family tree has no place. Consider my daughter's sister. How do I name the relationship between this child, the daughter of my child's birth mother, and me, my husband, and our other children? My sister has also adopted children, and they too have a birth sister who does not live with them. How is she related to *my* adopted daughter, let alone to her sister? "Cousins," my sister says, "they're all cousins." And that of course works. It's how families have resolved these tangled relationships from time immemorial. Anthropologists call them "fictive kin," those people to whom you feel related but with whom you have no "blood ties": the close family friends who are "aunts" and "uncles," the in-laws who linger on after the marriage that brought them into the family has dissolved, these various step- and adoptive- and birth-family relationships that defy neat lines on a family tree.

It's not just my family. More and more of us are choosing to live our lives this way, putting together families by choice and not by obligation. Adoption is not always done in secret now, as it once was, with families trying to "pass," but openly, proudly, with the families proclaiming themselves as of a different sort: families like mine, made interracially, or interculturally, or internationally. Gay and lesbian couples, committed to long-term, caring relationships, demand recognition of their families: their households, with or without children, are not alternatives *to* the family, but alternative *kinds* of family. Divorce, more and more people are realizing, does not have to "break" families, but can sometimes blend and extend them.

But while people are struggling to create a language to encompass these new relations, a way of expressing our connections that is neither the dismissive "just friends"[2] nor the archaic language of kinship, another language is being developed. It is a technical and legal language, reaching in the very opposite direction. With all of the caring and nurturance removed, we are hearing about "contracting couples," "surrogate mothers," "genetic parents," "gestational motherhood," "custodial" and "noncustodial" parents. Ovum and sperm and blastocyst, embryos and amnios, "state-of-the-art" babies and "boarder" babies have all entered into the public discourse in the past decade.

This language is a guide to a very different social reality. While on the one hand we are trying to think of children as people, deserving respect and needing care, on the other hand our society is also coming to think of children as products. There is a phrase that they use in medicine that intrigues me: *the products of conception*. It is medical language for what you get when sperm joins egg—in a loving waiting mother, in a frightened teenager, in a hired woman, or in a petri dish—the results are the "products of conception."

Interesting phrase, that. It is really a fine term for what we are talking about. Because we are in fact coming to talk about products and a production process. We are facing the expansion of a way of thinking that treats people as objects, as commodities. It is a way of thinking that enables us to see not motherhood, not parenthood, but the creation of a commodity, a baby. American society is involved now in the fixing of price tags for the separate parts of the procreative process. We are negotiating the prices for bodily parts, bodily fluids, and human services, energy, and lives as we produce "valuable" babies, "precious" babies.

This is the thread that I see running through all of the issues in the new as well as in the old procreative technologies.[3] Sometimes it comes right up to the surface, and we hear and read actual dollar figures: so many thousands of dollars for each in vitro attempt; $15,000 as the current market rate for a "surrogate" mother-for-hire; $20,000 to adopt a baby from one country, $35,000 from another. Sometimes the language of commodification, of pricing, goes back under again, and we talk vaguely about the "costs" and the "burdens" of rearing people with disabilities, how much we are "spared" with prenatal diagnosis and selective abortion. The talk of money and dollars comes to the fore and recedes to the background but always, through it all, when we talk about procreation now, we are talking about the commodification of life. It is not altogether surprising at this time that commodification is indeed the approach we take to procreation; some would claim that this is the approach we take to virtually everything. We talk about prices, bottom lines, and net gains and losses, what things are worth.

The commodification process is perhaps most clearly seen in the notion of "surrogate" motherhood. There we talk openly about buying services and renting body parts—as if body parts were rented without renting the woman. But pregnancy isn't a condition of one isolated organ. Women experience pregnancy with our whole bodies—from the changes in our hair to our swollen ankles—with all of our bodies and perhaps with our souls as well.

The commodification process is not unique to surrogacy arrangements. It was there long ago when we first began to experience some "shortage" of babies for adoption. While babies are not for sale in the United States, at least not openly, we all know perfectly well that the availability of a baby for adoption has a lot to do with the amount of money the potential adopters can spend. And we know that adoptable babies are themselves sorted as commodities, with the whiter, younger, and healthier carrying the highest price tags.

The commodification process has transformed pregnancy, as society encourages the development of prenatal testing. This process—genetic counseling, screening, and testing of fetuses—serves the function of "quality control" on the assembly line of the products of conception, separating out those products we wish to develop from those we wish to discontinue.[4] Once we see the products of conception as just that, as products, we begin to treat them as we do any other product, subject to similar scrutiny and standards.

As babies and children become products, mothers become producers, pregnant women the unskilled workers on a reproductive assembly line. Think of the anti-smoking, anti-drinking "behave yourself" campaigns aimed increasingly at pregnant women. What are the causes of prematurity, fetal defects, damaged newborns—flawed products? Bad mothers, of course—inept workers. One New York City subway ad series showed two newborn footprints, one from a full-term and one from a premature infant. The ads read, "Guess which baby's mother smoked while pregnant?" Another asks "Guess which baby's mother drank while pregnant?" And yet another: "Guess which baby's mother didn't get prenatal care?" I looked in vain for the ad that says "Guess which baby's mother tried to get by on welfare?"; "Guess which baby's mother had to live on the streets?"; or "Guess which baby's mother was beaten by her husband?"

Women are laborers producing the precious products, and management does not generally trust unskilled, poorly paid, disrespected workers. America is developing a legal and medical system to monitor pregnant women, control them, keep them in line with "fetal-abuse" statutes.

One very real concern about this ideology is what effect it will have on the "products of conception" to be dealt with in this way. And so we worry about the effects on the children thus created of artificial insemination with the use of sperm from paid donors, or "surrogate" motherhood and other purchasing arrangements. Certainly some worry about the fetus and its "right to life," with or without disabilities. But my chief concern lies elsewhere: in what this commodification process does to all of us, as a society, as individuals, and as mothers.

Why especially mothers? Mothers are not the only ones who can raise babies—adoptive parents, fathers, any caring committed person can successfully nurture a child, along with or instead of its "birth mother." The parent-child relationship is based not on hormones or on chromosomes, but on love and caring, social rather than physical characteristics. But many of the issues our society is facing today, issues brought up by new reproductive technology or new reproductive marketing, are not about childrearing, but childbearing: the conception, gestation, and birth of babies. And for that, there is no shared parenting. Only one person is pregnant with a baby, only one carries it in her body for all those months, only one births it. Biological motherhood is unique, and changing ideas about the procreation of children pose unique challenges for women as mothers.

Feminists are caught in an awkward position facing these new definitions of motherhood. The old definitions were so bad, we fought them for so long, and now the newer ones are worse. We have not yet claimed a language of our own for motherhood, a woman-centered way of looking at it.

The old definition saw motherhood as a status. Women were mothers. Mothering was not something women *did*, it was something women *were*. Long after men came to have occupational choices, motherhood remained the all but inevitable lot of most women. Motherhood was in fact a master status, and everything women did was seen in terms of our motherhood, or our potential for motherhood. Motherhood and its demands, babies and children and their demands, defined women. We had to be what they needed.

The new language sees mothering as an activity, as service, as work—and children as the product produced by the labor of mothering.

That is not acceptable. We cannot allow motherhood—the intimate, joyous, terrifying, life-affirming experience that is motherhood—to be reduced in this way.

Perhaps this is one of those moments of crisis a society faces, where there are two paths that can be taken. We can focus on nurturance, caring, human relations. We can come to accept and to respect a wider variety of family relationships and arrangements. Those qualities we have come to think of as maternal could become more widely shared, by both men and women. We could direct this nurturance, this maternal caring, not just to children, but to each other. The values and the experience of motherhood could come to shape the way we live in the world. That is, I suppose, the fantasy, the truly revolutionary potential of a recreated motherhood.

Or we can recreate motherhood to reflect the commodification of children. That, I am afraid, is the direction we have been heading in for a long time.

The commodification process came most strikingly to the surface for Americans with what was known as the "Baby M" case of the late 1980s. A woman named Mary Beth Whitehead was hired by Elizabeth and William Stern to serve as a "surrogate mother." Betsy Stern, as the wife was known, had multiple sclerosis and was afraid that a pregnancy would make her condition worse. Mary Beth Whitehead was artificially inseminated with Bill Stern's sperm and gave birth to a girl, a child the Sterns named Melissa. In the delivery room, Mary Beth Whitehead later told me, her husband turned to her and said "I don't think we can go through with this." And she couldn't. She reneged on the contract and wanted to keep the child, raising her as part of her family with her other children. The Sterns took her to court. The court first upheld the contract. The judge took away all of Whitehead's parental rights and allowed Betsy Stern to adopt the child and be recognized as her only legal mother. That ruling was later overturned by the Supreme Court of New Jersey. While Bill Stern remains the child's father, Mary Beth Whitehead remains her mother. The Sterns were given custody, but Whitehead, as in the aftermath of a bad divorce, has visitation rights.

This case involved no new reproductive technologies—artificial insemination has been used for over a century—but it raised many of the questions that the newer technologies do. What makes a mother? a father? Who has rights to a child? And have we gone too far in commodifying life if we sell pregnancies and make custody decisions in terms of contract law?

Case after case followed. When couples use the woman's own egg and hire a "surrogate gestator," a woman who will carry the pregnancy but not be the genetic mother of the child she bears, then who is the mother? The egg donor or the pregnant woman? If human cloning ever works, and a man has one of his own body cells cloned and hires a "surrogate gestator," will that child have no mother at all? Will the man be the father or the twin brother of the child he has created? Who will have the right to raise that child?

When embryos are frozen and the couples who produced the sperm and egg out of which they were created die, who owns the embryo? Is the embryo the property of the estate of the couple? Or its potential heir? When a couple divorce after they've created frozen embryos, then who owns those embryos? Can the embryos be sold? Sperm has been sold for a long time. What about eggs? Sperm is cheap and easy to produce; eggs involve risk and expense. For how much can you sell eggs? Can someone auction them off on a web site, as one entrepreneur attempted to do with the eggs of fashion models?

The questions keep coming, each new technology pushing new limits, forcing us to think about the relationship between parent and child. What makes someone a parent? What makes us family?

Mothering in America

Family sits at the center of almost every public debate in America. That's what we used to call "mom and apple pie" rhetoric—before the sugar and cholesterol in apple pie and the sexism in "mom" became apparent. Family is also the touchstone of our way of life—every community seems to call upon its image of family to justify itself, to proclaim itself. So why isn't this book called *Recreating Family?* In a way, of course, that's precisely what it is about. But when it comes to the actual living of family, its day-to-day work and pleasures, it's most often mothering that we're talking about.

When the mother is missing in a family, people seem to think a substitute woman is needed: grandmothers or housekeepers or somebody has to step in to *be* there. When a mother dies, the world of her children is shattered, and childhood itself ends.[5] When it is the father that is missing, our traditional answer has been to send in money to keep the family going. What we now think of as "welfare" of one kind or another mostly has its history in aid to widows and orphans: families without fathers. In the active years of parenting, when there are young children in a household, mothering of some sort has to be provided. I will argue that as true as that is, there is no particular reason why the work we call "mothering" has to be done by mothers or by women. And over the years, more and more people have come to see that. Stay-at-home fathers are still relatively rare, but they're out there, and they even hold conferences and conventions and celebrate what they are doing. But make no mistake: what they are doing is what we have called "mothering."

Mothering is an intimate kind of caring that has as its goal the creation of capable members of the larger community. It sometimes feels a lot like the kind of caring, intimate work we do with people who are sick or very elderly and frail. And in many ways it is the very same kind of work: a diaper is a diaper, after all, whether worn by a three-month-old or a ninety-eight-year-old. But there is a sadness in our care of the elderly, and sometimes of the very sick, because we know we are easing their passage out of life. Mothering—equally tedious, dirty, exhausting, isolating, frustrating work—has also the wild joy of creating the thing most worth creating in the world of people: people themselves.

As you can see, I love mothering. I am writing in passionate defense of mothering. I have screamed at my kids, wished myself far, far away from them, felt anger, frustration, moments of pure hatred—all the stuff anybody who is being honest will have to acknowledge plays a part in mothering. But I love it. I can afford to love it, afford it in every sense of the term: I have the middle-class services and environment that make it doable, let alone lovable. And I haven't had to do it alone. I've shared the mothering of my children, mostly with their father but also with grandparents and friends and even with "hired help," women who have come into our home a few afternoons a week and mothered. I cannot tell you how many hours of my life I have spent barricaded in this very office, pointedly unavailable to one or another of my young children, as I sit up here writing about motherhood while somebody else mothers them downstairs.

What I wish for the world is not that everybody should mother. No one who doesn't want to do this should have to do it. But every child does need to be mothered, and whoever is doing that work should have at least what I have had, the conditions that make it possible to love mothering.

All that is to explain, as if it needs explaining, why I am passionate about mothering. But why am I *defensive* about it? Does mothering need a defense?

In the early days of what is called the "second wave" of the feminist movement, mothering did need a defense. The mostly white, mostly middle-class, mostly college-educated women who made up that movement wanted access to the world that their fathers and brothers had and wanted out of the trap that had been laid for their mothers and sisters. A lifetime of what Betty Friedan famously called "the problem that has no name,"[6] an isolated, frustrated, suburban housebound life, was a thing to be profoundly rejected. So women marched and fought and sued and litigated and demanded—and to some extent got—the right to live men's lives.

For some women that did mean denigrating motherhood itself. "Liberation" came, for some, at the cost of giving up the joys as well as the burdens of traditional womanhood. I was pregnant with my first child in 1974, right in the middle of that wave, and the childless chairwoman of my department fired me, because, as she told my colleagues, "Some people are obviously not serious about their careers."

Within a few years that attitude changed. Feminists embraced not only contraception and abortion rights issues but also motherhood issues. Words like "pregnancy discrimination" entered our vocabulary to describe just what had happened to me. By the time I was pregnant with my second child in 1981, pregnant assistant professors were a dime a dozen (there were two in my department of ten people), and child care was available at professional meetings.

So it is not against feminism that motherhood needs to be defended. What then is the problem?

Mothering faces problems everywhere, and much of what I will be writing about applies to other countries. But this is a very American book about a very American problem. As much as we talk about "family" and "motherhood" and the "American way," we do not have a social policy or ideology that genuinely supports mothering. Rhetoric aside, America is shockingly anti-child, anti-mother.

I spent six months in the Netherlands once, on a Fulbright Fellowship. I took my two daughters, then aged thirteen and five, with me. It was my only experience as a single mother: my husband had to stay at his job and only came for visits. In some ways it was like being transported to 1950s middle-class America, a place in which I had never lived, having spent those years the child of a working-class widow. The Netherlands has an unusually high rate of full-time mothers and of women who work only part-time while child-rearing. School let out early, with long, long waiting lists for the little child care available. Elementary school children were dismissed at 11:30 every Wednesday morning, and I joined the huge crowds of mothers—and they really were almost all mothers, not fathers or hired care-givers—at the school gates. But the Netherlands is a rich country, as middle-class America once seemed to be, and one full-time salary is enough to support a household.

There are of course professional working women in the Netherlands as elsewhere. Some take some time off for early motherhood, some hire help, and some few men step in. But most women spend a lot of years as "mothers," tending their homes and families more or less full time. It is not a situation I am recommending as policy, but it is one way of supporting mothering.

From the vantage point of that country I could see my own afresh. Rare indeed is the American kindergarten child with a stay-at-home mother. The push is on here for longer school days, starting at younger ages. And that may indeed be a very good thing for both mothers and children. But then I look at my own neighborhood in Brooklyn, and see here, in this far-from-rich, mostly minority community, the kind of child care that is available. When I see mothers taking babies off at seven in the morning and picking them up at seven in the evening, I have to wonder. Just like the mothers who have been forced into low-paying work by "welfare reform," are these women "freed" from mothering or barred from it?

There was more to my outsiders' view of American family policy. Colleagues were shocked, and genuinely unbelieving, when I told them that I had had no paid time off for the birth or adoption of my children. I've always joked about my "academic babies," my two births planned for the summer. They didn't get it. Every Dutch woman has six paid weeks off before and ten paid weeks off after the birth of a child.

But it was the little things that got to me. We moved into an apartment building that was mostly filled with elderly people, mostly women as the elderly tend to be, who could no longer manage their own gardens and homes. Victoria was a very active, bouncy five-year-old. I took her downstairs to the apartment immediately below mine and introduced myself to our neighbor. I told her I wasn't sure how much noise carried, so please tell me right away when she was bothered by Victoria's running or jumping. She looked confused, and I thought maybe it was a language problem so I explained again more slowly and carefully. But no, it wasn't language: it was culture. When she understood what I was saying to her, the old woman looked concerned, reached out to me and said, "But dear, children have to run."

That children will run and be noisy and make a mess—it was okay there in a way it had never been okay here. I didn't have to keep apologizing for my children, and I felt the relief. Look at the glares a mother gets when a child is noisy in a public place. Now imagine mothering without that.

And imagine mothering, as most of the developed world does, without private expense for medical services or for education. Imagine the fabulous expenses of child-rearing, from pediatrics to universities, publicly shared. The Netherlands, like the rest of Europe and Great Britain, is certainly no richer than the United States. But when a society *cares* for its children, takes some collective responsibility for its children, mothering is a lot easier.

But how can I talk about America as an anti-child society when children are such a huge business? Children are, we are constantly reminded, a huge market. Money is spent on them, and they themselves have lots of money to spend—at least some children do. The extremes of class in this country are something else it is very hard to explain to others.

And people are desperate for children. The very word "desperate" has been irrevocably linked to the word "infertile" in our language. Americans spend unthinkable amounts of money getting pregnant or, failing that, traveling around the world adopting. And here too the race and class issues rear their heads. The United States has an enormous percentage of its children in foster care and in institutional care. Some children are precious and some children are not, and a rudimentary understanding of the American race and class system explains that.

But even if we, as a people, want children, or at least a certain kind of children, does that mean we want to mother them? Does that mean that we support the people who do that mothering? Mothering, the actual work of it, as I will show in this book, is underpaid and undervalued work. The child is the product, and the product of that work may well be valued, but that doesn't mean that the work itself, or the worker herself, is valued.

That is the tension that drives this book. There is indeed something about the having of children that is valued. People go to great lengths to have children. They risk their lives, their health, and their economic standing to have children. Industries have grown up around infertility services. New technologies show up in our newspapers as quickly as in our hospitals: we are interested in the new technologies of procreation and what they promise. And yet, mothering itself is not valued; it is done at great personal cost. Women like me who are well placed can afford the costs and enjoy our mothering enormously. Women who are not so well placed—women who are poor or very young or not well educated or of minority status or all of the above—suffer greatly in their mothering.

What is it about how we think and act in America that makes mothering the burden it is? What is the trap, and is there a way out?

Three Ideologies

I believe that modern American motherhood rests on three deeply rooted ideologies that shape what we see and what we experience: the ideology of patriarchy, the ideology of technology, and the ideology of capitalism. I shall look at each of these separately, but I know that they are not separate ways of thinking. Instead I see them as the strands of a tightly wound braid.

An ideology is the way a group looks at the world, a way of organizing our thinking about the world. As a member of a group or society, an ideology shapes the way you see the world, and consequently shapes the way you see yourself, the way you experience your own body and life. Thus an ideology may place you on the outside of your own experience, leaving you with extraordinary contradictions between what you are experiencing and what you are thinking about it. The horror of a dominant ideology, its evil, is its distortion of the reality of those oppressed by the group. Think of the black children who accepted the racist ideology of the dominant society, who internalized, took in as their own perspective, that black children were uglier, less suitable as playmates, less wonderful children than were white children. And of course think of the women who accept the dominant ideology of patriarchy and use it to view their own lives. There are women who believe that women are less complete, less full human beings than are men, that they live more trivial lives, lives of less worth than those of their husbands or their sons. Think of how women learned to think of their own sexual experiences in men's terms, starting with "fore*play*," proceeding to the *real* thing, "penetration," and ending with ejaculation. We are still struggling with what it means to view women's sexuality, fertility, and bodies with women's own eyes.

Ideologies are *political*; that is, they rest on a power base. When the entire system of values, attitudes, beliefs, and morality of a society supports the dominant order, the term *hegemony*, rather than ideology, is sometimes used. When people internalize that consciousness, it becomes part of common sense.[7] Think of how women have started to clear out all the "nonsense" we learned as "common sense" as a result of patriarchy.

The ideology of patriarchy is perhaps the easiest to understand of the three ideologies that shape motherhood. More than half the world has someplace else to stand, has another reality, women's reality, to contradict this particular ideology. But women's reality is not the dominant ideology, and women's view of the world is overruled by men's view. Motherhood in a patriarchal society is what mothers and babies signify to men. For women this can mean too many pregnancies or too few; "trying again" for a son; covering up male infertility with donor insemination treated as the deepest darkest secret; having some of our children called "illegitimate"; not having access to abortions we do want; being pressured into abortions we may not want.

The ideology of capitalism, that goods are produced for profit, is also something clear to us; we know that some societies avoid the profit motive, and that most societies feel there should be *some* limits to how much of life should be viewed as a commodity. It may seem farfetched to apply this ideology to motherhood and to children. But the family has always been an economic unit as well as a social and psychological unit. What is new, perhaps, is the shift from children as workers to children as commodities, accompanying the change in the family from its role as a unit of production to its new role as a unit of consumption.[8]

Finally, the ideology of technology shapes motherhood. No longer an event shaped by religion and family, having a baby has become part of the high-tech medical world. But as an ideology, a way of thinking, technology is harder to pin down, so pervasive has it become in Western society. The ideology of technology encourages us to see ourselves as objects, to see people as made up of machines and part of larger machines. It is this mechanization that connects the ideology of patriarchy with capitalism, to create the hegemony, the world view.[9]

The next three chapters discuss how these three ideologies shape the experience and institution of motherhood in America.[10]

Motherhood under Patriarchy

The term "patriarchy" is often used loosely as a synonym for "sexism," or to refer to any social system where men rule. The term technically means "rule of fathers," but in its current practical usage it more often refers to any system of male superiority and female inferiority. But male dominance and patriarchal rule are not quite the same thing, and when the subject is motherhood, the difference is important.

Patriarchal kinship is the core of what is meant by patriarchy: the idea that paternity is the central social relationship. A very clear statement of patriarchal kinship is found in the book of Genesis, in the "begats." Each man, from Adam onward, is described as having "begot a son in his likeness, after his image." After the birth of this firstborn son, the men are described as having lived so many years and begot sons and daughters. The text then turns to that firstborn son, and in turn his firstborn son after him. Women appear as the "daughters of men who bore them offspring." In a patriarchal kinship system, children are reckoned as being born to men, out of women. Women, in this system, bear the children of men.

The essential concept here is the "seed," the part of men that grows into the children of their likeness within the bodies of women. Such a system is inevitably male dominated, but it is a particular kind of male domination. Men control women as daughters, much as they control their sons, but they also control women as the mothers of men's children. It is women's motherhood that men must control to maintain patriarchy. In a patriarchy, because what is valued is the relationship of a man to his sons, women are a vulnerability that men have: to beget these sons, men must pass their seed through the body of a woman.

While all societies appear to be male dominated to some degree, not all societies are patriarchal. In some, the line of descent is not from father to son, but along the lines of the women. These are called "matrilineal" societies: it is a shared mother that makes for a shared lineage or family group. Men still rule in these groups, but they do not rule as fathers. They rule the women and children who are related to them through their mother's line. Women in such a system are not a vulnerability, but a source of connection. As anthropologist Glenn Petersen says, in a matrilineal system "women, rather than infiltrating and subverting patrilines, are acknowledged to produce and reproduce the body of society itself."[1] People are not men's children coming through the bodies of women, but the children of women.

In one such society, among the Trobriand Islanders, the man who rules or has rights of domination over children is not the father, but the mother's brother. The uncle rules as a man, but not as a father. Women are not the mothers of men's children: men are the children of women. The anthropologist Bronislaw Malinowski looked at this system and seemed to have some difficulty figuring out what was happening. He thought the Trobriand Islanders just didn't understand biological paternity. After all, it seemed to Malinowski, how could a man not have control over the children which are *his* if he knew they were his, and yet have control over those which are his sister's husband's children? For Malinowski, for Western society, what makes a child belong to a man, what makes it *his*, is that it grew from his sperm, from his seed. For the Trobriand Islanders sperm was not all that important. Later anthropologists have shown that the Trobriand Islanders understand the nature of biological paternity but that it does not have the same significance for them as it has for us.[2]

Our society developed out of a patriarchal system in which paternity is a fundamentally important relationship. Some of our social customs and traditions have their roots in this patriarchal system. To maintain the purity of the male kinship line, men had to control the sexuality of women, and ensure that no other man's seed entered her body. They had to control her virginity so that she came to the marriage bed unimpregnated. They had to control her in pregnancy, so that she could not destroy the seed of men. The "double standard"—the ideas about virginity for brides, abortion, "illegitimacy," about women's sexual and procreative freedom in all areas—reflects men's concern for maintaining paternity.

Remnants of this patriarchal system can also be seen in the way we name children: children take their "family" name from the line of the father. Half-siblings with the same father share a family name; those with the same mother do not. The name is passed down male lines: children of brothers share a name that came from the brother's father; children of sisters or of brother and sister do not share a name. They belong to the family line of other men. American children continue to take the name of the father, in spite of changes in the position of women. Even those women who have not taken their husband's family name for themselves almost always give their children the last name of the father.

In spite of all of these signs of patriarchy, the modern American kinship system is not classically patriarchal. It is what anthropologists call a bilateral system, in that individuals are considered to be equally related to their mother's and their father's "sides" of the family. We have in English, for example, no everyday word to distinguish a "paternal" aunt (father's sister) from a "maternal" aunt (mother's sister). We don't even have a common word to distinguish an aunt by birth (or by "blood") from an aunt by marriage: we use the same word, *aunt*, for the father's sister and the father's brother's wife. That is probably because these relationships carry very little weight. There are no legal obligations involved and few firm societally shared expectations, beyond showing up for major rituals like weddings and funerals. In actual practice, people do seem to take these relationships far more seriously than that, though, and the exchange of help, money, love, and social support between members of extended families is an important part of American life.

Underneath this casual, almost sloppy reckoning of kinship, there are certain fixed ideas about family and relatedness. Blood, we say, is thicker than water. Blood ties are the fundamental basis for reckoning kinship, and one of the few permanencies left in American life. In a society like ours, where people move every few years, where marriages last as long as they work, where job changes and career changes are expected, the family is a fixed point in a changing landscape. Who knows where they will be living or working, who their friends, neighbors, or colleagues will be in twenty years, but a sister is always a sister. Marriages may end, but children are forever. These relationships may be close or distant, loving or not, easy or tense. But they do not go away. They cannot be divorced, quit, annulled, fired, or dissolved. An estranged sister is still a sister.

So kinship reckoning in America still matters, still counts for something, even if it is a far cry from what it might mean in some tribal society. But this begs the question: *what is kin?* This is one of those commonsensical questions, something that "everybody knows" that shows the force of an ideology in shaping our understanding of the world's workings. Yet kinship and blood ties are reckoned differently in different cultures.

An interesting if bizarre demonstration of how very differently people reckon kin occurred in the 1950s. There was a disease that struck in the Eastern Highlands of Papua New Guinea, among the Fore people. Called kuru, it was a fatal neurological disorder.

> Because kuru seemed to run in families and was isolated to a small, interrelated population, a genetic basis for the disease was suspected. By the late 1950's it was proposed that kuru was a hereditary disorder, determined by a single autosomal gene that was dominant in females but recessive in males.[3]

That was a reasonable and very frightening hypothesis. It explained the transmission of the disease within families, and made a lot more deaths seem inevitable. The hypothesis was wrong, though, because what the Fore meant by family, by kin, was not at all what the Western physicians meant. The "sisters" dying in a family were often not, according to Western notions of kinship, in any way "related" to each other. It turned out that kuru is a slow virus, one that becomes active only after years of incubation. It is spread by cannibalism: kin ate the bodies of kin among the Fore. The right to eat the body, and the particular body part one ate, was determined by kinship lines—kinship as reckoned by the Fore.

The confusion between genetic kinship and social kinship occurs in our society, too. I've observed genetic-counseling sessions where the counselors tried to take a history using their language of kinship and clients answered using a different way of reckoning. In one case, after a long, involved description of a cousin's stillbirth, it turned out that the cousin was an aunt-by-marriage's child by another marriage. So we may get confused sometimes, this confusion being furthered by the inexactness of our kinship language, but we do have a fixed idea of what kin means: our society's definition of kin is based on genetic relatedness. In this sense, it harks back to the idea of a "seed." As soon as we hear the whole story, we understand the confusion: it's not *really* her cousin; in-laws are not *really* related. American ideas about "really" related people are based on genetic connections. It's a way of reckoning that makes us see adoptive parents as not the real parents, aunts and uncles by marriage as not real aunts and uncles, in-laws as not real relatives. Real kin, in our system, share a genetic tie.

What happens in a matrilineal system, when the genetic tie between a man and the children conceived of his sperm does not determine lineage? In this case the most "real" relatives are the ones that share what is called a "uterine" relationship: children and grandchildren of the same woman. Among the Nayar of Central Kerala of India, for example, marriage between half-siblings who share a father was considered "indelicate" but was not prohibited, and the children of brothers (first cousins on their father's side) are not considered related and might marry or not as they chose.[4] It was only the experience of a shared mother that defined "real" kinship.

In a patriarchal system, when people talk about blood ties, they are talking about a genetic tie, a connection by seed. In a mother-based system, the blood tie is the mingled blood of mothers and their children: children grow out of the blood of their mothers, of their bodies and being. The shared bond of kinship comes through mothers. The maternal tie is based on the growing of children. The patriarchal tie is based on genetics, the act of impregnating.

Each of these ways of thinking leads to different ideas about what a person is. In a mother-based system, a person is what mothers grow—people are made of the care and nurturance that bring a baby forth into the world, and turn the baby into a member of the society. In a patriarchal system, a person is what grows out of men's seed. The essence of the person, what the person really is, is there in the seed when it is planted in the mother. Early scientists in Western society were so deeply committed to the patriarchal concept that it influenced what they saw. One of the first uses of the microscope was to look at semen and see the little person, the homunculus, curled up inside the sperm. And in our era the director of a California sperm bank distributed T-shirts with a drawing of sperm swimming on a blue background accompanied by the words "Future People."

The Seeds of Women

Out of the patriarchal focus on the seed as the source of being, on the male production of children from men's seed, has grown our current, usually far more sophisticated thinking about procreation.

Modern procreative technology has been forced to go beyond the sperm as seed. "Daddy plants a seed in Mommy" won't work any more. Modern science has had to confront the *egg* as seed also. Modern scientific thinking cannot possibly hold on to old notions of women as nurturers of men's seeds. The doctor who has spent time "harvesting" eggs from women's bodies for in vitro fertilization fully understands the significance of women's seed. But that does not mean we no longer continue to think of the seed as the essence of being. It is not the end of the belief that the seeds, the genes, are everything, that they are all that really matters in the making of a baby, that they are what *real* kinship is based on.

The old patriarchal kinship system had a clear place for women: they were the nurturers of men's seeds, the soil in which seeds grew, the daughters who bore men offspring. When forced to acknowledge that a woman's genetic contribution is equal to a man's, Western patriarchy was in trouble. *But the central concept of patriarchy, the importance of the seed, was retained by extending the concept to women.* Valuing the seed of women, the genetic material women too have, extends to women some of the privileges of patriarchy. That is, when the significance of women's seed is acknowledged in her relationship with her children, women, too, have paternity rights in their children. In this modified system based on the older ideology of patriarchy, women, too, can be seen to own their children, just like men do. Unlike what happens in a mother-based system, however, this relationship between women and their children is not based on motherhood per se, not on the unique nurturance, the long months of pregnancy, the intimate connections with the baby as it grows and moves inside her body, passes through her genitals, and sucks at her breasts. Instead, women are said to own their babies, have "rights" to them, just as men do: based on their seed.

This does not end patriarchy, and it does not end the domination of the children of women by men. Instead, by maintaining the centrality of the seed, the ideology maintains the rights of men in their children, even as it recognizes something approaching equal rights of women in their children. Since men's control over women and the children of women is no longer based simply on men's (no longer) unique seed, men's economic superiority and the other privileges of a male-dominated social system become increasingly important. Children are, based on the seed, presumptively "half his, half hers"—and might as well have grown in the backyard. Women do not gain their rights to their children in this society as *mothers*, but as *father equivalents*, as equivalent sources of seed.

The Genetic Tie

What precisely is the physical nature of this highly valued genetic connection between parent and child?

Our bodies are composed of cells. The cells each have in them a nucleus. Within the nucleus are twenty-three pairs of chromosomes. In each pair, one chromosome came from the genetic mother and one from the genetic father. Located on the chromosomes are the genes, the basic units of heredity, composed of a kind of protein called DNA. Any particular gene of a parent may or may not be passed on to a child. A gene passed on may or may not be "expressed"—that is, a child with the gene may or may not have the characteristic. A child can carry one parent's gene for blue eyes, and yet have brown eyes.

The closest genetic connection a human being can have is an identical twin. Identical twins have the same chromosomes, the same genes. The next closest relations are those between parent and child, and between full siblings, including fraternal twins. If an individual carries a certain gene, the chances that a sibling will carry the same gene are fifty-fifty, the same as the parent-child relationship. Genetically, "there is nothing special about the parent-offspring relationship except its close degree and a certain fundamental asymmetry. The full-sib relationship is just as close."[5]

Using the word "inheritance" for genetic characteristics is misleading. It makes us think of genes as we do of other things that are inherited, such as royal titles, or titles to property. The word far predates modern genetics, and carries the older implication of things "passed on," a human chain of giving through generations and time. But that is not the way genetic inheritance works. First off, one doesn't lose the thing passed: more of it is created. Using one cell from the parent, the new being creates its own replicas of the genes.

Second, there is no intention here. Careful planning and good living won't give you a better genetic estate to pass on. There is no separating out of the characteristics you want to pass on and those you want to lose. The characteristics you pass on are not necessarily even the ones you've expressed: it may be your father's or mother's genetic trait, one you did not show, that shows up in your child. The only sibling to have escaped "the family nose" may be the only sibling whose child has it.

Third, there is something strangely ahistoric about these relationships of genetic connection that defies the word "inherit." Looking at two genes, there is no way to tell which came from the parent, which from the offspring. Looking at the genes, parent and child have the same relationship as do siblings: half their genes are shared in common. And half-siblings (only one parent in common, either mother or father because genetically it makes no difference) have the same genetic connection as do grandparents and grandchildren, with one- fourth of their genes shared. Genetic connections exist in these percentages: the 100 percent connection of identical twins; the 50 percent connection of siblings and of parents to children; the 25 percent connection of grandparents to grandchildren and of half-siblings to each other; and the 12.5 percent connection of cousins, and so on. In strictly genetic terms, your sister might as well be your mother. The genetic connection is the same.

But parenthood is not just a genetic connection, a genetic relationship. And it is more than the age difference that distinguishes the parent-child relationship: the social relationship of a seventeen-year-old sibling to a newborn baby is quite different than the relationship of a seventeen-year-old parent to a newborn baby. It may be six of one and half a dozen of the other genetically, but socially these are not interchangeable relationships.

The parent-child relationship is invested with social and legal rights and claims that are not recognized, in this society, in any other genetic relationship. That is because of our social heritage of patriarchy: that genetic connection was the basis for men's control over the children of women. The contemporary modification of traditional patriarchy has been to recognize the genetic parenthood of women as being equivalent to the genetic parenthood of men. Genetic parenthood replaces paternity in determining who a child is, who it belongs to. I believe it is time to move beyond the patriarchal concern with genetic relationships.

We can recognize and appreciate the genetic tie without making it the determining connection. We do that in most of our genetic relations. American society recognizes no special claims of a sibling on a sibling, or of aunts and uncles for nieces and nephews. We recognize the relationship, we allow people to make what they will of it, but it carries no legal weight. If my brother does not like the way I am raising his niece, so be it. Even though he is closely related to her genetically, even if she were to look more like him than like me, it gives him no legal claim to her. He has no basis to challenge my claim as parent, short of showing me to be unfit—and even then, no assurance that the child would be turned over to him. And if my son doesn't like the way I'm raising my daughter, even though he is just as closely related to her genetically as I am, there is no way he can challenge my custody, and that will still be true when he is over twenty-one. But my husband, as her father, can challenge my custody, without showing me to be unfit, as I can challenge his custody. We are parents, and that gives us special legal rights over the child.

When I argue, as I will repeatedly in this book, that we need to value nurturance and caring relationships more than genetic ties, that does not mean that genetics is a dirty word to me. Surely we have these genetic relations, and they can be a source of pleasure. I found myself grinning once when a new neighbor recognized me as "Leah's mother" because she looks like me. Or I like her. And no one on earth understands like my sister does what it is to go shoe shopping for these absurd feet our father bestowed upon us. I painted my great-grandmother's portrait from a photograph—and my cousin's face emerged from the canvas. This flash of connection, this recognition of genetic relationship—it's powerful. I can understand the adoptee's joy and astonishment to meet a genetic relation and find that "somebody looks like me."

But. Just how much weight do we need to give this tie? How much can it hold? Stripped of all the social supports, is that genetic tie sufficient to define a person? Am I my mother's daughter because of our chromosomes? If a woman donates an egg, or a man turns over to a lab technician a vial of semen, does that make the person a *parent* to a child created with those chromosomes?

Patriarchal Ideology and New Procreative Technology

The new procreative technology being developed is based on the patriarchal focus on the seed. The seed, the genetic material, is the one absolutely irreplaceable part of procreation, as science now approaches it. The procreative technology continues to substitute for one after another of the nurturing tasks but makes no substitute for the seed. Breasts became unnecessary quite some time ago, as artificial formula substituted for human milk. The act of giving birth becomes increasingly unnecessary, as doctors work on surgical removal of babies to the point now where one out of five American babies are born by cesarean section. The nurturance of late pregnancy becomes unnecessary as neonatal intensive-care units develop the skill to maintain ever younger and smaller premature babies or "extrauterine fetuses" in incubation. And the nurturing environment of the fallopian tube becomes replaceable as the nurturance of the glass dish, the in vitro environment, is developed.

None of these techniques of artificial nurturance works as well as the natural mothering experience, though as one or another becomes "faddish" there is a tendency for doctors to proclaim its superiority over the natural mother.

But once a substitute for a thing is possible, the thing itself loses its mystique. By their very existence, substitutes denigrate the original. What is the value of spelling skills in a world with spell check? Who needs to do long division in a world with calculators? What happened to oral history in a world that learned to write? Once a substitute, or just a "manmade" alternative is available, what's so special about the original? Think about how the mystical meaning of flight changed as airplanes streaked over eagles.

That is what is happening to mothering—as a physical and as a psychological experience—as we offer substitute after substitute, surrogate after surrogate. What is so *special* about motherhood?

I once listened to a group of lawyers trying to figure out if there was anything special or unique about a mother's relationship to her fetus, compared to anyone else's relationship to that fetus. The context was the issue of prenatal torts—the ever-present legal question of who can sue whom for what. If a child can sue someone, say a manufacturer of a chemical, for harm that was done to that child when it was a fetus, then is there any reason the child cannot sue the mother for harm she did to the child when it was a fetus? Is there anything that makes a mother's relationship to her fetus unique? They had a hard time thinking of anything.

We have focused on the seed, on the embryo, and then on the fetus, and reduced all of the nurturance, all of the intimacy, all of the *mothering*, to background environmental factors. And so as we substitute for this and for that environmental factor, substitute for this or for that mothering experience, we wonder what is so special about the original, what is so unique about the mother's relationship.

The problem has been brought to a head with the new procreative technology, which forces us to confront questions about mothering and the mother-child relationship. But these are not new problems or new questions.

People in our society have been substituting for aspects of mothering for a long time, always along the same patterns. Upper-class women have bought the services of lower-class women to provide one or another mothering service for their children. Or, it might more accurately be said in some circumstances, upper-class men have bought the services of lower-class women to supplement the services of their wives. Some societies have let men have mistresses while their wives mothered; some have let men hire servants to do the mothering so that their wives could be more like mistresses.

Wet nurses are the earliest example of this biological substitution of one woman for another in mothering. Sometimes wet nursing has been done in an exchange system between women—two or more women occasionally nursing each other's babies, substituting for one another. "Commercializing" wet nursing meant putting a price tag on that service. When the wet nurses were slave mammies, the price was factored into the cost of the slave. When it was a hired wet nurse, the cost was per feeding, per hour, or per week. In these cash exchanges, the breast-feeding relationship was considered unimportant. Milk became a product to be bought and sold, and not the basis of an intimate relationship. Once one buys the milk, the producer of the milk is reduced in status—her relationship is not a mothering relationship, not a relationship to the child, but a relationship to her product, to her milk. Her value lies in the quality of her milk, not in the quality of her relationship with the child. And so wet nurses were inspected, like animals, for the quality of their product.

Today we are more familiar with the nonbiological services that we hire from mother substitutes. We hire babysitters, day-care workers, nannies, and housekeepers to "watch" our children. The tasks are the traditional tasks of mothering—feeding, tending, caring, the whole bundle of social and psychological and physical tasks involved in the care of young children. When performed by mothers, we call this mothering. When performed by fathers, we have sometimes called it fathering, sometimes parenting, sometimes "helping the mother." When performed by hired hands, we call it unskilled.

We devalue these nurturing tasks when we contract for them. When we do them ourselves because we want to do them, we see them as precious, as special, as treasured moments in life. That is the contradiction that allows us to value our children so highly, to value our special time with them, to speak lovingly of the child's trust, the joys of that small hand placed in ours—and hire someone to take that hand, at minimum wage.

In sum, the ideology of a patriarchal society goes much deeper than male dominance. It means far more than just having men in charge, or men making more decisions than women do. The ideology of patriarchy is a basic world view, and in a patriarchal system that view permeates all of our thinking. In our society, the ideology of patriarchy provides us with an understanding not only of the relations between men and women, but also of the relations between mothers and their children.

In a patriarchal society, men use women to have their children. A man can use this woman or that woman to have his children. He can hire this woman or that woman to substitute for one or another aspect (biological, social, or psychological) of the mothering his child needs. From the view of the man, his seed is irreplaceable; the mothering, the nurturance, is substitutable.

And from the woman's point of view? We can use this man's sperm or that one's to have our children. With this or that man as father, our bellies will swell, life will stir, milk will flow. We may prefer one man's seed to another, just as a man may prefer one woman's nurturance to another for his child, but they are substitutable, they are interchangeable. For a man, what makes the child *his* is his seed. For women, what makes the child ours is the nurturance, the work of our bodies. Wherever the sperm came from, it is in our bodies that our babies grow, and our physical presence and nurturance that make our babies ours.

But is that inevitable? Did not some women substitute other women's bodies when they hired wet nurses? Don't some women substitute other women's arms, other women's touch, when they hire housekeepers and babysitters and day-care workers? And now the new procreative technology lets us cut our seeds loose from our bodies, and plant them in other women's bodies. Now the seed, the egg, of one woman can be brought to term in the body of another.

We have a technology that takes Susan's egg and puts it in Mary's body. And so we ask, *who* is the mother? Who is the surrogate? Is Mary substituting for Susan's body, growing Susan's baby for Susan? Or is Susan's egg substituting for Mary's, growing into Mary's baby in Mary's body? Our answer depends on where we stand when we ask the question. Right now we use that technology two different ways. John is the father, and if he is married to Susan, then

Susan is the mother and Mary is the "surrogate gestator." If John is married to Mary though, then Mary is the mother and Susan is the "egg donor." Who is socially recognized as the mother of the child? The woman married to the father.

But for whom are these substitutes available? Who can afford to hire substitutes for the various parts of mothering? The situation today is exactly what it has been historically: people of privilege, wealthy or fairly wealthy people, are the only ones who can afford these technologies. When people want to buy eggs, the prices vary considerably. Wealthier couples tend to be white and will not use the eggs of women of color, and that itself drives the price up. Tens of thousands of dollars have been offered for the eggs of Ivy League college women. Even the more typical egg donor/seller can get $5,000 to $8,000 for each cycle of egg donation. When people want to hire the services of a "surrogate gestator" on the other hand, using their own eggs and sperm, they come relatively cheap. "Surrogate gestators" earn far less than minimum wage for the nine months and the physical risks involved. But add in the medical and legal costs, and this, like much of one-on-one child care, is a service poor women sell, not buy.

Perhaps this is the ultimate meaning of patriarchy for mothers: seeds are precious; mothers are not.

Motherhood in a Technological Society

ONE DEFINITION OF technology is that it is just a tool—not good and not bad, just a neutral tool that can be used to whatever purpose. The purposes technology can be put to can be good or bad. But the technology itself? It's neutral.

Yet neutrality is not consistent with the other attribute we ascribe to technology: that it is *practical*. Science, we believe, is the acquisition of knowledge for its own sake, somehow "pure," but not really practical. Technology, the application of science, is useful and practical, there's a point to it. But as soon as one concedes that technology is *for* something, then it is no longer neutral. "In fact, no particular technology, construed as a technological object, gadget, process or system, or even as an isolated bit of technological knowledge or know-how can be morally neutral. It was designed or conceived for some purpose, and any such purpose is subject to moral or ethical evaluation."[1]

The simplest way to morally evaluate a technology is to ask what it is that it is in aid of. What's the point? We can look at the technology of motherhood, the old and the new reproductive technologies, the range of baby- and child-care technology, the objects, gadgets, processes, systems, and know-how—and try to figure out what it is they are *for*. I picture myself sorting through a heap of stuff—a rubber nipple, a baby mobile, a playpen, an IUD, a freezer chest of sperm, teach-your-baby-to-read flash cards, forceps, belly-button binders, Pampers, nursing bras, a case of Similac, a pile of sonographs—holding each one up and trying to figure out what it really and truly is *for*. That alone would be an enlightening experience. Take a simple Pamper—what *is* that thing for? To protect the baby? From what? And then why is the plastic on the outside? To protect the baby's clothes? To keep the dirt inside the baby package? Think of hours and hours of sorting—it is a rainy day as I write this and I picture myself on such a rainy afternoon in the world's attic—and trying to get to the root of it all, the point of it.

Like motherhood, technology is not just the tools and the know-how. It is more than the sum of its parts. When I make an "anti-technology" argument, it's not Velcro I'm complaining about, not this or that innocuous invention, not the typewriter or pen—both technological objects—with which I am writing that I'm objecting to. The ideology of technological society is more than this package of tools, gimmicks, know-how. It is a way of thinking about the world in mechanical, industrial terms.

Technological ideology grew as the industrial revolution profoundly changed not just the things we could make, but the way we think about ourselves and the world. One important clue to this ideology and how it influences our thought is the use of mechanical/industrial metaphors for *everything*: female "plumbing"; bureaucratic systems as "well-oiled machines"; an organization working like "clockwork"; people "programmed" to think in a certain way; intricate plots as "wheels within wheels." With changing times the prototypes for the machines change, and along with it our fears and fantasies: from the runaway conveyor belt of a Charlie Chaplin film to "HAL" taking over in *2001*.

Machinery, from the cotton gin to the pocket calculator, is an organized system for doing something. Whether it is the clackety-clack of a factory machine, or the faint hum of a user-friendly computer translating between English and "machine language," machines are there for a purpose, for a function, to be productive. As we think of ourselves, our bodies and our social organizations, as machinery, we think less about what we are, and more about what we are for, what we can make. We have a long philosophical tradition of distinguishing making from doing, material reality from doing or action. Aristotle distinguished making (*poiesis*) from doing (*praxis*) to focus attention on doing, the more valued. "We *make* ships, houses, statues or money; we *do* sports, politics or philosophy. The end of making is an object different from its act; the end of doing is the act itself. Life is a kind of doing" and "the fundamental question for man concerns what kind of doing or action is most properly human."[2] Aristotle concluded that that which is most proper to man (and he meant *man*) is the doing of philosophy, the free or detached contemplation of nature.

Aristotle's conclusion, the conclusion of antiquity, is not the modern conclusion. My pragmatic, career-oriented college students dismiss philosophy as "contemplating your navel." Making has far surpassed doing as the yardstick for evaluating our lives, ourselves, our society, our "worth." We value

what we "make of ourselves," value people who "make sor
selves." The world and all that is in it, including our own l
become potential resources, something to make something
bodies, sharpen our wits, and work on our relationships.

If things—even things like *us* and each other—are not valued in and of themselves, then where do we root our values? Caroline Whitbeck says:

> To regard everything, even ourselves, as a potential resource, is to implicitly regard all possible goals or ends as on a par. As a result, efficiency—that is, the efficient use of resources in the pursuit of goals—is implicitly taken as the overarching value. The determination of goals or ends appears as a matter of personal taste.[3]

Whitbeck would rather not call that an ideology of technology, but rather an economic ideology. She claims that is less confusing both because "technological innovations may be motivated by attitudes of reverence for nature and for life, and because the tendency to view everything as a potential resource is often carried to extremes in matters that have no connection with technology." The first argument is the "neutral-tool" argument—the products of technology, when they are good, can be very, very good. Shaker women, Whitbeck reminded me, invented the cut nail and the circular saw—have I got a problem with that? Am I about to object to Gutenberg's type? And would I give up my contact lenses? But it is not the *tools* I am talking about.

Whitbeck's second argument is really the more interesting, and the more telling. We do indeed come to see everything as a potential resource: the ideology influences our thinking even where it is not appropriate. And *that* is how we know that technology is an ideology, part of the hegemony, the total way of viewing the world, and not just a box of tools, an attic full of gadgets and how-to pamphlets. Whitbeck gives as an example of viewing *everything* as a potential resource, even in matters that have no connection with technology, the U.S. Court of Appeals judge, Richard Posner, who advocates eliminating inefficient adoption agencies and legalizing the sale of babies.[4] What is there in our way of viewing the world, in our values, ideas, beliefs, and culture, that enables us to think of a baby as a commodity? Even if we reject it, it was a "thinkable" thought: we know what he means. Is it because we have come to think of a baby as the product of our making, our bodies as the resources of which babies are made?

Whether "technology" is the best word or not, there is surely a long history of philosophical and social thought on what this industrial/technological, perhaps "economic," world view means. If we think of ourselves and our society as machines, then surely we aim to be well-oiled, efficient machines. The ideology of technology has as its consistent theme a connotation of order, productivity, rationality, and control. In my use of the term "technology" as a name for an ideology, I draw upon the work of Talcott Parsons, Paul Tillich, Elliot Krause, John Kenneth Galbraith, Jacques Ellul, Charles Anderson, Herbert Marcuse, Jürgen Habermas, and more. Some are more critical, some less. Anderson, for example, makes the "neutral-tool" argument, referring to the technological process of rationalizing, dividing, reducing, systematizing, and controlling, and saying that the process may be used for good or for evil.[5] Galbraith defines technology as the systematic application of scientific or other organized knowledge to practical tasks, with its most important characteristic the division and subdivision of tasks into component parts, thus allowing organized knowledge to be applied to performance.[6] Parsons focuses on efficiency and rationality as the key characteristics of technology.[7]

The critics of the technological ideology say it has gone too far, meaning that *people* are caught up in the technological embrace, used for technological ends. Like poor Charlie Chaplin, we get caught in the machinery. Krause calls this way of thinking an "industrial mentality," necessary for the processing of people as if they were so many widgets,[8] culminating in the dehumanizing power of technology, the ultimate mechanical self-image, the person viewing self as a machine, the person becoming in technological society "a thing among other things."[9]

What does this mean for motherhood? The social criticisms of technology are not concerned with the tools and know-how part of it, but with the larger issue that in technological society machinery serves as the prototype for organizing life. If the fundamental characteristic of technological society is the rational pursuit of efficiency (getting all the bugs out) then what is characteristic of motherhood in such a society? If experience becomes the value, then what is the value of mothering? For Ellul, an important critic of technological society, this value system is most distressing when applied to the "human techniques," such as medicine and education: "techniques appropriate to the arts of construction have been expanded, by way of an enlargement of the concept of efficiency, to the arts of cultivation. In the technological society, doing is planned and designed in the same manner as making."[10] As distressing as it is for education and medicine to be remade in the interests of efficiency, what does it mean for motherhood? How does a mother view her child as a thing among things, herself as an efficient maker of this thing, this product of her labor?

In technological society we apply ideas about machines to people, asking them, too, to be more efficient, productive, rational, and controlled. We treat our bodies as machines, hooking them up to other machines, monitoring and managing bodily functions. When a doctor manages a woman's labor, controlling her body with drugs and even surgery, it is to make her labor more efficient, predictable, rational. And so it is when mothers and fathers push their babies onto a schedule, so that feeding the baby meshes into the nine-to-five day. Books like *Toilet Training in One Day* show us how to "train" our children efficiently. When we think of parenting, or raising our children, of our *relationships* with our children as a job to be done well, we are invoking the ideology of technology.

To do these tasks efficiently, we divide them up into their component parts, organize them, systematize them, rationalize, *budget* our time, *order* our day, *program* our lives. All of this rationalizing, reducing, dividing, systematizing, organizing, all in the name of efficiency, does harm to the human spirit. It may or may not be the best way of "making" things—but not everything is best viewed as "made," not even everything best viewed as a "thing." It may or may not be the best way of utilizing resources—but not everything is best viewed as a resource.

There are apparent dangers in the inappropriate—no, make that *morally* wrong—applications of technological thinking, but the hegemony is maintained anyway. Marcuse argued that technology, a tool in the hands of the ruling class, helps guarantee the enslavement of the masses by its totally alienating rational objectivity. Marcuse's insight was to focus on reason/rationality as itself the culprit: "Technological control appears to be the very embodiment of Reason for the benefit of all social groups and interests—contradiction seems irrational and all counteraction impossible."[11] How very often mothers have been accused of being "irrational" or "unreasonable" in the depth of their feelings about their children and their motherhood: their feelings of love, anger, pride, joy, grief, all too often dismissed as either "hysterical" or, more patronizingly, "sentimental."

Maybe we should not use the word "technology" for this system of domination—maybe it does make people think we are throwing out the baby with the bathwater, rejecting the "techniques," the tools. Of course there are wonderful, life-affirming techniques, ways of doing things. But the critique of technological society is not an indiscriminate throwing away of the tools. It is an objection to the notion of the world as a machine, the body as a machine, everything subject to hierarchical control, the world, ourselves, our bodies and our souls, ourselves and our children, divided, systematized, reduced. And all to what end? Controlled for what purpose? For whose purposes?

The Mechanical Mother

My focus in the next few pages is going to be on the physical part of motherhood, because people often think that biology is beyond culture, beyond ideology. The "mechanism" of contraception, the "mechanics" of labor, the "programming" of genetic development—these things are often seen as simple biological givens with which we must cope. But remember, that is the nature of ideology: the constructs look like common sense, the ideas are obvious, the descriptions are simply how things are, "naturally."

In our society, when we look at what we know, what our taken-for-granted reality is about physical motherhood, we are looking at medical ideology, a particular type of mechanical thinking, of technological ideology.[12] Medical ideology is deeply rooted in the mind-body dualism expressed by Descartes: the body is a machine, the structure and operation of which falls within the province of human knowledge, as distinguished from the mind. The way I first saw this was:

> The Cartesian model of the body as a machine operates to make the physician a technician, or mechanic. The body breaks down and needs repair; it can be repaired in the hospital as a car is in the shop; once "fixed," a person can be returned to the community. The earliest models in medicine were largely mechanical; later models worked more with chemistry, and newer, more sophisticated medical writing describes computer-like programming, but the basic point remains the same. Problems in the body are technical problems requiring technical solutions, whether it is a mechanical repair, a chemical rebalancing, or a "debugging" of the system."[13]

Emily Martin has since pointed out that while doctors may once have been lowly mechanics, their status has certainly risen. Looking specifically at childbirth, she says the metaphors of industrialization and technology now work more like this:

> Medical imagery juxtaposes two pictures: the uterus as a machine that produces the baby, and the woman as laborer who produces the baby. Perhaps at times the two come together in a consistent form as the woman-laborer whose uterus-machine produces the baby. What role is the doctor given? I think it is clear that he is predominantly seen as the supervisor or foreman of the labor process.[14]

Martin shows how the image of childbirth as production and women's bodies as factories for the making of babies is there in the way that menstruation and menopause are described as well. In her review of medical and college textbooks on menstruation, she found repeated use of negative language; words like *degeneration*, *decline*, *withdrawn*, *weakened*, *deteriorate*, *disintegrate*, *debris*, and finally, *repair*. *A Textbook of Medical Physiology* reports that "the cause of menopause is the 'burning out' of the ovaries."[15] The hierarchically organized, factory-like body fails with each menstrual period to produce a baby, as the lining weakens, disintegrates, degenerates, and produces debris. With menopause comes the ultimate failure and breakdown of a system of authority, complete burnout. But must menstruation be viewed as failure to produce? Is it just straight logic to see the menstrual period as a waste product following the failure of production?

Here is where Martin shows us that it is not just the ideology of technology that influences the view of women's bodies, but also the ideology of patriarchy. For there are other circumstances in which the body produces a lining it continually sloughs off and replenishes: the lining of the stomach must also be constantly replaced. In describing that, however, the medical texts stress something very different: rather than using images of breakdown and repair when discussing stomachs—which both men and women have—the images presented are of continual production and replenishment.[16] The ideology of technology informs us that all bodies are machines; the ideology of patriarchy says that men's bodies are better machines.

Consider the way spermatogenesis is described, with glowing words about the "remarkable" transformation to mature sperm, the "amazing" character of the process, and its "sheer magnitude" as the normal male manufactures hundreds of millions of sperm a day:

> It is surely no accident that this "remarkable" process involves precisely what menstruation does not in the medical view: the production of something deemed valuable. Although this text sees such massive sperm production as unabashedly positive, in fact only about one out of every 100 billion sperm ever makes it to fertilize an egg: from the very same point of view that sees menstruation as a waste product, surely here is something really worth crying about.[17]

What does it all mean for the woman, conceptualized as a machine, a container, holding the precious sperm? What is it like to be the laborer in such a factory? Sheila Kitzinger, the extraordinary childbirth educator, says:

> Grateful as most women are for all this care and awed by the advanced technology, it is not difficult to understand how a woman can feel that she is merely a container for a fetus, the development and safe delivery of which is under the control of obstetric personnel and machinery, and that her body is an inconvenient barrier to easy

> access and the probing of all those rubber gloved fingers and the gleaming equipment, and even—ridiculous, but we are talking about *feelings*—that if she were not around the pregnancy could progress with more efficiency.[18]

When we look at what happens as a result of the combined ideology of technology and patriarchy, we find a depersonalized mother-machine[19] being manipulated to efficiently produce babies out of valued sperm.

Technological Society and Liberal Philosophy

It is not only the body that we treat as a machine, as mechanical, but the social order as well. Rather than seeing society as an organic, deeply interconnected whole, technological ideology encourages us to see society as a collection of parts. Liberal philosophy, the intellectual underpinning of the American Revolution and of American government, is the articulation of the technological ideology in the social order.

Carolyn Merchant's work *The Death of Nature* traces the development of a mechanical order in Western society to replace the organicism of earlier times. Whereas in the time of the Renaissance the earth was perceived as "alive and considered to be a beneficent, receptive, nurturing female,"[20] by the seventeenth century the world view had changed, and the machine became the metaphor. "As the unifying model for science and society, the machine has permeated and reconstructed human consciousness so totally that today we scarcely question its validity. Nature, society, and the human body are composed of interchangeable atomized parts that can be repaired or replaced from the outside." This "removal of animistic, organic assumptions about the cosmos constituted the death of nature—the most far reaching effect of the scientific revolution."[21]

The rise of mechanism, as Merchant calls what I think of as technological ideology, laid the foundation for a new social order, as the relationship between mind and body, person and society was reevaluated. "A new concept of the self as a rational master of the passions housed in a machine-like body began to replace the concept of the self as an integral part of a close-knit harmony of organic parts united to the cosmos and society."[22]

The difficulty in reconciling the image of people as "atomized parts" with our very real desire for community, for interconnectedness between people, remains one of the ongoing problems of liberal society. This was addressed in *Habits of the Heart*, a book about the conflicts American society has structured between individualism and commitment. The authors describe modernity as a "culture of separation,"[23] America as a world in which "it became clear that every social obligation was vulnerable, every tie between individuals fragile."[24]

As individuals, separation and compartmentalization form a central theme in the lives we lead. We "change hats," "shift gears" as we move from one mechanical social order to another. We carry these separate selves around, experiencing not only the compartmentalization between people, but *within* ourselves as well. We have "work lives" and "home lives." We change clothing in our different roles, we change style, we change tone.

And against this, we have motherhood, the physical embodiment of connectedness. We have in every pregnant woman the living proof that individuals do not enter the world as autonomous, atomistic, isolated beings, but begin socially, begin connected. And we have in every pregnant woman a walking contradiction to the segmentation of our lives: pregnancy does not permit it. In pregnancy the private self, the sexual, familial self, announces itself wherever we go. Motherhood is the embodied challenge to liberal philosophy, and that, I fear, is why a society founded on and committed to liberal philosophical principles cannot deal well with motherhood.

In what follows, I will consider the particular problems that liberal philosophy creates for mothering, the ways that liberal policy works against the interests of mothers. I begin with the implications of this view of the "rational mind" housed in a "machine-like body."

When the authors of the American Constitution declared "All men are created equal," they were drawing on this philosophical tradition of the Enlightenment. What made that statement reasonable was that the equality they spoke of was of the mind, of the rational being. Certainly some men were weak and some strong, some rich and some poor—but all share the human *essence*, the rational mind. The extension of such "equality" to blacks and to women is based on the claim that these groups, too, share the essence of humanity, the rational mind—housed, in the "accident of birth," in the body of the black, the body of the woman. And it is that same belief that underlies the endless stream of movies and stories about the computer or robot, the machine, that learns to think and to feel, and so becomes essentially human—and ultimately tragic.

If we believe, then, as this liberal philosophic tradition holds, that what is especially valuable about human beings is the capacity for rationality, then the ordering, rationalizing, and purposeful efficiency of technology will be seen as good. But hand in hand with the valuing of rationality is a "theoretical disdain for the significance of the body," and a disdain for physical work in preference for "mental" work. The latter, dividing the physical from the mental work, and then using machines and people interchangeably to do the menial physical work, is the essence of technological organization.

In American society, "blue-collar work" is less valued than is managerial work. The "white collar" is a status symbol for having risen above the work of the body. The repair people who work on office copiers come in dressed as managers—white shirt and jacket, carrying a briefcase. To do the work, the briefcase unfolds to a tool bag, and the white shirt-sleeves get rolled up. But dressing in washable work clothes and carrying a tool bag, however much more practical, would be relatively demeaning. Physical labor, the work of the hands and the bodies, is of low prestige.

This division of labor is a particular problem for women as mothers: mothers *do* the physical work of the body, we *do* the "menial" work of body maintenance. Thus women become identified with the physical, the body, and men with the higher, the rational. The distinction between menial physical labor and highly valued rationality goes a long way toward explaining the utter disdain with which a laboring woman may be strapped down and ignored or even insulted, while the doctor who "manages" her labor—reading her chart and ordering others to carry out his decisions—is held in such high esteem. Or similarly, why the woman who produces perfect nourishment from her body is seen as cowlike, animalistic in a negative way, while the pediatrician who "prescribes" a "formula" deserves such respect—and high pay.

The mind-body dualism has consequences at the macro level as well: viewing the body as a machine encourages us to see it as a resource to be used. If the mind and rationality are held as "above" the body, it becomes relatively easy to see the body as a resource for the use of the mind, and specifically, women's reproductive bodies as "societal" resources. So if the factories or the armies need fodder, women's bodies are the resources from which the young are produced. And if there are too many mouths to feed, then the bodies are to be idle, like factories closed until inventories are reduced.

And here we have the ubiquitous problem of reconciling individual freedom and social order. In China, an increasingly technological society without the liberal tradition, the solution is simple: the needs of the society determine the rights of the individual, and the "one-child" policy is enacted. In the United States, such a policy would not be tolerated. And yet the birth rate does fluctuate with social need. In all kinds of ways people do what society needs them to do, and do it seemingly out of choice. What can we make of the choices of women to be used by the social order?

Because of their respect for the individual judgment of rational people, in principle "liberals are committed to the belief that individuals are fulfilled when they are doing what they have decided freely to do, however unpleasant, degrading or wrong this may appear to someone else."[25] The hook here is the notion of *freely chosen*. Thus, "informed consent" becomes a crucial American legal concept: if one consents or agrees to something *rationally*, then one accepts the consequences. But liberal thinking with its emphasis on rationality does not seem equipped to understand the more subtle forms of coercion and persuasion, whether psychological or economic, so the "choices" people make out of their poverty or need, choices individuals may experience as being coerced, liberals tend to see as being freely chosen. To take a simple example: advertising campaigns that are shown to be highly effective in getting a targeted population to start smoking, such as those campaigns aimed at young women, are legal—as long as the ads include the information that cigarette smoking may be hazardous to your health.

The liberal position on prostitution is an even better example of how these ideas about mind-body dualism and individual choice come together:

> Liberals do not conceive one's body to be an essential part of oneself, so there seems to be no reason why one's sexual services may not just as well be sold as one's other abilities. Indeed, the propriety of selling one's intellectual capacities might be more problematic, on liberal grounds, than the sale of one's sexual services.[26]

The liberal vision of a better world does not inherently preclude people experiencing their bodies as salable commodities.

The extension is easily made from sexual prostitution to what some call "reproductive prostitution," the hiring of "surrogate" mothers. Here is what John Robertson, a liberal legal scholar, has to say about that:

> Baby selling laws prohibit fees for adoption in order to protect the child from unfit parents and the mother from exploitation and coercion. But these concerns do not apply to surrogate gestators who freely choose this reproductive role before pregnancy occurs, uninfluenced by the stigma of illegitimacy or the financial burdens of single parenthood. An acceptable system of paid surrogacy must assure that the surrogate is fully informed, has independent legal counsel, and has made a deliberative choice. There is also a fear that surrogates will be drawn primarily from poorer groups, who will serve the rich with their bodies as well as their housekeeping and childrearing services. Indeed, money is likely to be a prime motive in the decisions of women to serve as surrogates, but other factors are reported to play a role. It is not apparent that only poor women will select that occupation, much less that the operation of a labor market in this area is more unjust than labor markets in other areas.[27]

Surrogacy is then an "occupation" and a "reproductive role," freely chosen. The only protections needed are to make sure that the surrogate is operating "rationally"—informed, with counsel, making a deliberative choice. The patent absurdity of claiming fairness because wealthy, well-educated women have the same rights to be surrogates and poor women have the rights, although not at all the means, to hire surrogates slides by.

In sum, liberal philosophy is an articulation of the values of technological society, with its basic themes of order, predictability, rationality, control, rationalization of life, the systematizing and control of things and people as things, the reduction of all to component parts, and ultimately the vision of everything, including our very selves, as resources.

As Whitbeck said, efficiency becomes the overarching value, and the determination of goals or ends appears as a matter of personal taste. So if a woman wants her body to be used, if she chooses to use her body as a means to an end, so long as she does so rationally, fine. If babies are products and mothers are workers selling their resources, then that is their choice. Whether mothers sell those resources explicitly to purchasing, contracting couples in surrogacy arrangements, or implicitly to their husbands or to the state—these are all personal decisions women make about their goals. As long as she is acting rationally (and what could be more rational than having a lawyer and a contract?) in her means, her goals are beyond analysis, and her personal and private choices are just a matter of personal taste.

And so we come back to questions of rationality, of order and reason, ideology and hegemony. Marcuse is right: "Rationality" has become the culprit. Technological control, dividing motherhood into parts, organizing and systematizing intimate relations, separating out menial physical labor from higher, rational, contractual intent—all of this becomes the very embodiment of reason for the benefit of all.

All that remains to be done is to affix the price tags.

Motherhood under Capitalism

The ideology of technology dehumanizes people by encouraging a mechanical self image—people viewing themselves as machines. Capitalism adds that not only is the body a collection of parts, its parts become commodities. In the United States the essential fluids of life—blood, milk, and semen—are all for sale.[1]

THAT IS MY basic starting point in understanding the meaning of capitalism as it exists in the United States: there is a price tag on everything. This chapter will explore what the experience of motherhood comes to mean when prices are affixed.

From the standpoint of the ideology of technology, we have seen that motherhood is perceived as work, and children as a product produced by the labor of mothering. Mothers' work and mothers' bodies are resources out of which babies are made. From the standpoint of the ideology of patriarchy, it is men's babies that are being made. From the standpoint of the market, not all work is equally valuable, and not all products are equally valued. There is not a direct relationship between the value of the worker and the value of the product. What is essential to capitalism is the accumulation and investment of capital, of wealth, by people who are in a position to control others. Under capitalism, workers do not own or control the products of their own labor.

Babies, at least healthy white babies, are very precious products these days. Mothers, rather like South African diamond miners, are cheap, expendable, not-too-trustworthy labor necessary to produce the precious product.[2]

This is where it is all heading: the commodification of children and the proletarianization of motherhood.

This is the end result of the evolution of these three ideological perspectives. This is what ties together the new technology and the old technology, the legal, the medical, the political, and the psychological recreation of motherhood.

We are no longer talking about mothers and babies at all—we are talking about laborers and their products.

Capitalism alone is not responsible for the deep trouble motherhood is in, but it is a very important part of it. Societies that have resisted the commodification of life tend to look at the situation in the United States as a kind of warning. Responding to work of mine on new procreative technology, Margaret Stacey called it a warning that should be well heeded, lest the United Kingdom go the way of the United States: "Although the UK, like the US, is predominantly a capitalist society, we have hitherto consistently sought to prevent the intrusion of capitalist values into our health and welfare services. In the UK, issues associated with health and reproduction are less blatantly exploited for profit than in the US."[3]

Exploitation, profit, and motherhood: an unseemly combination. How do capitalism and market values fit into the re-creation of motherhood?

While there is much disagreement about the relation between patriarchy and technology on the one hand, and patriarchy and capitalism on the other hand, clearly capitalism and technology are intertwined ideologies. One can envision a technological society without capitalism—though many would claim that the technological societies which claim to be socialist really practice state capitalism. But it is possible to envision people as cogs in a wheel, without the wheel turned to profit. It is harder to picture full-blown capitalism without the technological ideology.

But my goal here is not to answer chicken-and-egg questions about the relationship between these three ideologies. Rather, I am going to take this ideology as a given right now—in America we do live in a society in which capitalism is an economic system and a guiding principle, shaping the way we see life. Ideas such as supply and demand, cost-benefit analysis, and profit permeate our lives. We think of the profit motive as if it were a basic human desire, greed as if it were part of "human nature." It is the nature of capitalism to raise the motive for making money and owning goods above all else: that is not an inevitable part of the human spirit, but very much a part of American life.

This chapter will focus on one essential aspect of the capitalist ideology, the extension of ownership or property relations in ways that are at best inappropriate, and too often morally wrong. There is a great deal of modern social criticism that makes exactly that claim, including, for example, the ecologists.

They argue that it is inappropriate to think we can own the land, the waters: the earth, they claim—significantly—is our *mother*, not our property.

But what happens when we start thinking of motherhood itself in terms of property? As wrong as it is to think of the human relation to the earth this way, it is worse when we start thinking about our relations with each other in the language of property.

The actual word *property* gets used relatively infrequently in discussions of human relations. More often the key term is *rights*. "A right can be interpreted as an entitlement to do or have something, to exclude others from doing or having something or as an enforceable claim."[4] There are two directions in which property rights have extended that are directly relevant to motherhood: rights of ownership of one's own body, and rights to one's own child.

The way an ideology works is to force our attention in certain ways, to give us a point of view, a perspective—often expressed in language as metaphor. People do not necessarily talk of or even actively think of their bodies or their children as *property* in the sense of real estate. But what Janet Farrell Smith says of parenthood can be said equally of bodily ownership:

> In applying a property model to parenting, it is important to remember that a parent may not literally assert that a child is a piece of property, but may work on assumptions analogous to those which one makes in connection with property.[5]

Women are not just passive victims of capitalist ideology: we *use* it in our interests as well. Women, like men, lay claim to their own bodies and to their own children, and call on the basic values of capitalism to support those claims. As I shall discuss in the next section, feminists have been able, in some sense, to capitalize on the value of ownership to gain certain rights for women, particularly what are called "reproductive rights." But there have been attendant costs, with regard both to the owned body and to the owned child.

The Owned Body

Within a capitalist system we cannot legally force or forcibly prevent people from doing something with their own property without very compelling reasons. The right to own, and therefore to control, property is among the most valued of rights.

In technological society, I have argued, the body is treated as a thing and as a resource. In capitalist society, where the emphasis is on private ownership, the body is viewed not as a resource for the community or the society, but as private property, a personal resource. Rights of privacy are in a sense just a variation on other rights of ownership, of private control.

Given the view of the body as owned property, the extension of ownership to all of our body parts allows women some measure of control over the use of our bodies in procreation. If women are full persons, then we are moved out of the category of owned property, and into the category of owners of our own bodies. Men can no longer entirely legally barter in women's bodies.

Feminists have made use of this concept of bodily ownership to make American society recognize that, just as we cannot force a woman to have some particular surgery, we cannot force her to have an abortion—even if either one, the abortion or the surgery—would save her life, or save the state much money or save other people much difficulty. And we have as a society also concluded that we cannot stop her from having an abortion, just as we cannot stop her from having, say, her gallbladder removed, even if we think it is unnecessary surgery, bad for her, or risks a loss to the society or to her family and friends. It is, after all, her body.

But while ownership is a useful legal analogy for one's relationship with one's "own" body, it is certainly far from the essential experience of being embodied people.

Often we do not feel as if we own our bodies. If we view them in ownership terms at all, it may be as rented space. John Quincy Adams said, shortly before his death: "I inhabit a weak, frail, decayed tenement; battered by the winds and broken in upon by the storms, and, from all I can learn, the landlord does not intend to repair."[6]

Sometimes we feel as if we *are* our bodies: intense physical sensation or effort can have that effect. In pain, sex, and athletics one can sometimes achieve—and some people strive for—a true unity of mind and body. But such intensity of physical experience can also make a person feel as if there is a distinct inner self, the owner of the outer body, "distanced" from physical sensation. And people can strive for that experience too, to step outside the body, to "rise above" the body. The experience of bodily change over the life course can also distance us from our bodies—is this middle-aged woman really me? Or am I in here somewhere, looking at a weathered hand working a pen across a page? It is a hand I control, I own, a hand that is *mine*, but surely not *me*—not the *me* that played with clay, that learned to hold a crayon. And sometimes—with terror or with humor or both—we experience the body as inhabited *without* any of the control of ownership. The loss of strength or agility with age or illness can make a person feel trapped inside the body.

That last, Adams's view, is close to an essentially religious view that our bodies are ours to use for a while, but that our bodies, and our souls, come from a god-force and do not belong to us. That perspective does not give the individual infinite control over his or her body, since the body is not the person's but God's property, and God sets the rules of tenancy. We speak of tenancy but we know we have no coin with which to pay our rent but our own subservience.

There is another way of seeing the body as not "ours" to own, but as not coming from God. That is to see the body—and perhaps the mind and soul as well—as part of something much larger: the stream of life, the gene pool, the evolutionary chain, the fatherland or motherland, the family.

In American society we may be able to talk about and think about the body in all of these ways, but legal recognition goes only to the view of the body as individually owned. That is an idea deeply rooted in our liberal political system and our capitalist economic system. And it is not a bad way of *legally* viewing the body. Every time a society removes individual ownership of the body, it opens the way to state control. So viewing the body as property, privately and individually owned, protects each of us from all of us, protects us as individuals from the power of the state.

Given the present economic and political system it would be dangerous to argue against this view of the body as privately, individually owned, legally expressed as a right to privacy. "Privacy, as it is connected with a model of property relations, is not only an ability to deny others access to certain aspects of one's life, but also a right of entitlement to exclude others."[7] Other views of the body, even if more satisfying ethically or spiritually, are dangerous politically. As Janet Farrell Smith points out:

> Since some of these rights (to form a family, to decide whether or not to have children and to raise those children) are now established in U.S. constitutional law on a basis of the right to privacy, it would be a strategic mistake to extract that basis from procreative choice.[8]

Within the American system, intelligent feminist use of the individualist ethos has been invaluable in assuring women's rights in procreation. Once women themselves are recognized as full citizens, then individual women must be accorded the same rights of bodily autonomy and integrity that men have. For women, that means sexual and procreative autonomy. Because it is her body, she cannot be raped. Because it is her body, she cannot be forced to bear pregnancies she does not want. Because it is her body, she cannot be forced to abort pregnancies she does want.

This does not mean that women are not forced by circumstance into these very situations and eventualities. It only means that the society will not use the official power of the state to force her. Women are in fact prevented from having abortions they might want by family pressure, by economic circumstances, by religious and by social pressures. And women are forced into having abortions they might not want to have because of poverty, because of lack of services for children and mothers, because of lack of services for disabled children and adults. By offering amniocentesis to identify fetuses who would have disabilities, and by cutting back on services for disabled children and their families, we effectively force women to have selective abortions.

Because of our current battles over the right to abortion, Americans tend to think of the state as "permitting" women to have abortions, as if the drive for continuing pregnancies came from the state, and the drive for abortions from women. In fact, the legal protection works also to permit women not to have abortions. When women's ownership rights over their bodies are lost, the rights to have and the rights *not* to have abortions are likewise lost. Such was the case in Nazi Germany, where some abortions were indeed forced, but it is equally true that women lost the right to have the abortions they themselves chose, the abortions they as individual women felt they needed.

In American society, when we bring it back to the simple legal questions—who can force an abortion or forcibly prevent one—we wisely retreat to safety, calling forth our most sacred value. It's *her* body. We invoke a higher power, the power of ownership.

This then is the way that women have been able to combine dominant American liberal philosophy with capitalist ideology to our benefit. We've made use of the mind-body dualism, to allow a view of the body as owned, like a shelter which houses the more important mind. If one claims rationality for women—the essential liberal claim for all people—then simple fairness gives women the same rights of bodily ownership that men have, and the very high value of ownership, of property rights, is then turned to the advantage of women who can claim exclusive rights to our own bodies. In the name of ownership, women have demanded access to contraception, sterilization, and abortion. And given the prevailing liberal philosophy, we've gotten those rights to control our fertility—although given the capitalist class system, we have fared less well with access to the necessary means.

While the "owned-body" principle has worked for women in avoiding motherhood, it is less clear how it can be made to work to empower women as mothers. Our bodies may be ours, but given the ideology of patriarchy, the bodies of mothers are not highly valued. The bodies are just the space in which genetic material matures into babies. In a patriarchal system, even if women own their bodies, it may not give them any real control in pregnancy. Women may simply be seen to own the space in which the fetuses are housed. This is the argument on which attempts to control women's behavior during pregnancy are based: owning her own body is not enough to assure her civil liberties if her body is believed to contain the property of someone else, somebody else's baby.

Of course, if women's bodies are understood to be the space in which sperm and egg grow to be a baby, and women are understood to be the owners of that space, then the acceptance of "surrogacy" follows logically, almost inevitably. The woman can rent out space in her body just as she can rent out the spare back bedroom. And she will have no more ownership rights over the inhabitants of that space in her body than over the boarder in her home.

The combination of patriarchy and capitalism explains the powerful reluctance to engage in the open sale of babies by their mothers, while permitting surrogacy. The baby is considered precious, even beyond sale, but it is not owned by the mother. The mother's capital is her body; it is her property but it is cheap. In the surrogacy contracts only about a third of the total cost paid by the potential adoptive parents goes to the "surrogate" for her "service." The legal and medical fees take the rest. Those services are of course highly valued, and a few hours of work by an attorney cost more than months of gestation.

Is it possible to make the legal concept of the owned body work in the interests of mothers? We could take advantage of mechanistic thinking, and claim "sweat equity" for women in their babies: they are ours because we have done the work to make them. We would then have made the connection between the owned body and the owned child. But the "sweat equity" idea will work only if women's labor, the "sweat," is valued. And because pregnancy is bodily work, and because it is women's work, it is not likely to be highly valued in American society.

What is valued is the child. In patriarchal ideology, the child is the extension of the man. In capitalist ideology the child is the repository of wealth.

Mothers may not be much valued in America, but children are.

A Child of One's Own

When people talk about becoming parents, about wanting a child, they often use the word *own.* They want a child of their own. They want, it sometimes sounds, to "own" a child. The word *have* gets used in its blurred meanings: they want to "have" a child. They want to have it to *own* it, and they want to have it to, well, to *have* it.

What exactly is it that people want when they want to "have" a baby? I will now explore what it has come to mean to want to have children in a market-oriented society, and how that wanting is experienced and met.

Having a child *is* a lot like owning something. It's more complicated than the sense of possession of a pretty little object, a vase or a painting. Rather, it's like the complicated owning that goes with a house—you own it, but it takes an awful lot of energy, or work. The demands make one sometimes feel more owned than owner.

When a woman gets pregnant easily, readily, she doesn't have to think about what it means to "have" a baby. But when a woman, or a couple, cannot readily have a baby of their own, on their own, they take the complex whole of "having" a child and start sorting it out into the parts they can and the parts they cannot have for themselves.

Some people want the opportunity to be part of a child's life, to help a child or children. They want the good times—the trip to the circus, the help with the science fair project—and they want the bad times, to be there psychologically, physically, financially for a kid who needs them. Some of these people realize that they don't have to "have" a child to be there for a child. Many of us have had the experience of the childless aunt or uncle or family friend, the one who was not all tangled up with his or her own kids, who saw us as real people, who went to bat with our parents for us, who came up with the extra time or energy or money when our parents' supply gave out. Mostly it is people who are not tied up with kids of their "own" who can do that. Sometimes it is people who never had kids, and sometimes it is grandparents and older people whose parenting is, basically, behind them.

Some people, when they say they want to have a baby, are talking about the having of it, the actual act of bearing the baby. That is a life experience a woman may very well want, and more than once, for herself. When we offer such a woman adoption as an alternative, it does not meet all of her needs. An adoptive mother may feel exactly in every way the same about her child as does a mother who gave birth to her daughter or son. But she may feel differently about herself, about her body. "Having" a baby is something a woman may want for herself, for her own experience, independent of her relationship with her child or children. When I think about that personally, I know that the depth, the intensity, the quality of my feelings toward my child by adoption are no different than my feelings toward my children by birth, but I am sure that I relate differently to my own bodily experience than I would have had I never been pregnant and never given birth. And while it is not my own experience, I can imagine that a man may well want that experience of pregnancy as well—he may want the experience for himself of a pregnant wife, a pregnant lover, of feeling the baby move against him through her.

For some people that physical experience of bearing a baby matters, and for some it doesn't much matter, and for some it matters, but negatively—

that's the part of "having" a baby they'd prefer to avoid. I've talked to men who are just starry-eyed over their wives' pregnancies, who want home births and the most intimate physical connection with the entire pregnancy and birth experience. And I've talked to men who have resented every moment of the demands of the pregnancy and the birth on their wives. And it is just as true of women—I've talked to women who fantasize about going through pregnancies and births and suckling again and again, just for the sheer joy of it. And to women who feel revulsion at the thought of it all.

The genetic tie is another part of having a baby, a baby of one's "own." Part of having a baby is reproducing part of oneself. Whatever it is that is genetic in who or what we are, part of that part gets passed on to our children. For myself, I feel that it's just the physical body that gets passed on—the shape of a nose, body build, tendency toward diabetes, a bad back, strong legs. Other people feel that it is also intelligence, wit, sometimes even "character." But whatever it is, some of us want very much to reproduce parts of ourselves in this world.

Being involved in a child's life, physically experiencing pregnancy, having a genetic tie, a feeling of "owning" a baby—all of these are aspects of the experience, but they are not all of the aspects of what people mean when they say they want to "have" children.

In a capitalist system, when people want to have something, they become a "market" for it. When people want something simple, the path of success is to find a cheaper way of producing more of that thing. If people want, say, coffee, one could just grow more coffee cheaper. But one can also start thinking about what it is about coffee that people like and don't like, want and don't want, and start marketing different products to meet the coffee need: decaf, instant, coffee substitutes like chicory, herb teas, and instant broth, caffeine tablets.

And so it is with babies. Since there are a lot of things people want when they want to "have" a child, there are a lot of ways of marketing parenthood. Just looking at these few meanings of "having" a child, we can see the potential and the actuality of a range of marketing strategies.

When people want a child to help, to take care of, to be involved with rather than to "have," it doesn't lend itself to commercial exploitation, but it certainly does open up nonprofit "marketing." Donations to many good causes rely on pictures of children. Physically disabled and mentally retarded adults are probably more needy as individuals than are children with the same problems—after all, the children most often have parents tending to them, advocating for them, buying for them. But it is poster children, retarded children, children on crutches that we are shown when asked to help people with disabilities. Grown-ups starve in families too, but oh, those children's eyes and swollen bellies just tear us up. We give. Arthritis is not just an old people's disease, the arthritis foundations tell us—so we give. Villages in underdeveloped nations need fresh water supplies, so we "adopt" a child and mail off our $16 a month to save the children. These are all good things to do, but it is easier to get people to do them when the pitch is helping children. And so it is a kind of marketing that goes on. Some say it is an exploitation of children to use their sad faces, their large eyes, their skinny braced limbs to make us give.

When people want a more direct relationship with children, more than just sending money, another kind of nonprofit marketing steps in. "Big Brother" and "Big Sister" and "Foster Grandparent" programs all address the needs of people who want to relate to a child in a real and direct way. Foster parenting does the same, with more of the demands of the full parenting experience.

All of these ways of giving—of money and of ourselves—address part of what it is people want when they want to have children in their lives.

When people want children to "have," children of their "own," then the potential for more directly commercial marketing takes over. The current push in reproductive technology can be seen as ways of segmenting this market into different parts of "having" a child, and addressing these various needs.

When it is the pregnancy experience that people want, and then all the parenting that follows, the focus is on creating a pregnancy and allowing parenting to follow from that. Most of infertility research has been directed at exactly this: how to get the woman pregnant. If the problem was her blocked tubes, unblock them or—with in vitro fertilization—bypass them. If the problem was his sperm, fix whatever caused the problem, replace the sperm with artificial insemination, or use fertilization techniques—in vitro fertilization again—that require fewer viable sperm. The treatment is a success if the woman is pregnant and going to "have" a baby.

Treatments for infertility that promise to do this have been very successfully marketed. Sadly, the marketing success far exceeds the pregnancy successes. By the late 1980s we had seen an incredible expansion of in vitro clinics, most of which had never produced a baby, and a top success rate hovering around 10 to 15 percent. More than a decade later, the success rate is still only 22.9 percent according to the American Society for Reproductive Medicine, which represents the doctors and clinics who provide IVF. The felt desperation of infertile couples has been used to sell a high-risk, high-cost, low-success treatment.

Achieving a pregnancy is not always the answer for people who want to "have" a baby—even for those who very much want the pregnancy experience, the technological fix may not work. And for others, the pregnancy is not the issue. When the need is to "have" a child to parent, then the focus is on getting a baby. I sometimes hear infertile people say that quite clearly: "I just want a baby to hold, to love; I just want a baby in my arms." Getting the woman pregnant with all sorts of high-tech, invasive procedures is not the only way for infertile people to "have" a baby. There are nontechnological ways of obtaining babies; they are being produced all over the place. One possibility is to tap into that overproduction and effect some redistribution. Non-market adoption aims to redistribute the babies some people "have" but don't want to "have" to other people who want to "have" babies but cannot "have" them. A little juggling around between the "haves" and the "have-nots" and everybody's happier.

Most of the people in the private adoption sector are not "brokering" babies, but just trying to match up babies with families. When that works, it works well. Non-market adoption started to break down into its current chaos when the demand for healthy white babies—the standard "replacement" baby for the white majority of couples with infertility—far exceeded the supply. When there were more potential adopters than there were babies, we had a "market" with unmet needs. It was inevitable in this society at this time that more traditional marketing strategies would take over. Profiteers sell babies. Some of the profiteers are the mothers themselves, women who have extra babies that they don't want to have, but would like to sell. Some women have gotten pregnant deliberately, just to sell a baby and make a profit.

More commonly, the profits are made by the brokers. Often these are lawyers who make the profit out of their charges for adoption services. Money is changing hands, but no one is technically selling a baby. When the whole project slips right out of the legal sphere, and "black marketing" takes over, babies are simply sold for whatever the market will bear.

In this situation so-called "surrogacy" adoption began. While the commodification of babies, treating them as products, has gone a long way in our society, it probably still feels—and almost certainly felt in the mid-1970s when the first surrogacy contracts were drawn up—inappropriate to simply say that the time has come to put babies up for sale. Such sales would also raise the difficult question of ownership; of who owns a baby in the first place. What the brokers did instead was to say that if a wife cannot carry a pregnancy and have a baby of her own, a man can hire a surrogate to carry a pregnancy. He hires someone to substitute for his wife in bearing the husband's "own" baby.

This strategy sidesteps the laws against selling a baby because, as Noel Keane, the "founder" of surrogacy-for-hire in the United States and the man who brokered the contract between William Stern and Mary Beth Whitehead, says, "You have to look at who the baby is sold to." The contracts are between the man, the sperm donor, and the woman, the mother. How, Keane asks, can a man buy his *own* child? Keane says the woman gives the baby "*back* to the father," as if it came from him in the first place. And so here we have the marketing of patriarchy: the mother just incubates the man's child, for a fee. For Keane, the child is at least as much the father's (the sperm donor) as the mother's because not only is his genetic contribution equal to hers, but it is his by intention, by contract.

When one starts dealing with parenthood in terms of sales and contracts, and most especially broken contracts, questions of ownership loom large. When the "surrogate" changes her mind and wants to keep the child, the question we ask is "Whose child is it?" We talk as if the child were indeed property, as if it belonged to someone.

Most often we get trapped into a discussion of mother's versus father's ownership rights over their children. We talk as if the child were the property of just two people, as if the genetic tie to the parents were the only defining relationship for the child. The child is seen as the product of the sperm and, perhaps reluctantly conceded, the egg, and that defines *who* and *whose* the child is.

But is that how any of us define ourselves—as the product of an egg and a sperm, as the property of the egg and the sperm donors? The children we produce are people, who like us see themselves as individuals in a social context, in relationships, including the very important but not *defining* parental relationship.

The idea of owning children as property is more closely tied to the traditional *rights* of fathers in patriarchy than it is to the ongoing *responsibilities* of raising a child. The need is far more pressing to extend the responsibility ethic than the rights ethic to the care of children in America.[9]

It is not that the view of children as property is totally unrealistic, or inevitably evil and manipulative. Given our great respect for property, there are ways in which, in this society at this time, it works in the interests of children to treat them as property. But the combined forces of capitalism, technology, and patriarchy encourage us to commodify children in some of the least desirable ways.

Part II

Introduction

An Alternative Vision

So far in this book I have tried to show the ways in which American motherhood is being recreated, to show how legal, social, and technological changes are being used to devalue motherhood, to commodify children and parents' relations with children. In Part I, I explored the ideological bases for this construction of motherhood. In Part II, I will look at what is happening in selected, key institutions or areas of concern for motherhood.

My goal is to present an alternative vision. I want to suggest how we as a society might incorporate technological and scientific "advances"—if such they are—and how we might structure social and legal changes in an affirmation of motherhood and the mother-child relationship, and do so in a way that is not at the cost of a woman's personhood.

In the next chapters the influence of the three ideologies will be heard as a chorus, as first one ideology predominates and then another.

Patriarchy has blinded us to the *relationship* that is pregnancy. It is as if looking at pregnancy with men's eyes we see, well—nothing. We see a baby "not here yet," a baby "expected." It is that blindness to the presence of the baby for the woman that allows us to discount the loss of the birth mother who gives a baby up for adoption. As long as she hasn't held it with the *outside* of her body, we say she never held it at all. But it is not the fetus that is denied: the fetus is increasingly seen and valued, while the relationship with the woman in whom it resides is disvalued. And so the fetus becomes a patient, a captive, an "unborn child," needing protection—including protection from its mother. Patriarchal ideology also focuses the discussion of infertility, so that the problem becomes how to get George's baby growing in Martha's body.

In treating male infertility, the woman's body comes to be treated as an extension of her husband's—her body on the table for his infertility.

The influence of the ideology of technology becomes most clear when medicine is on the scene. The technologists step in and humanity becomes a nicety, a luxury. Parts of people are harvested, collected, stored, frozen, rented, purchased. People are hooked to machines and the attention and care go to the machinery. Abortion becomes an assembly line, childbirth no less so. Human, spiritual, social meaning is held aside, while the *real* work goes on. Things that can be quantified are made real; those that cannot be quantified come to seem unreal. Infection rates are an observable measure for childbirth; joy is not. The blood gases of a premature baby in a neonatal intensive-care unit are real, charted, dealt with. The child's pain and anguish are denied. Insanely, doctors have declared that babies do not feel pain. There was no place for that in their calculations. The isolation and desolation of the newborn in an Isolette were denied.

And through it all can be heard the rustling of dollars.

Other themes sound in these chapters as well, minor notes as accent.[1] One is the theme of solutions emerging that are worse than the problems. Technology that started off trying to solve infertility finds itself creating orphans: embryos of dead people are put in deep freeze. The tragedy of a miscarriage or stillbirth is changed to the tragedy of months or even years of agony. Middle-class women declare life has more to offer than diapers and dishes—and poor women get a lifetime of diapers and dishes, without even the recognition of their mothering of "other people's children." Problems are matched up, but not solved: one family's poverty becomes another family's "affordable" child care; one woman's lack of access to contraception or abortion becomes someone else's joyful adoption.

Another recurrent theme is the danger of placing yet more power in the hands of institutions rather than individuals. We face some hard choices. What do we do with pregnant women who use drugs or refuse medical treatments? How much treatment should a sick newborn have? Who is going to set the standards of care for childbirth? When is abortion the right thing to do, and when is it wrong? The temptation is to make law, to create standards, and then to hold people to those standards. Proposed "fetal-abuse" statutes, court-ordered cesarean sections, Baby Doe legislation, all of these are understandable but misguided attempts to deal with our fears. But the lawyers know better than anyone: do not use the law this way. Reproductive-rights attorney Janet Gallagher has said: "I beg you, do not use the law as the solution to your fears."[2] Bioethics consultant and attorney Lawrence J. Nelson echoes the thought: "Do not turn to the law."[3] To use the law for these complicated moral decisions is to lose the nuances, the idiosyncracies, and the individuality that protect us from fundamentally untrustworthy political institutions.

A third theme running through these chapters is the dialectic between ideology and social structure. Out of the beliefs, values, and ideas we create social structure and social institutions. And then those institutions reify our ideology. We believe, for example, that genetic ties are the real ties, the only permanent, irreducible connections. And then we create a world in which those ties are indeed valued, recognized, and attended to—made real socially. Paternity based on a single sexual encounter stands on the same legal ground as the paternity of a loving husband and father, a man committed for the long haul. And that recognition of a man's genetic tie at the same time undercuts the recognition and support of his social, emotional, and nurturing ties. *Paternity* has more social support than has *fathering*. Our beliefs about genetics similarly limit the ways we can think about infertility, with some solutions seen as real, and some as alternatives, second best, making do. And so we create social structures that reinforce those beliefs: the modern creation of the anonymous adoption, the "matched" child substituting for the "real" child.

And finally there is the theme in motherhood that is perhaps the central theme of modern life: alienation. The concept of alienation is essential to my understanding of what is happening to modern American motherhood. "The central feature of alienation is that things or people which in fact are related dialectically to each other come to seem alien, separated from or opposed to each other."[4] These chapters will point out ways in which women are alienated as mothers, are cut off from their bodies, their children, the fathers of those children, and other mothers.

A great deal of what I am trying to do is put together that which patriarchy, technology, and capitalism have taken apart: mind and body; public and private; personal and political; work and home; production and reproduction; masculine and feminine. I want us to move beyond the mind-body dualism, with its disdain for the body and its esteem for narrow, rational linearity. I want us to move beyond the division of the world into a public sphere (the world of men, work, and production) and a private sphere (the world of women, home, and reproduction).

There is much in the experience of motherhood that fights against alienation, that fights against seeing things and people as separate, but rather fosters a vision of connection. Motherhood is an experience of the body and of the mind: women have come to feel "in touch with" their bodies, maybe for the first time since childhood, in pregnancy. Motherhood is an experience of interpersonal connection. The isolated, atomistic individual is an absurdity when one is pregnant: one is two, two are one. Motherhood is an experience of connection beyond the human community: a cow with her calf, a cat with her kittens are part of the same world, sharing the same experience. And while motherhood can alienate women from men and place women more firmly under the domination of men, motherhood can also be a bridge, a connection with a man.

And so the rest of this book is about the ways we can put motherhood back together again.

Pregnancy as a Relationship

It is time to take another look at the nature versus nurture argument—one of the many false dichotomies out of which motherhood has been created. A newborn baby is neither a tabula rasa, a blank slate on which nothing is yet written, nor a bundle of genetic predispositions, tendencies, and instincts. Between the moment of zygotic zero, when sperm and egg fuse and genetics are set, and the time of birth, there have been months of development. Even at birth, babies have a history, months of experience which shape who they are and what they bring to their new life.

One of the implications of our dismissal of the importance of the body, and of pregnancy, is that we fail to see the significance of gestation as an experience for the potential child as well as for its mother. In certain ways we act as if the child first springs into being at birth. The pregnancy is thought of as a time of "expecting" for the mother—its future the only thing that counts, its present having meaning only for its future. Consider the differences in meaning between the archaic term *with child* and the more contemporary *expecting*.

When we think of the newborn child as having just gotten here, we ignore where it has come from. But children do not enter the world from outside the world; they do not come from Mars or out of a black box. By the time they are born they have been here, in this world, for nine months: not as children, not as people, but as part of their mothers' bodies. A baby enters the world already in a relationship, a physical, social, and emotional relationship with the woman in whose body it was nurtured.

The Physical Relationship

Medicine and science have recognized the significance of the physical environment provided in pregnancy relatively recently. It was not until the late 1800s that physicians began to provide prenatal care. "Neither the providers of health care nor pregnant women themselves considered routine medical supervision necessary."[1] How the baby came out, that it could be hurt on the way out—doctors were interested in this while they still believed that as long as the baby was in the womb it was beyond the influence of the environment and, consequently, beyond the influence of doctors and medical care.

It took the thalidomide tragedy to completely destroy that idea. The birth of hundreds of babies with serious, obvious physical impairments directly traceable to a drug mothers took (which doctors prescribed for nausea in pregnancy) changed forever the medical view of the uterine environment and the meaning of pregnancy. The placenta, once thought of as an impenetrable barrier, came to be seen as a "bloody sieve."

But the more things change, the more they stay the same. Doctors could have used this new information to come to the same conclusion I have come to: fetuses are part of their mothers' bodies, no safer than any of her organs from damage done to her. Like every other part of her body, the fetus has special susceptibilities and special resiliencies. That is, poisons which damage the kidney may do no direct damage to the heart. Things which do direct damage to the heart may not directly harm the kidney. But the whole is connected: ultimately, poisoning someone's kidney or heart is poisoning the person. Some organs we can live without—one kidney is adequate. Some we cannot—we only have one heart. The fetus we can live without, so it is possible to destroy the fetus and not kill the mother. And for most of pregnancy, the fetus is enough part of the mother that it is impossible to seriously damage the mother and not damage the fetus.

But the medical profession did not come to the conclusion that fetuses are fundamentally a part of their mothers' bodies. They stayed instead with the essentially patriarchal view that fetuses are seeds growing up, entirely separate beings "planted" in the mother. But now, instead of seeing the mother as a safe haven, they began to see that there was, as the old spiritual says, "no hiding place down here." Previously the uterus was thought of as a protected nest, but now the nest seemed unsafe, inadequately protected. The fetus was vulnerable to harm as we all are. The all-powerful, protective mother had failed.

Before this fall from grace, when the mother's body was believed to do the work of protection, the mother's mind was of little importance. Once the mother's body could no longer be trusted to protect the fetus, once the nest was shown to be open to danger, then the mother's job became guarding the nest. The mind, as distinct from the body, became important. Women had to know, consciously, what the fetus needed, and what would harm the fetus. Women had to be taught how to nourish and how to protect their fetuses. And women had to be willing to learn.

The notion that there are dangers pregnant women must avoid is of course not at all new. All cultures seem to have pregnancy taboos. What Western medicine did was make the shift from dismissing all taboos as old wives' tales to instituting its own taboos.

The more that doctors learned about the unique vulnerabilities of the fetus, the more importance they placed on "compliance," the willingness of a patient to "follow doctor's orders." The focus on compliance actually started before the thalidomide revelation when doctors feared toxemia, a disease of late pregnancy, the causes of which are still not clear. *Williams Obstetrics* notes that everyone from "allergist to zoologist" has proposed a theory.[2] The symptoms are a dramatic rise in blood pressure, the accumulation of enormous amounts of water so that the woman swells up, and the spilling of protein into urine. Unchecked, toxemia can cause convulsions, which can either directly kill the fetus or bring about a premature birth. The mother, too, can die. Prenatal care is organized around screening for toxemia: blood pressure, urinalysis, and a weight gain check are all that a standard monthly visit normally monitors. Since a symptom of toxemia is sudden weight gain from accumulated water, doctors began to check weight very carefully. Somehow the idea of weight gain as a *symptom* slipped over into weight gain as a *cause*, and doctors began to put great emphasis on women keeping their weight down during pregnancy. By the 1950s and 1960s this idea had gotten so out of hand that medical authorities were recommending that overweight women lose weight while pregnant. The July 15, 1962, issue of the *American Journal of Obstetrics and Gynecology* had four full-page ads for drugs to be used to control weight gain in pregnancy—drugs including phenobarbital and amphetamines to suppress appetite.[3]

There were important social and psychological effects of this medical emphasis on weight. Even now that the idea of restricting weight so severely to prevent toxemia has been totally discredited, we are left with its residue of distrust.

Doctors had set up a nearly unachievable goal: it was very difficult for a woman with adequate access to food to keep her pregnancy weight down to no more than the prescribed twenty to twenty-four pounds. It was virtually impossible for women who were a few pounds overweight to keep their weight gain down to even fewer pounds, much less to lose weight while pregnant. So all through the course of pregnancy women under medical care—virtually all middle-class women—had the experience of a monthly evaluation of their competence as mothers: the majority failed. Doctors, believing that women were putting their health and their babies at risk by overeating, began to see women as foolishly self-indulgent.

The medical writing and advice books of the 1940s through the 1960s do not talk about the very real hunger many pregnant women experience. The picture they paint is of childlike women indulging in cake and candy. I think instead of a story my mother tells about her pregnancy with me. Always a very slim woman in her youth, pregnant as a "skinny teenager," my mother became ravenous while pregnant. She walked into her mother's kitchen one afternoon to find a roast chicken cooling on top of the stove. She reached out and tore off a piece. Then another. She didn't realize what she was doing until my grandmother called out, "Marcia, please, at least take a plate!"

A hungry young woman devouring a whole chicken right out of the oven is a very far cry from the image of the bored, lazy woman eating bonbons while watching soap operas—the stereotype of the era.

By setting up an unattainable—and as it turns out entirely inappropriate and ultimately dangerous—goal, both mothers and doctors learned not to trust mothers. Try as they might, women could not put what they were told and believed was in the best interests of their babies into action against the messages they were getting from their bodies. They learned not to trust their bodies: they may have felt hungry, may have felt the *need* to eat (as indeed they did), but they believed what they were told, that it was dangerous to eat, bad for the baby. The doctors, for their part, learned that women could not be relied on to follow advice as to what their babies needed.

The thalidomide disaster occurred in 1961, while this battle of the bulge was still being fought. The cultural lesson that was learned, the lesson that passed into popular knowledge, was not what now seems most obvious: that doctors can make terrible, terrible mistakes. In the United States there was one woman, Frances Kelsey of the FDA, who was concerned about chick embryo studies that showed that thalidomide interfered with limb development. By preventing its sale here, she not only saved countless babies from loss of limbs, she also saved the American medical profession from serious loss of face. Had she let thalidomide through, it is hard to imagine that American doctors would have been any more reluctant than their European counterparts to prescribe it, or more reluctant to prescribe that than they were DES, Bendectin, or any number of other drugs since proven dangerous—including the heavily advertised diet drugs.

But the fact remains that in the United States women did not get thalidomide from their doctors. And so the message that came through was not that doctors can be hazardous to pregnancy, but that *mothers* can be. Women can take things that will hurt their babies. Not only are mothers not protective, mothers are a potential source of harm. Babies need protection, not *by* their mothers, but *from* their mothers.

Ever since the thalidomide disaster it seems we have been learning about one thing after another that pregnant women should avoid. In my first pregnancy, it was cats and rare beef. Toxoplasmosis was the danger, and it could be caught by eating rare beef or by breathing in particles of infected cat feces. As taboos go, that one was okay—changing the cat's box became my husband's job, and I somehow never reclaimed it after that. Then I remember the year of the potato—some research had linked a possible virus carried by bad potatoes to neural tube defects. Pregnant friends avoided commercially prepared potatoes and picked through raw ones for only the most perfect and unblemished. In my second pregnancy, caffeine was the danger. I never drank more than one cup of coffee in a day, never more than three or four (well, maybe four or five) in a week. Alcohol and tobacco of course have been major taboos for a while. I've never smoked, fortunately, and rationed alcohol like a teetotaler right to the end. Then it was good: alcohol was being used to delay premature labor and an evening of hard Braxton-Hicks contractions earned one a glass of wine. Hot water is a relatively newfound danger: hot tubs and hot baths can raise the uterine temperature to unsafe degrees.

The list goes on and on. All kinds of things, known and unknown, can harm babies in utero. Mothers must watch themselves. And we all must watch mothers. The signs that have been put up in New York bars and restaurants are indeed indicative of the times. They warn that drinking alcohol in pregnancy may result in fetal defects. Pregnant women sipping a wine spritzer have been harassed by total strangers. A man lurching out of a bar looking for his car keys certainly poses a greater threat to the health of children than the average pregnant woman having a social drink, or even two. The constant exposure to exhaust fumes from cars and buses is certainly a greater hazard to fetuses than the occasional glass of wine, the odd beer.

I am not trying to argue here that these taboos have no basis: probably except for the potato episode, these things are not good for the developing fetus and are best avoided by pregnant women. The issue I am raising concerns not the taboos, but the ways in which they are being enforced, the spirit in which they are held. It is one thing for a loving community to protect a pregnant woman from things they believe will harm her and her baby. It is another thing for a city to cut funds for services to pregnant women while running ad campaigns to show how dangerous women are to their fetuses. And it is surely cause for alarm when a society begins, as ours has, to contemplate legal action against pregnant women who violate taboos. My husband's gifts of assorted herbal alternatives to coffee (each one worse than the next) were acts of kindness, as was his taking over the cat-box job. My sister-in-law's gift of a bottle of alcohol-free sparkling apple cider to celebrate my pregnancy was given in the spirit of love. But the signs in the bars and restaurants seem to me to be mean-spirited. The introduction of fetal-abuse laws are very much in the spirit of meanness, not love or kindness.

The Social Relationship

Mothers and fetuses are not just connected chemically. The placenta is the point at which their fluids meet, but there are other points of meeting: heads rest on bladders in pregnancy, feet dance against ribs. The mother holds her fetus within her.

The relationship between a mother and her fetus is not just a chemical relationship, an exchange of nutrients and wastes. Nor is this relationship purely mechanical. The ideology of technology would have us draw on all kinds of mechanical metaphors for the physical relationship of the mother and her fetus. But neither is a machine. It is not a question of so many inches of head circumference fitting into so many inches of pelvis.

The mother, as a social being, is responding socially to the experience of carrying her baby. Her reactions are not mechanical, but social. I am not talking here about women reading Latin poetry to their fetuses in the hopes that they will enter Harvard on scholarship. I am saying that *any* mother is engaged in a social interaction with her fetus as the pregnancy progresses. The pregnancy is a social as well as physical relationship. Women are not "flowerpots" in which babies are planted,[4] but social beings, giving social meanings to their experiences. When a baby uses her bladder as a trampoline, the woman responds. She responds not only by making another trip to the bathroom; she responds socially, with annoyance, amusement, irritation, anger, sometimes even with pleasure at the apparent liveliness of the baby, and most often by the end of pregnancy with a longing to end this phase of the relationship. But respond she does, not only to the physical experience, but to the social and emotional overlays of meaning given to that experience.

Negotiating sleep in the last weeks of pregnancy is an even clearer example. It is not an easy thing to fall asleep with a six-pound jumping bean in your belly. But the fetus is not simply a mechanical irritation. Mothers need to find ways of soothing fetuses to sleep when they want to sleep. With a great deal of thought, or with no particular conscious effort at all, women learn how to lie in bed and what to do to ease the fetus into quiet—or when to give it up, and get out bed for a while.

The fetus, for its part, is not yet a social being: these interactions with its mother are its first social experiences. In acting as if the baby "arrived" from outside, "entered" the world, we are making it sound like children start as separate people, arriving in our lives as babies. But there is a continuum from the single cell to the newborn child to the youngster. The fetus/baby/child's actions affect others, who respond socially. In the course of these interactions, the child eventually becomes a social being as well, someone with a sense of self. Women's experience of this growth from a cell to a person is continuous; men's experience is discontinuous—in goes a seed, out comes a baby.[5] As a patriarchal culture, making men's reality our ideology, we deny the continuity that women experience, and in denying it we violate the continuity. By acting as if it were not there, we destroy what was there.

Again, let me take the relatively simple example of sleep. In the earlier part of pregnancy, the embryo/fetus has no sleep-wake experience that we could recognize. It cannot, until it has developed sufficient brain capacity. But by thirty-three weeks—about two months before they are born—fetuses have developed rapid eye movement (REM) sleep, during which dreams take place, and deep, or non-REM, sleep. As the fetus takes up more and more space in its mother's body, as it becomes more capable of responding to its environment, mother and fetus have to come to some kind of shared cycle. While babies can, we all know, sleep through anything, presumably the mother jumping up to a loud alarm clock, taking a shower, listening to music, banging pots around the kitchen, and taking a subway ride to work are bound to have some effect on the fetus. Sounds do penetrate, and movement of course is felt. On the other hand, when she lies down at night, she does what she can to get the fetus to sleep. Lying on her back presses the baby against her spine: a lumpy mattress against which the fetus may protest. She may learn—she may be taught by her fetus—to lie on her side. Her slowed, even breathing and her general relaxation ease her fetus to sleep. They accommodate each other.

The accommodation goes on through the night. No one "sleeps through the night." We all have periods of relative wakefulness and periods of deeper sleep: sleep researchers have shown us that there are regular cycles to deep sleep, REM sleep, and wakefulness. In pregnancy, mother and fetus have to share the same rhythms. When babies are born into their mothers' own beds, there is a continuity in this sleep-wake cycle. Right at the time of birth both babies and mothers, if undrugged of course, are wide awake. In babies this initial period of quiet alertness is a very special time, and part of what the fuss about immediate "bonding" is about. I remember particularly with my son, my firstborn, a long time of looking into his eyes, of other people, family, there at the home birth, holding him and looking into his eyes. But then babies—and their mothers—fall asleep, exhausted from the birth. For days, even weeks after my son was born, my husband and I used to call to each other to come look if his eyes were open. He woke up a lot, certainly, but never with that clear stare, that thoughtful gazing.

When, from birth, babies sleep by their mothers' sides through the night, as is the case throughout most of the world, the transition from inside to outside is part of a continuum of change. The sleep-wake cycle of mother and baby can stay "in synch." I kept my babies in bed with me at night. Only very, very rarely do I remember being awakened in the early months of infancy by a baby's cry pulling me out of a sound sleep. But often, so very often, did I roll over during the night to find the baby just stirring, just starting to search for the breast.

In American society, it is customary for babies to be born in hospitals, and put immediately on hospital schedules. For a few days, mother and baby are kept separate, particularly at night. When they are "brought home" (as if for the first time) babies are often put into separate rooms, almost always into separate beds even if in the same room. Whatever synchronization of sleep cycles that there was is gone, destroyed because it was discounted to begin with. The mother finds herself awakened out of deep sleep at seemingly random times during the night. New parenthood in America is experienced as above all else an exercise in sleep deprivation. That is not a biological fact of life: that is a cultural creation.

If we were to recognize the continuity, the continuing connection between a mother and her fetus/baby, we would not destroy their intimate rhythms. We would not treat the baby as if "delivered" from outside, and bring that baby home from the hospital as if it came from the hospital to start with. But American mothers are specifically told not to take the baby to bed. We try to avoid intimacy, any hint of sexual intimacy, in the most profoundly intimate and essentially sexual of experiences. We ignore the fact that the baby has been sleeping in its mother's bed, and in its mother's body, all along. We act in every way as if the baby were foreign, and we make of it a foreigner, an alien, a "little stranger." But it is *not* alien, it is part of its mother, a newly separated part, coming into its own separate existence.

The fetus enters the world not only as part of its mother's body: it is part of the life the mother lives, part of the rhythms of her day and of her household as well as of her body. Again, starting with the simple example of sleep-wake cycles, throughout the day as well as the night pregnant women have periods of activity and periods of rest. Fetuses are *there*, sharing these experiences. When they "arrive" on the outside, they come with this shared background. One of the clearest examples is the dinnertime experience so many new parents have. Before the baby was born, the time right before dinner was consistently, for many women, one of the most active times of the day. Most women seem to retain responsibility for the kitchen and cooking, whether they have outside jobs or not. Getting dinner ready, whether it is following a commute from work, or while chasing a toddler around the house, or both, tends to be a busy, noisy time for mothers in many households. Pots bang, water runs, the mother is calling out to children or to other members of the household. Lo and behold, after the baby is born, it is wide awake during this general dinnertime bedlam. If parents try to fight it, put the baby into a quiet room, dark and alone, and hope it will go to sleep, they sometimes succeed, but often they end up with a crying baby on their hands. People seem to have more success with moving the baby right into the middle of the action *where it is used to being*, either strapped to a parent in a baby carrier or propped on the kitchen table.

The baby outside is not a creature entirely different from the baby inside. We may deny the continuity, but we live with its effects. Patterns learned inside are expressed outside. Not only sleep-wake cycles, but even habits: some babies learn to suck their thumbs in utero and continue doing so; some do not and may never learn. What the baby was inside is part of what the baby is outside. Its capacities for social interaction begin to develop in the months before birth.

By thirty-two weeks the fetus's hearing functions much like it will after birth. The fetus hears and responds to speech, learning the rhythm of human speech long before the words. Babies show movement, almost a dance, to the sounds of speech. And newborns can recognize their mothers' voices, something that mothers have often felt to be true, but knew could not be true. Now we have experimental evidence supporting this knowledge, so now we can indeed know what we knew. A baby younger than three or four days old prefers a recording of its mother's voice reading a story to another woman's voice reading the same story. In an experiment, babies were given "pacifiers" to suck. By changing their rate of sucking, they got one of the two recordings. Within twenty minutes, babies learned what rate of sucking provided their mothers' voices.[6]

These late-pregnancy experiences the fetus has shape the baby, just as the experiences a baby has shape the child it becomes. Some of these are near-universal experiences: they shape the near-universal experiences of baby care, the singing, rocking, swinging, swaddling, holding close that show up in all cultures in various forms.

Babies are soothed by singing; singing is probably most like the way fetuses hear their mothers' and others' voices, strong on rhythm, weak on distinct words. Babies are soothed by being held firmly: the uterus was a tight swaddle, the contractions of pregnancy providing frequent "hugs." Babies are soothed by being held close to the heart. By now it is common knowledge that babies calm down to the sounds of the adult, seventy-two-beats-per-minute heart rate: this has been turned to profitable use by selling teddy bears that play a recorded heartbeat. Babies are soothed by rocking: the rocking chairs, cradles, and hammocks used all over the world duplicate the rocking of the pelvis when the mother walked while pregnant. Babies seem to *need* to be rocked or walked: they are coming out of an environment in which they were rocked for hours each day.

When the new reproductive technologists talk about creating artificial wombs, they are talking about creating a very different environment for a fetus. What would a baby be like that had grown without being held close, without an adult heartbeat surrounding it, without the sound of speech, without being rocked? Or would the artificial womb come provided with the mechanical mother: some rocking, a recorded heartbeat, recorded voices (saying what?), artificial contractions of the artificial womb. Grown outside of a woman, outside of the human community, we could indeed create an alien baby, a little stranger, the living reification of our ideology.

It is with mothers, of course, that fetuses have the most direct relationship. And it is on mothers that fetuses have the most direct effects: when they move, the mother feels it. But it is not only to mothers that fetuses relate. The movement of the fetus within is also felt by people in physically intimate contact with the mother, especially her lover and other children. The closer—literally, physically closer—other people are to the mother, the closer they are physically and socially to the fetus. When they hold the woman close, they too feel the fetus within. It reaches out to them, and that too is a social experience. It is also an interaction. Surely it is a very different experience to be the lover of a woman whose fetus lies with limbs facing outward, kicking, prodding, pushing against her belly, than to lie with a woman whose fetus lies facing her back, offering only its own back, its smooth rolling motions against her belly. There is an interaction between the fetus and these others, varying with how active a fetus is, how it lies, how it moves, and how the other responds, whether moving away repulsed, prodding back, crooning, laughing, or leaning in for more, or pulling back from this intimacy.

Mothers use this movement of the fetus to create bonds between the fetus within and the rest of the family: how many women, how many times, have pulled the father's hand close to the belly and said, "Feel that." How many women have held one of their children against them and said, "Listen, feel the baby move."

Some fathers reach out for this contact themselves. In his book *The Nurturing Father*, Kyle D. Pruett describes his interview with Peter and Susan about their experience with pregnancy:

> . . . he could not keep his hands off his wife's body, especially her swollen abdomen. "She was so beautiful and so huge." Once Susan felt the quickening of life within her, Peter would spend "what seemed like hours" with his hands on Susan's belly just "waiting to feel something happen." He became convinced that his unborn child was "tapping back messages in code" when he tapped rhythmically on his wife's abdomen; "I could make him kick back, I really could." . . . He even began singing to the fetus in the last trimester because Susan thought his voice "calmed the baby down. Probably me, too," she added later.

And then, holding his newborn son in his arms minutes after his birth:

> "I remember when he kicked his brand new little feet against me as I held him in my arms that it felt almost familiar, like when we were tapping out code back and forth while he was still inside Susan."[7]

These relationships with babies begin to form before birth. Certainly they are relatively one-sided: the tapping had a meaning for the father it could not have had for the baby. All relationships with babies, for quite some weeks or months after birth, are relatively one-sided. But they are relationships, and they are the beginnings of social interactions. My son treasures, and has shared often with his sister, his memory of the time, resting near me, he put his cheek against my belly and she responded to the pressure with a clear, swift, strong kick. Was that a "social" action on her part? No more so than when after birth she would grasp tightly to his offered finger. But these reactions, social or not, call forth a wealth of social meanings. They are responded to socially—and that in turn calls forth more responses. It takes years of this, years of this "calling forth" in Caroline Whitbeck's beautiful phrase,[8] before a baby becomes a social creature. It goes on for years, for a lifetime, but it begins before birth.

Redefining Abortion

IF PREGNANCY IS A developing relationship, if a fetus is part of its mother's body, gradually becoming an other, then what is an abortion? For some women, and maybe for most women early on in pregnancy, an abortion is much the same as contraception: a way of not entering that relationship. And for some women, and maybe for most women as the pregnancy progresses, abortion is a way of ending a relationship, and with that, of stopping the growth of the other. The difference between avoiding and ending a relationship is not simply a matter of weeks of gestation. An abortion at, say, ten weeks may mean different things to different women, and different things to the same woman in different pregnancies. One woman schedules an abortion with less emotional involvement than she has in scheduling dental work. Another schedules an abortion and begins a lifelong grieving for the death of her baby.

Is this the contradiction it appears to be? No, not if we take a genuinely woman-centered view of pregnancy and of abortion, and recognize that abortion, like pregnancy itself, takes its meaning from the woman in whose body the pregnancy is unfolding.

Nor is it a contradiction that women take motherhood very seriously, and yet may have abortions relatively "casually." Abortion is one way a woman prevents herself from entering into an unwanted relationship, a way she can avoid the serious commitment of motherhood. Women understand motherhood to mean a lifetime commitment, a central relationship: we must have ways of avoiding such a commitment precisely because we do take it so seriously. In this way, the relation between abortion and motherhood is like the relation between divorce and marriage. In those societies that take marriage most seriously, that view the marital relationship as the central one in life, the divorce rate is the highest: people have to have a way out of such an important commitment. In those societies in which husband and wife are not expected to be all to each other, divorce is relatively rare: it matters less to whom you are married. If women took motherhood casually, abortion would be much less important. We could abandon, sell, or just ignore our children. Motherhood would not take over our lives.

But for the most part women do take motherhood seriously. And it is because of that, not in spite of that, that some abortions are easy, avoiding motherhood, while some are hard, ending motherhood. It is the meaning of a pregnancy for a woman that shapes the meaning an abortion holds for her.

A very young woman, after a few hurried sexual encounters in her boyfriend's car, finds her period two weeks late. All she wants is to get out of "trouble" and fast. Another woman weighs the hassles of an occasional abortion against the hassles of careful contraception, and decides to take her chances. Another woman chooses a diaphragm as the best compromise between safety and efficiency—and knows that this choice of contraception over her reproductive years could mean at least one and maybe several "accidental" pregnancies and abortions. A couple of abortions over the next twenty years are part of her contraceptive planning. And yet another woman learns that the baby she carries—a baby for whom she has rented a larger apartment, refused a job transfer, and knitted a receiving blanket—would be born with a fatal disease. She aborts, packs away the blanket, takes the job transfer after all, and mourns the death of her child.

Abortion truly is all of these things: the death of a wanted baby, a way out of trouble, a contraceptive technique. As part of contraception, abortion expresses an unwillingness to make a baby, stopping the division of self, stopping a bit of oneself from going on to become someone else. In this sense abortion is not fundamentally different from contraception. Each month that a woman ovulates she releases one particular egg, an egg with an already limited range of potential. This month's egg is capable of becoming a different baby than last month's, than next month's. The egg not fertilized when it comes forth in time for the new year is September's baby not to be. The egg that carried a particular dominant gene is a brown-eyed baby not to come. Let that egg be fertilized and then stopped, aborted rather than "contracepted" into nothingness, and it is a still more specific baby not to be.

Why do we make such an enormous distinction in modern society between abortion and contraception? One answer lies in certain philosophical premises about the nature of embryonic life. And yet some contraceptives—the IUD, some pills—are technically abortifacients. They do not prevent sperm from joining egg and creating a zygote, the genetically unique potential person, but prevent the very early embryo from implanting. So why is it that abortion planned and recognized by the woman, abortion deliberately controlled by the woman, is said to be distinct from, and less acceptable than, contraception?

The History of Abortion

The more pragmatic answer as to why abortion and contraception are perceived as being very different comes from a look at the historical development of contemporary abortion and contraception practices.

Women of ancient times have left few written records. Most of what we know about the early history of abortion comes from the responses of men. Early Greek and Roman law put restraints on abortion, both to protect women from mutilation and to guarantee that wives not deprive husbands of children. Jewish law is largely silent on the subject. In Christian thinking, Augustine in the fourth century concluded that the soul was not present until the time of quickening, when the woman felt movement. Abortion prior to that point was therefore not the destruction of a human life. In the thirteenth century Thomas Aquinas placed the presence of the soul as Aristotle had: at forty days after conception for a male, and eighty days for a female. It was not until the seventeenth century that the Roman Catholic Church crystallized its strong stand against abortion.[1]

The Catholic Church's current position is both internally consistent and, ironically, essentially the same as the argument I am making from the other side: abortion and contraception—and for that matter in vitro fertilization and artificial insemination—are fundamentally the *same*. But in contrast to what I am saying, the Church objects to all of these efforts to control our reproduction. Both the Church's position and mine focus on *control* rather than technique as the important issue, a control I value and the Church deplores.

In America, abortion has always been a personal problem for women, a problem of safety, access, and control, but as a political issue it dates back only to the mid-nineteenth century, when physicians used abortions as one more stepping stone toward gaining their professional status. Abortions were widely available in America at the time, advertised in newspapers and performed by people with a variety of backgrounds. In driving out the "quacks," physicians were in one sense doing what they were doing in other areas of practice. They replaced midwives at childbirth in the same way: by attempting to redefine the services provided as "medical" in nature. But with abortion, another dimension was added. Physicians argued that their knowledge of embryonic and fetal development, minimal as it truly was at the time, enabled them to know what the women having abortions presumably did not know: that the embryo was a baby. Having made this claim, doctors were able to say that the abortionists were not only incompetent, dirty, and backward—all the charges they leveled at the midwives and their other competition—but also that what they were doing was wrong and immoral, a kind of murder.

Physicians did not, however, want an absolute ban on abortions. What the doctors claimed, a contradiction highlighted in the work of Kristen Luker,[2] was that abortion was wrong, but physicians alone could determine when it was necessary. For example, abortion was necessary when the pregnancy threatened the life of the mother, a determination over which doctors claimed technical expertise. Thus there were two kinds of abortions: the ones the doctors did not do, which were "immoral," and the ones the doctors did do, which were both moral and, almost by definition, therapeutic.

The argument the physicians made, in sum, was that abortion was a crime against the fetus, the potential baby, made acceptable only when doctors thought it was necessary. But the standards of necessity the doctors applied were not the same standards that women—especially poor women without access to the sympathetic ear of a private physician—would necessarily apply.

Partly because of the lack of skill of the medical doctors themselves, and partly because the abortionists were indeed driven "underground," there was another powerful argument to be made against abortion; it was dangerous; it threatened the life and the health of the woman. Relatively early on in her crusade for available contraception, Margaret Sanger addressed this issue of the threat to women's health posed by abortion and the lack of contraception.

It is informative to look at her 1920 distinction between contraception and abortion: "If no children are desired, the meeting of the male sperm and the ovum must be prevented. When scientific means are employed to prevent this meeting, one is said to practice birth control. The means used is known as a contraceptive. If, however, a contraceptive is not used and the sperm meets the ovule and development begins, any attempt at removing it or stopping its further growth is called abortion."[3] There is no mention here of fetus, embryo, or unborn child, let alone murder, killing, or destruction—yet she is making a strong argument for the superiority of contraception over abortion.

There is, in the contemporary context, a striking lack of moral argument here: the superiority of contraception over abortion is presented as a safety issue, not a moral issue. "There is no doubt," Sanger wrote, "that women are apt to look upon abortion as of little consequence, and to treat it accordingly."[4] Here, one used to the 1980s' right-to-life rhetoric expects a condemnation of "unthinking unfeeling women who abort casually." But no, Sanger is talking about the health and safety of the woman herself: "in an abortion there is always a very serious risk to the health and often to the life of the patient. It is only the women of wealth who can afford the best medical skill, care and treatment, both at the time of the operation and afterwards. In this way, they escape the usual serious consequences."[5] After reviewing the dangers of abortion, and its widespread practice in America at the time, she concluded: "There is the case in a nutshell. Family limitation will always be practiced as it is now being practiced—either by birth control or by abortion. We know that. The one means health and happiness—a stronger, better race. The other means disease, suffering, death."[6]

In the almost seventy years since Sanger's writing, the right to contraception has been widely accepted. We have gone beyond that, in fact, to think of contraception as more a *responsibility* than a right. Only immature, thoughtless, irresponsible people fail to use contraception, most Americans have come to think. Sanger's arguments about the relationship between too many mouths to feed and poverty have been accepted, and more. There is a film about children living in poverty that I often show to my undergraduate sociology students. Two of the three families depicted are small, just one or two children. One family is large, with both parents, eight children, and a grandchild. Students get angry at that: the other people are poor in spite of limiting family size, but these people are poor, it would seem, because they didn't use contraception. It's their own fault, self-righteous young students tell me. Why did they have those children if they couldn't afford them? Children, they believe, are luxuries you shouldn't indulge in, especially not in quantity, if you can't afford the upkeep.

So the idea of controlling fertility is now accepted as a moral good: for most Americans it is the responsible, mature, right way to behave.

But abortion—abortion is not just a way of controlling fertility, a form of "family limitation" to be compared with other forms on the basis of safety. Those same undergraduates get just as angry when we talk about women having repeated abortions. Abortion today is not just a less safe way of avoiding unwanted births. In fact, diaphragms with backup abortions are safer than the more effective contraceptives, the pill or the IUD. Safety is simply no longer the issue. The woman's life or health is not *seen* as threatened. The entire focus of the anti-abortion argument has shifted from the woman to the products of conception, the "life" for which they claim a right. It is not what she is doing to herself that the modern anti-abortion argument asks, but what she is doing to her embryo, to her fetus. And it is not her physical self or her safety that the pro-choice argument most often addresses, but her moral status, the issue of her moral agency, *her* right to life, to control her body, her motherhood, her self that is argued over and against the rights of the products of conception.

While Sanger and the birth-control activists won and birth control itself became widely available, the larger debate underlying the legalization of birth control did not get fully resolved. The underlying argument is about the relation between womanhood and motherhood: how much control over her motherhood a woman can exercise and still be acceptable as a woman. Much of this is now being argued out in the context of abortion. In 1920 Sanger wrote:

> Today . . . woman is rising in fundamental revolt. Even her efforts at mere reform are . . . steps in that direction. Underneath each of them is the feminine urge to complete freedom. Millions of women are asserting their right to voluntary motherhood. They are determined to decide for themselves whether they shall become mothers, under what conditions, and when. This is the fundamental revolt referred to. It is for women the key to the temple of liberty.[7]

For our today, too, reproductive freedom often seems to be the fundamental revolt, the key to women's liberty. Abortion today, like contraception in 1920, is the touchstone for understanding motherhood, and womanhood. Is there a "new woman"? Is the experience of motherhood changing? In America today, abortion—the experience, the institution, the ethics, the *existence* of abortion—has become the starting and the stopping point for such discussion. People argue to and argue from abortion in their understanding of motherhood and of womanhood.

"But if a woman has the right . . . ," people say, and then argue toward or away from abortion. "Then what stops . . . ?" and "Then why can't . . . ?" they ask. Heated discussions of Baby M and Baby Doe, of birth control and controlling birth, of maternity leaves and paternity suits come back again and again to abortion as the point of reference.

And just what does abortion itself mean to modern America? Does it signify the two competing images of woman, the independent, person of the world on the one hand, and the nurturant, sacrificing, center of the home on the other?[8] Or is the competition not between the women a woman could be, but between the woman as real, flawed, genuine life in progress, and the fetus as fantasized, perfect, imagined life potential? Abortion signifies all of this and more, of course—individual and collective decision making, bodily autonomy and societal control, personal needs and social policy, rights and needs and responsibilities, connections and separations.

Constructing the Fetus

It is the separations that capture my attention: the separation of women from motherhood, of pregnancy from birth, of sexuality from reproduction, and of fetuses from mothers. The most fundamental change I hear between the arguments that Sanger and her contemporaries were making and today's debate is that the fetus has been brought into the discussion, the fetus not as part of its mother, but as separate, a little person lying in the womb. A woman's conflict about motherhood is not new; her need to balance the needs of her life as it is, her children that are, against those that are not yet, that too is not new. What is new is this cultural creation, the fetus, the "unborn child."

There is today, it seems, a cultural fascination with the fetus. Janet Gallagher compares it with whale watching[9]—the fetus, like the whale, symbolizes something pure, something of the world and innocent of the world. Both, fetuses and whales, have been made "real" for us by science, by an invasion of their watery worlds with recording equipment. People who live hundreds of miles from the sea can picture the sounding whale, see its smooth back, its spouting blowhole. And people who have never been pregnant, never shared anyone's pregnancy intimately, can visualize the fetal head shape, fetal hands, fetal movement in utero.

The ability to penetrate the hidden world of the fetus has been used—with great passion and power—on both sides of the abortion debate in the United States. "Right-to-life" advocates have used these techniques to make the fetus visible, real, a being who can capture our compassion. The most dramatic example of this was the film *The Silent Scream*, which purports to show via sonogram (an ultrasound picture) a twelve-week fetus during an abortion. With the use of special effects (dramatic slowing and speeding up of the film to make fetal movement appear to change in intensity) and powerfully suggestive language (the "child" in its "sanctuary") the audience is asked to share the identification with the fetus within, and to ignore entirely the woman—never shown—in whom it resides.

On the other hand, these same techniques are being marshaled in support of the right to abort. Women are being encouraged to have more and more prenatal screening tests to ascertain the condition of the fetus, and to abort when the medical determination is unsatisfactory. Abortions where the fetus would be "defective" are among the most socially acceptable of abortions in America. Fears of disability, extreme repugnance toward the mentally retarded, and firmly embedded cultural ideas about health combine to shape our attitude toward abortion for "fetal defect." These abortions, "selective" abor-

the old abortions to save the life of the mother, these are the abortions of which doctors approve. But this argument for legalized abortion, unlike the earlier one, focuses not on the woman, but on the fetus within.[10]

It is important to remember that not all arguments for legal abortion are feminist arguments. The feminist pro-choice voice has been only one of the forces for legalized abortion in America, and not, I think, necessarily the dominant one.

In fact, not everyone who is in favor of legalized abortion is necessarily pro choice—that is, not all would have the decision to abort be entirely the decision of the woman herself. There are those who think a single woman or a married couple who want to have an abortion should be able to do so, but that a married woman whose husband wants the child should not have the individual freedom to abort. There are those who claim that it is morally wrong to bring to term a baby who would have some particular disease or suffer in some way. They are not speaking of a woman's right to choose, but of a moral obligation to abort. And there are those who would like to see "welfare mothers" be required to abort their third—or fifth, or twelfth—pregnancy and be forcibly sterilized.

One of the unresolved problems of the feminist reproductive-rights movement is what to do with these non-feminist allies in the abortion movement. This, too, is not a new problem, but one that the early birth-control movement faced. Sanger made her alliances with the eugenics movement and with the population-control movement. The contemporary feminist reproductive-rights movement does the same: making uneasy alliances with the new eugenics movement which looks at embryos and fetuses as products suitable for quality-control testing, and with the population-control movement, with its often implicit classist and racist agenda. At the clinical level, the focus is on the fetus; at the policy level the focus is on the population. The woman is lost.

The Medicalization of Abortion

Sanger and the birth-control movement made alliances that were probably necessary, but there are costs, and we are still paying them. For Sanger, the most powerful allies were the doctors. The compromise she made was to give doctors control over contraception, to medicalize birth control. Fitting a diaphragrn is no harder than fitting a shoe. Women can do it for themselves. Yet birth control for women was incorporated firmly into the practice of medicine—a diaphragm requires a prescription. Women coming for birth-control information and services are "patients."

So it is with abortion. The legalization of abortion in America has been as much a reaffirmation of the rights of doctors to practice medicine as they see fit as it has been an affirmation of women's rights to control their reproduction. Abortion, *Roe v. Wade* told us, is a decision between a woman *and her physician.*

For all of its power as metaphor, the actual practice of abortion is strangely stripped of its meaning. As experience and as institution, abortion is medicalized, constructed as a medical event, under medical control, and with the culture of medicine providing the meanings, defining women's experiences. Abortion occurs in clinics, in settings removed from women's lives, by people removed from women's lives. The medicalization of abortion—giving doctors absolute control over the procedure itself—means that "a woman's right to choose [abortion] is always circumscribed by the physician's right not to perform it."[11] By what the profession of medicine is and is not willing to do, doctors continue to shape the availability and the experience of abortion in America.

Doctors do not like to do abortions. That, Jonathan Imber, in a recent book on doctors and abortion, clearly demonstrates. Their objections are not primarily phrased as moral or ethical issues. Early abortions are boring; they have "low priority in terms of medical knowledge and technique." But late abortions? Here Imber shows us the contradiction in the doctors' positions: "Most doctors were unwilling to perform second trimester abortions precisely because of their technical challenge."[12] Obviously, something else is at stake here. Imber says it is an effort to avoid controversy. As one of the doctors he interviewed said: "But the real reason we try to avoid them is that I don't want to be known as the local abortionist, I want to be known as a doctor who loves mommies and their babies."[13]

For this doctor—and I think he speaks for many—there is a distinction to be made between the women who get abortions, whom he dislikes, and the "mommies" whom he loves. There are, of course, not two groups of women—those who have abortions and those who have babies. These are the same women at different moments of their lives.

Abortion to serve the needs of individual *women* is not a high priority for many doctors. Abortion for eugenics or for "social" reasons is. While at least one of the doctors Imber interviewed recognized the threat "not only Jews need worry about" of using abortion as a way to "keep the numbers of dirty, poor people down," others contended that "family planning services were reaching the wrong people," and that "the population problem is not caused by the offspring of young engineers or doctors." These views were, Imber says, "generously offered," a point of pride, an example of the medical profession serving the community.[14]

If doctors do not themselves want to do abortions, but tend to think some people ought to be having them, and if they don't want to be known as "abortionists," but some of the good mommies do come in with unwanted pregnancies, then what is the solution? As Imber convincingly demonstrates, it has been to move abortion outside of the private practice of medicine and into the clinic. Doctors do not do abortions—*clinics* do.

And what are the consequences of relying on referral to clinics as the solution? "Practitioners have reinforced the market stronghold that the larger clinics maintain over abortion," creating a system of mass-production abortion services.[15]

This solution, as it is practiced, is a very far cry from the feminist vision of abortion that was offered in the late 1960s and early 1970s, in which women's need for abortion was seen as connected to women's lives, as occurring in the context of who a woman is and how she lives her life. Abortion was a political issue, personally experienced, and a personal issue, politically ensnared. Clinics today revolve around the procedure of abortion, with the political work largely absent, and the counseling relegated from the heart of the event to a support service for medical staff. Counselors serve the clinic and the medical workers as much as or more than they serve the women—who themselves are relegated to the status of "patient."

We now see the legacy of legalized, medicalized abortion, and it is a legacy that troubles many people. Abortion counseling has shifted from illegal political work—work highly valued by the counterculture in which it was performed and strongly disdained by the society at large—to the more mundane work of easing women through legal and often profit-making clinics. What has this medicalization meant for the workers, and consequently for the women using the services? For an answer, let us compare what Carol Joffe found in a study of abortion counselors conducted shortly after legalization[16] with what Melinda Detlefs[17] and Wendy Simonds[18] saw in two separate and more recent studies of abortion-counseling services.

Very few of the current counselors have been doing abortion counseling for even as long as four years, so most of those working now entered the field long after the legalization and medicalization of abortion were settled issues. These women were not, unlike the earlier counselors, drawn into a political cause. Counselors Detlefs interviewed said they "stumbled" into it, got involved "accidentally." They feel, as one put it, "no real firm commitment" to doing abortion work. In marked contrast to the way it was seen by those interviewed by Joffe, abortion counseling today is more likely than not "just a job." The political commitment, the sense of doing something important for women, those feelings that motivated the counselors Joffe interviewed a decade ago, are strangely lacking now. One of the counselors Detlefs interviewed spoke almost longingly of how things were in the years before she entered the field, the years Joffe wrote about, when people were "adamant about it. And that's gone. . . . after a while it's easy to start forgetting what's going on here and why you're doing it. . . . The awareness is gone, lost. At least here and a lot of places—now it's just shuffle, shuffle, shuffle the people."

What has happened in these intervening years to change things so? Some of the changes are the result of the work the early abortion counselors accomplished. In the early years, the activism, the energy, came from the pro-choice groups. But with the legalization of abortion, the energy shifted. These days, the pro-choice people are holding a defensive line at best—and doing a good job of it, but most of the activism comes from the right-to-life people. Joffe predicted that the pressure of the right-to-life movement would have the effect of stifling whatever discomfort counselors might feel about abortion. But that is not what happened. Counselors themselves are no longer uniformly pro-choice. Doubts come creeping in in two ways. Some of the people who "fell into" abortion counseling as "just a job" came without pro-choice feelings, certainly without strong pro-choice commitment. Others find themselves swayed by the right-to-life arguments, or just the right-to-life presence. As one counselor Detlefs interviewed said, "When you see people fighting so hard, you wonder."

And Wendy Simonds points to the conflicts the birth-control movement itself has created for attitudes toward abortion. Her research was done at a clinic which offered contraception and abortion services. There, she found, despite a stated insistence on value-free counseling, "The staff has definite views about abortion, and definite goals which it hopes to accomplish with each patient. . . . Though the guidebook (for counselor training) says that a counselor should 'help' the client choose a contraceptive, what is really expected of the counselor is that she impress upon the client the importance of contraception, which employees assume. Underneath the talk of objectivity, the organization exists to supply contraception." The clinic staff feels that abortion should not be used as contraception. Simonds says that when staff members talk about patients among themselves, they often whisper the word *abortion*, or call it "the procedure." They are dismayed by women coming for repeated abortions—for clinic workers these are contraceptive failures, not birth-control successes.

It does not have to be that way, as Simonds found in yet more recent research.[19] In a thoughtful and powerful ethnography of one of the few remaining avowedly feminist abortion clinics, she found a continuing commitment to feminist ideals, to demystifying medical practice, to encouraging women to make the best choices for themselves.

But relatively few abortions are provided by feminist centers, and the medicalization of abortion has meant that medicine defines the meaning of the experience for all of those involved, for the other health workers as much as or more than for the women seeking abortions. What comes to be seen as being of significance is not a woman taking control over her life, making decisions for herself, but the medical procedure. The actual abortion, the physical act of suctioning, becomes the heart of what happens. The women counselors do the "people work" for the doctors and technicians, who do the "real work" of the clinic. The counselors mediate between the institution, which encourages a speedup to get the women on and off the tables as quickly as possible, and the human being who is being "processed." Rather than simply giving orders—sign on the dotted line, undress here, lie there, pay on your way out—the counselors are engaged in face-to-face interactions with the clients, easing them through the clinics. Even in nonprofit settings, the institutional goals of processing as many women as possible, of avoiding lawsuits, and of freeing doctors to do only highly valued technical work are met by having low-paid, nurturant women mediate between the client and the institution. The counselors are there, but the feminist goal of what the counselors were to do—helping a woman take charge of her life—has given way to the institutional goal of taking charge of the patients.

So the reproductive-rights feminists of the 1970s won, and abortion is available—just as the reproductive-rights feminists of the 1920s won, and contraception is available. But in another sense, we did not win. We did not win, could not win, because Sanger was right. What we really wanted was the fundamental revolt, the "key to the temple of liberty." A doctor's fitting for a diaphragm, or a clinic appointment for an abortion, is not the revolution. It is not even a woman-centered approach to reproduction.

Reconstructing Abortion

In 1965 *Life* magazine published the first photos of "life in the womb"[20] and we embarked on the cultural creation of the fetus. Now when we look at a pregnant woman, in our heads we look through her, to the fetus we know lies in there. If we were to look at the *woman*, at what she is *doing*, we could say that she is starting to make a baby. We could indeed think of her as a "little bit pregnant," as starting the pregnancy, beginning her entry into motherhood. But if we focus on the seed, focus on the fertilized egg, we come to think that the baby is there already, inside her, not the creation of her body but its captive. And then it comes to seem only reasonable, what ethicist Daniel Callahan calls a "balancing rights perspective,"[21] to weigh the rights of this fetus against the rights of *its mother*. But by creating this fetus, this unborn child as a social being, we turn this woman into "its mother"—defining her in terms of the fetus even as she seeks to avoid making a baby, avoid becoming a mother.

If women controlled abortion, controlled not only the clinics, but the values and the thinking behind abortion, would we make such a distinction between contraception, not letting this month's egg grow, and abortion, not letting this month's fertilized egg grow? Or could we put early abortion back together with contraception, into the larger idea of birth control, and say that until we feel we've made a baby, an abortion is stopping a baby from happening, not killing one? Seeing women as creators, not containers, means seeing abortion as refusing to create, not destroying that which we contain.

That standard, that there is a baby in there when the woman in whose body it exists feels it is a baby, is very close to the traditional cultural acceptance of quickening as the standard for abortion. Until a baby had quickened, that is, until the woman felt it move, abortion was her private business. Once the baby communicated itself to her, and through her to the society at large, then abortion was no longer generally acceptable. *Then* a "balancing" of rights was necessary.

A woman-centered understanding of abortion would return to a woman-centered standard. It would not look to the gestational age of the fetus, to its "viability," or to any other fetal standard for judging the meaning or the acceptability of an abortion. We would not feel obligated to counsel some women to take their abortions "more seriously," nor would we deny, or feel threatened by, the very real grief of other women. We could accept the fact that for one woman, in one pregnancy, an abortion is a minor inconvenience and a small price she expects to pay now and again for an active sex life and a safe barrier contraceptive; and that for another woman, or for the *same* woman in another pregnancy, an abortion is the death of a baby.

The Give and Take of Adoption

THE INSTITUTION OF adoption is the embodiment of all of our deepest cultural contradictions about motherhood. Shame, secrecy, and sexuality: the stigma of inappropriate, "illegitimate" fertility and the stigma of infertility. Pride, pleasure, and responsibility: adoption as a moral solution, both to illegitimacy and to infertility; doing a good deed in giving up a baby to those who can "better care for it," and doing a good deed in taking in a baby "as one's own." The recognition of the social relationship of parenthood: the forging of the bonds of family out of legal rather than blood ties. The continuing concern with the "seed," the endless pseudo-science reports about how adopted children are "not the same." The fascinating convolutions of class relations: rich people adopting poor people's children and hiring other poor people to care for them. The business of adoption: the brokers, the fees, the black market, the gray market, and the white-baby-only market, the international wheeling and dealing in children.

If we could come to understand adoption, perhaps we could come to understand motherhood.

To adopt is to take as one's own; to adopt a child is to make of that child one's own child. When we think of adoption, that is what comes to mind: the waiting arms, the welcoming parents. But for every pair of welcoming arms, there is a pair of empty arms. For every baby taken in, there is a baby given up.

If we can make ourselves believe that babies arrive in the world at birth, if we can make ourselves ignore the meaning of pregnancy, then we can ignore those empty arms. We can tell a woman who will be giving a baby up not to see it or hold it, so that she won't miss it. We can tell her not to "bond" with the baby, but to give it up right away. But if we recognize the absurdity of dismissing months of physical intimacy, then we have to recognize that adoption is also someone's loss: perhaps a chosen loss, perhaps even a full-hearted relinquishment, but always a loss.

Recognizing the reality of the relationship that is ending takes nothing away from the reality of the relationship that is about to start. This is not a zero-sum game. The question is not, should not be, and need not be "Who is the real mother?" We can acknowledge the ongoing grief of a woman who has given up a baby without saying that that makes her the real mother, or more the mother than the adoptive mother or father who gives ongoing love and care. A woman who has carried a baby in her body is a mother. Her motherhood is part of who she is, who she will always be to herself, if not to the child. She may give up the child, give up its care, give up its responsibility, end forever the relationship. Yet she is changed by what she did, by her mothering of that child. It shapes her.

And a woman who adopts a child is the mother of that child. There was never any question in my mind but that adoptive parents are true, real parents to their children. And now that I too am an adoptive parent, I know in my heart, in my soul, what I always knew in my head. Parenthood is a social relationship, not a genetic connection. Adoption is not a second-best, almost-your-own way of making a family. Adoption is what all parenthood is: an intimate social relationship. A woman—or a man—who raises a child is the parent of that child. Her motherhood, too, is part of who she is, who she will always be. She, too, is changed by what she does, shaped by her mothering of that child. And a man who raises a child becomes part of that child and his fatherhood becomes part of his identity, changes him, shapes him.

Because I believe it is the intimacy, the relationship that makes a parent, and not the genetics, I fully recognize *both* the adoptive relationship *and* the loss that is the birth mother's—and it is the unique loss the birth *mother* feels that I address. I am not able to use the gender-neutral language "birth parent" that I saw so often in reading the social science literature about adoption. What, after all, is a "birth father"? If it is not to be genetics that ultimately determines parenthood, but nurturance, then a genetic father who does not nurture is not, in a sense that is meaningful to me, a father, a parent. On the other hand, I am comfortable with the gender-neutral "adoptive parent," because any adult, man or woman, can be the parent, the nurturer of a child. But in adoptive families, no less than in those formed by birth, it is predominantly women who do primary parenting, who "mother," and it is adoptive mothers who feel their motherhood most threatened by the motherhood of the birth mother.

We need a way of recognizing the significance of both of these women's relationships to the child and, more important, the significance of the child to both of these women. Children know who their parents are, understand the social, psychological parents to be "real." But unrequited love is real, too: the birth mother feels the significance of the child, even when the child would not know her, when she means nothing to the child. That someone else is mother to her child does not erase the birth mother as a mother: the motherhood of one woman does not cancel out the motherhood of the other.

Under the best of circumstances, the women themselves can recognize the sharing that has gone on. It's been expressed in the heartfelt poetry of birth mothers and adoptive mothers:

> Our child
> Can never be not yours
> Nor not ours.
> . . .
> Thank you for
> Caring deeply,
> For trusting enough
> To place your babe into a small secure ark,
> To float into the rushes of life
> Without even a Miriam at watch
> To tell you where
> His growing path will be.
> We honor that trust,
> And we shall love and cherish him
> As strongly and surely as you do.
>
> —Chris Probst[1]

And from the other side of the giving, from a birth mother to her child:

> I loved you and still do
> But I can't let that love in my life.
> I gave you life so your mother could love you.
> I signed papers that said I was "Abandoning" you,
> But with love,
> With the knowledge that a family waited for you,
> Waited with joyous outstretched arms.
> I've seen the joy of families with special babies
> Like you.
> It is matchless.
> I've no regrets.
>
> —Anon.[2]

But rarely is the giving and taking done under the best of circumstances, and all too often there are regrets:

Sign the paper here
We need your heart and soul
And your reward is
DOIN TIME
You will forget
You can have other children
Don't be selfish
You won't regret
You have nothing to offer.
. . .
In the night we feel
Sorrow, the twisting, churning
Of nothingness
The madness of giving, and not
Knowing to whom
No one ever told us
About
DOIN TIME.

—Helen Garcia[3]

The grief of the birth mother is there because grief is a fully normal response to loss. Some regret may be part of grief, the feeling of sorrow following loss. But regret also implies a feeling of being sorry for some act, some choice of one's own. Grief may be inevitable in life, but by acting wisely, with foresight, we think we can avoid regret. The birth mother without regrets may express and come to terms with her grief. The loss is there, but she can live with it, take satisfaction in the joy she created, the life she created and gave away. The birth mother with regrets feels punished for her choice, feels she is eternally "Doin Time."

In Garcia's poem we hear the pressure the birth mother experiences: pressure, forced choices, and ultimately regret. It is not this choice that leads to the regret, but the *force*. We also hear regret in the stories of women who would have chosen to give a baby up, but were forced away from that, into raising the child or to abortion, and of women who would have chosen abortion but were forced into raising the child or to adoption. Regret will be a theme in the lives of women wherever we are without power to make the choices we need to make for ourselves.

The reality is that birth mothers do not always give up their children with a deep sense of the rightness of what they are doing, but because they are pressurd into it. Birth mothers who give up babies for adoption suffer the powerlessness of their youth, of the stigma of their inappropriate fertility, and most often they suffer the powerlessness of poverty as well.

If we step outside the psychological dynamics of adoption, if we look for a moment at the class relations in adoption, some ugly facts emerge. "Poor countries export children to rich ones, black parents to white, poor parents to better off."[4] And if we take a thoughtful look at the mechanisms established for facilitating adoption, we can also accurately say that "adoption agencies are a system for redistributing children from the poor to the middle classes."[5] Thirty-two-year-old attorneys living in wealthy suburbs do not give up their children to nineteen-year-old factory workers living in small towns. Whether we look at the birth mothers who go through adoption agencies and compare them with the adoptive couples who go home with their babies, or look at the open marketing of babies as practiced via newspaper ads and brokers, we see that adoption is as much a class issue as it is anything else.

Adoption in America is a competitive market situation. In her 1980 exposé *The Baby Brokers* Lynne McTaggart traced the very open selling of white babies.[6] Want ads are placed in economically depressed towns. Brokers want cash only for certain transactions. International trafficking in babies is rampant. Certainly this system sits side-by-side with the very legal, very open, very legitimate work done by the adoption agencies. But the agency system operates in its own chaos, and creates its own marketing. In the 1980s, at one of the well-respected, genteel, long-standing adoption agencies in New York, my husband and I were told that there was a sliding scale for adoptions, going up to $9,000 for people earning $70,000 a year. That money, we were told, was most certainly not to be thought of as purchasing a baby. It was a fee to cover the costs of the agency's services. And although there were homeless newborn non-white infants within walking distance of where we sat, the "boarder babies" abandoned in New York City hospitals, the agency did not work with the city: the city does not pay its bills. Those babies, the babies of women of color who were not sophisticated enough, well enough, or "together enough" to get themselves to the agencies that would handle black babies, well, those babies would go into the foster-care system. The city itself reflects no urgency in placing those children for adoption.

Children are commodities in a competitive market, and the ironies abound. Potential adopters with the most resources—two parents, solid income—can get the "cream of the crop," the healthy, white newborn. Older, single, or in any way disadvantaged prospective parents find themselves on a waiting list for the leftovers: older children, children with known disabilities, children who have been in and out of foster care. "The most difficult children tend to be placed in situations which have more than usual stress and fewer than usual resources. While this paradox is widely acknowledged, the competitive nature of the adoptive situation in the United States makes it inevitable."[7]

McTaggart concluded that the new adoption business, the brokering of babies—and I would add the even newer business of brokering "surrogate" services to create babies to order—"magnifies what is wrong with the old one, most particularly the roles assigned to each member of the adoptive triangle: the child as merchandise, the biological mother as manufacturer, the adoptive parents as potential customers."[8] The true miracle of adoption is that out of all this ugliness, beautiful families are formed. Once the brokers, the wheelers and dealers leave, children cease to be merchandise and people forced into the role of purchasers are able to grow into parenthood. It is not only the birth mothers who are abused: this system punishes everyone. "It is only the most extreme manifestation of the way we abuse the rights of unwanted children, disregard the needs of teenagers in the area of sexuality and fertility, and punish those people who cannot produce their own children."[9]

But while all of the members of the adoption triangle are made to suffer, they do not suffer equally. The last group, the ones who are infertile, have social power that the others lack. Infertility, after all, does happen to rich people, to white people, to well-educated people, and adoption may be their only choice if they want to share the joys of childrearing. Unwanted pregnancies may happen to rich, white, well-educated women, too—but adoption is rarely their only choice. If they make that choice, those are the birth mothers most likely to have no regrets, whatever their sense of loss may be. It is the young, uneducated, poor birth mother who is most likely to feel the pressure, the loss of choice. The system is weighted heavily against her, as her ability to create something precious is turned into her liability.

Solving Problems with Problems

There is an enormous difference between what works on an individual level and what works as a social policy. As a public policy, adoption cannot be the long-range solution for infertility, even though it obviously works for many individuals. It does not work as a social policy because it makes us dependent upon the grief of one group of people to solve the problems of another group of people.

In a better world, in the world I would want us to have, there would be virtually no women giving up babies: contraception, abortion, and the resources to raise their own children would be available to every woman. But in a better world, we would also devote our energy to solving infertility, solving it on its own terms, curing physical problems with physical solutions, and, most important, preventing these physical problems wherever possible. Safer contraception, a cleaner environment, better preventive health-care services—these would go a long way toward avoiding infertility in the first place.

While attention has focused on the infertility of wealthy whites, in fact infertility, like virtually all illness and disability, is class and race related. Poor people and people of color are much more likely to be infertile. For people of color, adoption, informally arranged through families or more formally through agencies, remains available. The very factors that go into making so many children of color in need of adoptive homes, however, also go into making it harder for people of color to adopt. And the complexities of race relations in the United States make it very difficult, and often entirely inappropriate, for white people to adopt black babies. An all-white family in an all-white community, however much love it offers, cannot meet the social needs of a child growing up black in America.[10] But there are many families like mine, white people living in mixed communities with friends or relatives who are black, who can and do raise well-adjusted black children.

There have been recent attempts to deal with the inflexibility of the adoption system that left children with no permanent placement rather than placement in an "unmatched" family as part of larger shifts in adoption policy. The Multiethnic Placement Act of 1994 made it illegal for states to delay or deny the adoption of a child based on attempts at racial matching. In 1997 the Adoption and Safe Families Act changed the balance in decision-making in adoption from the preservation of the families the children were born into to the "health and safety of the child." My brother, Jeff Katz, who was head of Adoption Rhode Island, the agency that handles "special needs adoptions" in that state, expressed his confidence that as a result of that law "tens of thousands of children are going to be adopted by loving families . . . parents who will fight like hell to make sure their children receive the education and services they need."[11] Jeff, understandably enough as director of an agency responsible for placing these children, focuses on the needs of children in foster care; while I—and it makes for interesting family dinner conversation—focus on the poverty, sexism, racism, and capitalist individualism that pushes those children into foster care and creates a society in which the only children who get their needs met are those whose parents can "fight like hell."

With economic justice and an end to racism, with a feminist revolution, these problems would mostly go away. Right now we are not living in that better world, and right now adoption makes enormous sense, especially but not exclusively as an individual solution to infertility. Taking in a baby that needs parents is surely more reasonable than risking one's life and health in low-success infertility treatments.

But we are left with the painful contradictions that adoption presents: creating a family in joy, helping others to create a family in joy, being humiliated in public agencies because of one's infertility, being humiliated in those same agencies because of one's fertility, giving a baby, losing a baby, adopting a baby, buying a baby—adoption is all of those things. Since it is the infertile, would-be adoptive parents who have the most power, they are the ones whose definition of adoption has the most power. For them, adoption is a solution to infertility, their creation of a family, a way of having children of their own. And that becomes the cultural understanding of adoption, as we focus on the welcoming arms and turn away from the empty arms.

Beyond the moral dilemma of relying on one problem, women who have to give up babies, to solve another problem, people who are infertile wanting babies, there are practical problems. For a brief historical period, using one problem as the solution to the other problem seemed to work, partly because as a society we turned a deaf ear to the anguish of the birth mother, and partly because the birth mother also often felt this was her best choice. But pragmatically, two problems cannot be used as a solution to each other, because if the two are not kept "in synch" solving one problem comes to look like the creation of the other problem.

And that is precisely what did happen. We have come a long way toward solving the dilemma of American women being forced to give up babies. We solved it with legalized abortion, making it possible for women with unwanted pregnancies to avoid creating a baby only to lose it. And we solved it by making it more acceptable for a woman to raise a baby by herself, without a husband.

But solving the one problem intensified the other. So now some people talk about how awful it is that young women raise their babies alone, when there are such deserving couples waiting. And some people talk about what a tragedy it is that women are having abortions when there are so many homes waiting for babies—or at least for white babies. Others step in to solve the problem: some by importing babies from other countries, relying on their problems as our solutions. And some solve it by deliberately creating empty-armed mothers, making a business of baby brokering and of "surrogacy" encouraging women to have babies for the sake of giving them up to solve other people's problems. If the problem of an unwanted pregnancy is no longer sufficient motivation to create willing birth mothers, then the problem of poverty can be turned into the motivation.

It could have gone the other way, of course. Picture what would have happened had we somehow managed to find solutions to the problem of infertility first, and were able to get almost any woman pregnant at will. Then we would have been left with the problem of "extra," unwanted babies. Perhaps we would then speak disparagingly of couples having children, especially those having large families, while other children go homeless, with no one to care for them.

The painful irony is that we do have that problem, too—we do have children, not so much babies as children, going homeless. Although adoptions from foster care in the United States increased from 31,000 to 36,000 in the first year after passage of the Adoption and Safe Families Act, there are still at any given time 100,000 children in foster care waiting for families.[12]

Orphans Real and Imaginary

Adoption is a triangle. The third side, the one I have not yet discussed, is the child. For an infertile woman or couple, adoption is a route to parenthood. For a birth mother, adoption is a way to solve an unwanted pregnancy, or to provide care for a child she cannot raise herself. For a child, adoption is survival. It is parents, a family, a place in the world. In Eileen Simpson's autobiographical account of her orphanhood, *Orphans Real and Imaginary*, she recounts how she and her sister lost their mother to TB shortly after Eileen's birth.[13] Their father, faced with raising two very young daughters, shuffled them around in foster care, finally placing them, prophetically, in an orphanage. A few years later, he too died. She writes of her life in the orphanage, later in a "preventorium" to treat "pre-tubercular" children, and still later with battling relatives who apparently wanted the small legacy that went with them more than the children. In her book, Simpson places her own orphanhood in larger context. She discusses orphans in history and in literature, from Charles Dickens to Little Orphan Annie and more. She discusses "half" orphans, people who lost one parent (how horrified I was to think of myself, who lost a father in childhood, as any kind of orphan at all), and "psychological" orphans, people whose parents were physically present but psychologically absent. The category broadened, became meaningless. Is there anyone who has never felt orphaned—abandoned, unloved? We move from true orphanhood, the pathetic inhabitants of a Dickensian please-sir-may-I-have-some-more orphanage, to existential loneliness, the orphanhood of all modern people.

A basic theme of Simpson's book, expressed in her essay on orphanhood but more poignantly presented unstated in her autobiography, is the manipulation of children in the interests of adults, and the achingly sad ability, in the face of such manipulation, of children to continue to love.

The father moved the girls from one foster home to another whenever people spoke of splitting up the two sisters, but he also moved them when foster parents, "equally distressing to my father," hinted at adoption.[14] He preferred the orphanage. Several times a year he came and whisked the girls away, straight to Best and Company, where they were transformed with new clothes and haircuts into the daughters he wanted, and photographed the way he liked them. But each year, by the time the photos were framed, the girls were back to being orphans, returned to the institution.

Their father was unwilling to make the sacrifice it would have taken either to keep his children with him or to give them up. Instead, he kept his apartment in Greenwich Village, his life of independence. And he kept his two children—as stored property. These are the things *I* saw as I read this book. These are not the things Eileen Simpson always saw. A loving daughter, she never questioned her father's abandonment.

I have been thinking about this book, about orphans, as I have been attending meetings on the new procreative technology. Infertility specialists announce with pleasure that they have broken the age barrier: with egg donations even old women can have babies. We know scientists have helped to complete the pregnancies of women who have died: the bodies of brain-dead women have been kept functioning to bring a fetus to term and then been unplugged after the birth. Doctors are helping to solve the infertility problem of older men: men in their fifties and over, often starting second families, make up a sizable segment of infertility patients. At a recent meeting I attended one specialist said he'd solved the infertility problem of a seventy-one-year-old man. Another topped it: he'd helped a seventy-eight-year-old become a father. But the first took the prize: he'd twice (twice!) removed live sperm from men after their death. They do it all the time with prize bulls, said the veterinary scientist at the meeting, describing the technique. "Just how we did it!" said the doctor who had just solved the problem of death, let alone age, as a cause of infertility.[15]

In her discussion of orphans in history and literature, Simpson talked about "posthumous" children, children born after their father's death. Now we have children born after their mother's death, children conceived after their father's death; now we can create orphans to order with the freezing of embryos.

But *why*? Why would a man want his sperm to live after him? Is this the route to immortality? Is virility, aliveness, so tied up with motile sperm that if those little tadpoles can still wriggle a man still lives? What can it mean to be a child created, brought forth into the world, just so a sperm could live?

What of Baby M and the other children of "surrogates"—children brought into the world not just because someone wants a child to rear and to love, but because a "genetic link" is needed. No orphan, Baby M—she suffered from too many, not too few, parental claims. But still her situation highlights the contradictions in our relations with children. Stern, her father, claimed intent: he *planned* on that child. Whitehead, her mother, claimed love: she had *not* planned on loving that child. Like countless women before her, however a pregnancy began, she fell in love with her baby. Relatively few of us had parents who so carefully planned us; most of us were lucky enough to have had parents who grew to love us.

Is intent a substitute for relationship, for love? Simpson shows us not. Her father's intentions, his bursts of attention, made her love him. But far more did she need ongoing care, the matter-of-fact love of parenting. She missed parents, seen from the outside as people who

> had the power to soften the discipline, slow the tempo, make exceptions. They bestowed affection on their children, offered them special tidbits at the table, selected their clothes with an eye to what suited them, took account of their preferences, and were indulgent about defects of character (especially those that reflected their own). Parents felt no need to disguise their preferences: they unashamedly preferred their own children.[16]

Those are the needs of children: preference, specialness, daily love. And what are the needs of adults for children? Sometimes to love and be loved, so the needs of parents and of children match. Mostly it works out.

But now we can separate out our genetic material from ourselves, from our lives, in space and in time. Now we can create children with whom we have no tie but the genetic. We can deliberately create abandoned, orphaned children. We can do it out of our own sense of orphanhood, as Mr. Stern, who had no "blood kin," had Baby M produced, so he would have a genetic relation. Certainly he intended to raise the child, to love her. But what of the old men who want a baby? What of the scientists rescuing sperm from dead men's testicles?

To overcome our adult orphanhood, our existential loneliness, we create orphans: the children of intention, not of love.

The orphanages are opening up again, Simpson reminds us. Not filled with the indirect victims of TB, but of the newer diseases of poverty: drugs, crime, abandonment. Children still move from foster home to foster home, finally to the orphanages, the state unwilling to terminate parental rights and genetic claims, even after years of neglect and abandonment. So some orphans sit, abandoned property, while others are created—from the living or the dead—so that genes may live on.

Infertility

THE TREATMENT OF infertility needs to be recognized as an issue of self-determination. It is as important an issue for women as access to contraception and abortion, and freedom from forced sterilization. There is no contradiction in assuring access to both infertility services and abortion services for all women who would choose them. Not only do different women have different needs, but the same women have different needs at different points in their lives. A woman who had an unwanted pregnancy and abortion at eighteen may very well need, for unrelated reasons, treatment for infertility at twenty-eight. Being infertile at twenty-eight, or thirty-eight, does not necessarily make a woman regret abortions she may have had at eighteen—what the woman wants is to have a child now, not to have spent the past decade of her life raising a child she didn't want then.[1] And a woman who needed to have medical treatment for infertility at one point in her life may very well have an accidental, unwanted pregnancy at some later point, and want an abortion. The issue is not getting more women pregnant or fewer: the concern is women having as much control as they can over entry into motherhood.

Of course the issue of individual control is inherently complicated. It raises the basic questions of free will, individual choice in any social structure, and our limitations as embodied beings whose bodies do not always accede to our will.

Feminists have been struggling with all of these questions in one area or another. In regard to motherhood, we have become particularly sensitive to the loss of individual choice in a pro-natalist system. There is no question but that women have been forced into motherhood, and into repeated motherhood, when that is not what they themselves wanted. And it is also true that social systems create our wants as surely as they create the ways in which we meet them. Women have been carefully trained to want motherhood, to experience themselves and their womanhood, their very purpose in life, through motherhood. And that is wrong.

And yet. Wanting children, and wanting our children to want children, is not such an awful thing. I am frankly at a loss as to how I could possibly raise my own children in a way that was not pro-natalist. I love them, I love having them in my life, my children bring me joy—and I share that with them. I love friendships, and long talks—and I share that with them, too. And it delights me when I see them developing their own friendships, learning the pleasures of conversations with friends. How can it delight me less to see them develop their own interest in children? I love it when someone brings a baby around, and my son is eager for his turn to hold and play with it. I love to watch him teaching his sister and her friend how mirrors work, or helping them work a problem through. I look at him and I think, He's going to be a great father. It's not that I insist on this for them, or insist that they experience children in the same way I do, as a parent, but I want them to have the pleasures life can bring, and to me children are one such pleasure.

Certainly a world in which nobody much cared whether or not they had children would be a sad place. So pro-natalism, in a general, joyous, but not coercive way, is a good thing.

Like all the things we teach our children, some lessons are learned more powerfully by some children than by others. Some of our children will learn from us the joys of having children to raise, and will want that for themselves very much, and some won't. How much a person wants to have children, how well they learned that lesson, is not connected to the condition of their tubes, their exposure to infection, or to any other cause of infertility.

In this sense, infertility is just like any other adult-onset disability. I have a good friend who ultimately had to have a leg amputated. He fought it as hard as it could be fought, for years. He endured great pain, repeated prolonged hospitalizations, the loss of a business he had developed, risks to his health from drugs, and repeated surgery. I thought he was crazy. It's only a leg—use crutches. Other people thought *I* was crazy to suggest such a thing. It's his *leg*, they'd say, how can he not fight to save his leg?

I watch women go through painful, dangerous, expensive, life-encompassing infertility treatments, and hear the same kinds of discussions among their friends and family. Some say, "So she won't have children, what's the big deal. She can join 'Big Sister,' take her nephews to the circus. It's nice to have children in your life, but it's not worth risking all this." And others say, "If there's a chance, the slightest chance that she could get pregnant, how can she not take it?"

If we are to recognize and respect choice, we have to respect these choices as well: the choice to accept infertility and the choice to fight it.

Infertility as Disability

Thinking about infertility as a disability does give us a particularly useful model for developing social policy.

We begin with the "simple idea that society defines, implicitly, a population of 'normal' people; that is, people tend to think of the 'standard human model' as able-bodied, having what are considered typical functional abilities."[2] Disability then can be understood only in the context of normal abilities, and is inherently a *social* and not a *medical* concept. The relevant medical concept is impairment, defined as "the expression of a physiological, anatomical or mental loss or abnormality. . . . an impairment can be the result of accident, disease or congenital condition."[3] Examples of impairment which result in infertility include scarred fallopian tubes, congenital malformations of the uterus, testicular damage done by mumps, and so on.

Disability is most often based on an impairment, and is a " 'dis' (lack of) 'ability' to perform certain functions. . . . Disabilities apply to generic or basic human functions: walking, speaking, grasping, hearing, excreting and so on."[4] Procreation—sperm production and ejaculation in the male, the ability to ovulate, conceive, and gestate in the female—can certainly be considered a basic human function, and the loss of ability to perform such functions a disability.

The third level of analysis, beyond impairment and disability, is handicap, defined as a "socially, environmentally and personally specified limitation. Aspirations or life goals must be taken into account when defining or identifying a handicap."[5] In the case of infertility, a person who does not want (any or any more) children is not handicapped by an impairment in procreative capacity—surgical sterilization is in fact the purposeful creation of such an impairment. But for a person who does want a child, the same impairment constitutes the basis for a handicap.

Even under these circumstances, the handicapping effects of any given impairment vary, depending on the social environment. For me, a very sedentary person, a below-the-knee amputation of one leg would not be particularly handicapping—I don't think it would change my life dramatically, provided I had an adequate prosthesis, good banisters to hand when I needed them, cars with hand controls, etc. For my friend, the loss of a leg was experienced as handicapping. For a professional athlete or dancer, it would be even more profoundly handicapping.

Similarly, an infertile person who can adopt a baby, and so enter into the social role of parent, may not be handicapped by infertility. The handicap depends on how goals are defined (having a baby rather than having a pregnancy) and the societal resources (babies available for adoption) to which the person has access. For a man who is infertile, the availability of a sperm donation, enabling his mate to become pregnant, can offset the handicapping effects of his impairment and resulting disability.

An advantage of thinking about infertility as a disability is that we can see the proper place for medical treatment. Some treatments can cure the cause of the impairment: blocked tubes can be unblocked, ending an impairment, whether it's a fallopian tube and the impairment caused infertility, or the eustachian tube and the impairment caused hearing loss. Other treatments can bypass the impairment and prevent the disability: in vitro fertilization offsets the disability effects of tubal impairment. But there are equally important, non-medical ways of managing disability, ways that address the handicapping effects of the disability—like learning sign language, having wheelchair ramps, adopting babies.

This analysis leaves two unresolved issues, however. One is deciding which ways of overcoming the handicap are socially acceptable. Kidnapping newborns would also ameliorate the handicap of disability. That is quite obviously not an acceptable solution, any more than buying a human slave to carry around a person without a leg or purchasing corneas from starving people to cure blindness would be acceptable. So while the principle of providing services to overcome a handicap is not unique to infertility, there remains with all handicaps the problem of deciding which services, medical or other, are socially acceptable.

Second, we have to remember that not all ways of solving the handicap are equally acceptable to the *individual*. Returning to the example of the leg amputation, a wheelchair, crutches, and various levels of sophistication in prosthetic devices will all help overcome the handicap. But some (technologically sophisticated replacement leg) may be better than others (crutches). With infertility, as with other disabilities, ways of overcoming the handicap that most closely approximate normal functioning are usually the most acceptable: donor insemination or in vitro fertilization rather than adoption, for example. But these are individual decisions: some people with an amputated leg might find adjustment to a prosthetic too difficult, painful, or aesthetically unappealing, and prefer crutches. And some infertile couples might prefer adoption to the risks and discomforts of infertility treatments, especially those of in vitro fertilization.

For now, while there are babies needing homes, adoption is the preferred solution of many infertile couples. But adoption is problematic, for the reasons discussed in the preceding chapter. As a long-range feminist social policy, we cannot rely on adoption, but are going to have to address directly the prevention and treatment of the impairments that cause infertility.

As a rule, prevention generally makes more sense than treatment when designing social policy. On an individual, clinical level, we certainly have to respond to a crisis with appropriate treatment, but as a plan, we can put our efforts into avoiding crises.

Much infertility is avoidable, though no one knows quite how much. We need more basic research on the causes of infertility, with particular attention paid to the neglected areas of environmental and iatrogenic causes. Infertility is approximately one and a half times as common among women of color as among white women[6]—access to good nutrition, a generally higher standard of living, and better medical care, high priorities in any feminist agenda, would prevent some infertility.

But a focus on prevention has its negative side as well, in that it may lead to a "victim-blaming" stance, individuals being held accountable for their own infertility. Consider the attention paid in recent years to the infertility problems of the so-called delayed-childbearing women, the women who "put off" motherhood until their thirties or forties. One reason their infertility gets so much attention is that precisely because they are older, and put off child bearing to develop careers, they are the ones who can now afford the high tech, high-cost treatments. But their infertility is often blamed on their own choice, as if they're now paying the piper for their carefree years in graduate school or the years establishing jobs, businesses, and careers rather than making babies.

Besides its unkindness, there are at least two problems with holding women accountable for their own infertility. In the first place, the data are not all that clear on just how much fertility is actually lost as originally fertile women enter their mid to late thirties. While common sense tells us that infertility must increase with age, simply because each year of life presents that many more opportunities for damage to fertility, it is very difficult to get an accurate measure of the extent of this loss.

Until recently, fertility data were collected on married women only. Particularly prior to the legalization of abortion, a period which covers the early reproductive years of today's "delayed-child bearing" women, many of the most fertile women became wives and mothers. Many highly fertile young women were the pregnant brides of thirty years ago, pushed into marriage and motherhood by fertility. On the other hand, among those who avoided early motherhood and early marriage were those women who were markedly less fertile. Simply put, young married women have been likely to be fertile—it's one of the reasons they've married young. Older women who have never had children are likely to have higher rates of infertility—it's one of the reasons they were able to avoid having had children. It is not altogether clear what percentage of women discovering infertility at, say, thirty-seven were any more fertile at twenty-two.

Second, and I think even more important, this blaming of the women themselves ignores the context in which women have "chosen" to delay childbearing: a lack of maternity leave, of child care, of shared parenting by men, and so on. Shall we blame the woman for putting off childbearing while she became a lawyer, art historian, physician, set designer, or engineer? Or shall we blame the system that makes it so very difficult for young lawyers, art historians, physicians, set designers, and engineers to have children without having wives to care for them? Men did not have to delay entry into parenthood for nearly as many years in the pursuit of their careers as women now do.

It is easier to blame the individual woman than to understand the political and economic context in which she must act, but it does not make for good social policy. If we want to decrease infertility in part by having women concentrate childbearing in their twenties and early thirties, we have to make that possible for them.

Unfortunately, we have no reason to think that we can prevent all infertility: even if everyone had excellent health care, a safe working environment, good nutrition, and tried to get pregnant at twenty-four, we'd still have some people experiencing infertility. If prevention won't solve it, and adoption should not be relied on as a long-range solution, then we're left with medical management.

One school of thought among feminists has been to do away with high-technology infertility treatments. For all of the reasons I have outlined, I don't think that is acceptable policy.

But neither is business as usual. Infertility treatment embodies all that is bad in our medical care: it is available only to the well-to-do, it is male dominated, and it is offered in a way that is totally divorced from the context of one's life. And worse, it doesn't work. In vitro fertilization (IVF) fails more than three-quarters of the women who try it.

Much has been written about the skewed reporting of IVF clinics. Some of it is like the psychological self-protection in which many medical workers engage. Calling a "chemical pregnancy" (a positive pregnancy test even if the woman "miscarries" in time for a normal period) a success is a way of shifting blame for the failure to achieve a baby from the clinic staff (*we* got you pregnant) to the woman (*you* lost it). Blaming the patient for failing when the treatment was "successful" is a fairly common medical practice.

Some of the reporting, I think, is deliberately misleading. Some clinics cite the best success rates available for IVF even if they themselves have never achieved a baby. Half of the IVF clinics in the United States have not, in fact, ever gotten a baby born. There are more subtle misleading reports, too: dividing the number of babies by the number of women; for example, as if two sets of twins and one set of triplets among twenty women was the same as seven out of twenty women having babies. I've only seen one IVF clinic, but I'd be willing to bet that its wall of baby photos near the intake area is a near-universal feature. A few minutes of study and I realized that the same babies were pictured repeatedly—here at birth, there dressed for "First Christmas," over in the top corner showing off a new tooth. Innocent enough—grateful parents send photos, pleased staff puts them up—but the image is one of lots and lots of babies, a misleading image of lots and lots of "successes."

IVF clinics are having more success these days, getting more women pregnant and more babies born. But I fear it has as much to do with a change in admissions as anything else. Where the original candidates had no other chance of a pregnancy—no tubes at all, for example—today IVF and the related procedures are being used with less and less indication, earlier and earlier in the infertility workup. That is, IVF is now being used with women of greater fertility, women who might very well have conceived on their own in another few months. There are now women who do get pregnant while on the waiting list for IVF treatment, and we see more and more cases of women who "failed" IVF and then later became pregnant spontaneously.

The most significant shift in IVF use, however, is that it is now being used to treat male infertility. A man with a very low sperm count, or with other fertility problems, can use IVF to have his sperm fertilize an ovum. This means that fertile women, women who could get pregnant readily with another man, or with insemination with donor sperm, are being subjected to IVF treatment, including hormonal stimulation, sonograms, and surgery, to maintain their husband's genetic paternity.

The medical community likes to talk about infertility as a problem "of the couple." Since fertility level is a continuum (some of us get pregnant very readily, some less so, some men have higher sperm counts, some lower) this often makes sense. Two people of lower fertility will have more trouble conceiving with each other than either would with a highly fertile partner.

But if a man has a high sperm count the infertility problem is treated entirely as the woman's, whereas if the man has a low sperm count, the problem is *still* treated largely as the woman's. Further, Judith Lorber reports that most women who are undergoing IVF or GIFT for male infertility are told about "some little thing wrong" in themselves as well.[7] Which of course is probably quite true. Even very fertile people aren't perfectly fertile, and nobody seems to get pregnant at every possible opportunity.

This inclusion of "some little problem" of the woman's in the treatment makes the treatment of the woman as the patient for male infertility "more acceptable medically to the couple and to the staff."[8] All of this is particularly problematic when "sexual dysfunction seems to be a common reason why couples present themselves for infertility treatment, and why there are so many 'waiting list pregnancies.' It may also be the reason why the husband's inability to masturbate to ejaculation on demand is a perennial problem in IVF clinics the world over."[9]

A couple may be a social unit, but it is not a physiological unit. If a man cares deeply enough about an impairment which prevents him from producing adequate sperm, that impairment should be treated. We do therefore need more research on *male* treatment of *male* infertility, an area now neglected in favor of female treatment of male infertility. But if a man is more concerned about simply overcoming the handicapping effects of his impairment, insemination with donor sperm should be encouraged.

Many men do care less about the infertility per se than they care about what it is doing to their lives and to their wives.[10] Women have been very protective of men, and ultimately of themselves and their potential children, concerned that the man may not feel he is the social father to a child if he is not the genetic father. Doctors have colluded with women to protect genetic paternity, at the cost of women's safety and health. I think that a focus on men's nurturing capacities is more than appropriate, and that many more men would in fact accept the use of insemination with donor sperm (that is, accept the loss of their own genetic paternity) if it were recommended by infertility specialists as a relatively inexpensive, quick, and safe way to achieve a pregnancy and, as so many infertile men and women have expressed with longing, "get on with their lives." The more we learn to think of fathering as a social, emotional, nurturing, loving relationship, the less important genetic paternity will be.

In sum, I think we as a society need to think about infertility as we need to think about any other disability. We need to see it as a multifaceted problem. Some of it can be prevented, some can be cured, and some needs to be lived with. Part of the solution to any disability problem is a change in societal attitudes; part is a change in societal services. Disability is not doom, life is not over, and one does learn to cope. But recognizing that blind people can live wonderful and full lives neither excuses us from preventing and treating that blindness which is preventable and treatable nor gives us cause to deny the sadness in loss of sight.

We can recognize and acknowledge and fully appreciate the depth of grief that may accompany infertility, just as such grief may accompany the loss of a leg or of sight. To say that women are more than just mothers, that we are persons in our own right, does not mean that we have to deny the sadness of loss of motherhood.

Medicalizing Motherhood[1]

WHILE INFERTILITY, *not* getting pregnant, is a form of disability, strangely enough, more often pregnancy itself has been thought of as a disability. And just as infertility has been medicalized, so too have pregnancy and childbirth been treated as fundamentally medical events, with consequences no less damaging to women than the medicalization of contraception, abortion, and infertility.

The medicalization of childbirth occurred in two areas. One is the direct management of maternity care, with physicians taking over from midwives and from birthing women themselves the control of pregnancy and of childbirth.[2] The second area is in the occupational arena, where we can see once again the consequences of the uneasy alliance of feminists with the medical community.

In America, as a society founded on the liberal principle of equality, a major focus of feminist thinking has been the achievement of equality between women and men. This concern has encouraged some feminists to think of pregnancy and childbirth as comparable to other experiences that men can and do have. Thus some feminists would have society view pregnancy as a disability condition, comparable to other disabilities, so that women workers can be made comparable to men workers. Childbirth, they claim, should fall under sick-leave provisions. Workers can become disabled, they can be sick, but when they recover, they regain their prior status. Jobs are to be held open until the worker recovers, whether the recovery is from a pregnancy or, say, a broken leg. This way of minimizing the uniqueness of the pregnancy and birth experience does not always serve women well.

Actual "recovery" from birth is a matter of days. A woman can certainly return to a clerical job within a few days of a normal, healthy vaginal birth. The fact of the matter is that she is not sick. Biological motherhood, however, occurs in a social context. A day or so after the birth a new mother is usually in no mood to be sitting at a computer in an office. She is busy, tired, exhilarated, and entranced with her new baby, with more important things than her paid job on her mind. At a month or six weeks, when the sick-leave or disability coverage begins to run out, the baby is not sleeping through the night—and so usually neither is the mother. And the baby is beginning to smile at her. A woman may not *want* to leave the baby to spend the day typing, filing, or doing factory work. Even women in personally fulfilling jobs, women artists, lawyers, physicians, actresses, have been known to prefer spending their time with the new baby. And this is not a matter of physical health or disability.

For many women, fully paid but brief pregnancy disability leave and then child care—even free, high-quality child care—are not always the preferred solution. Even if you convince a woman that the baby will be just as well off, the *mother* may not be. Women who do not want a maternity experience essentially comparable to what men's experience with fatherhood has been may find that the dominant thinking in the feminist movement does not represent their concerns.

These work issues have been addressed by feminist attorneys. At a feminist conference on women and the law,[3] for example, participants debated "Pregnancy: Equal Treatment vs. Special Treatment." They "struggle[d] with the question of whether, and if so, how, pregnancy, a unique physical condition of women, can be incorporated into a theory of women's equality under the law." Those at the workshop discussed whether pregnancy "can or should be compared, as a legal matter, to other physical conditions that similarly affect how a person functions, as required by the Pregnancy Discrimination Act, or whether a doctrine of special accommodation to pregnancy should be developed." Dominating the discussion was the awareness, by all concerned, that *either* way of treating pregnancy, given our society in which women are placed at a disadvantage, can be used *against* women.

The danger in recognizing pregnancy and childbirth as unique female events is that women will be defined by their biological status, and forced into traditional social roles. The danger in the egalitarian approach, which minimizes the difference between men and women—pregnancy is similar to a twisted ankle and birth comparable to gallbladder surgery—is that women's lives will be limited, not expanded, by nontraditional roles.

Recent political gains by women have been made mostly by emphasizing the egalitarian approach. In our society, where the rights of individuals (rights to try rather than to succeed) dominate, collective solutions are rarely available. There is no free, high-quality child care, so that whatever changes have been made in occupational opportunities, women still remain largely responsible for the care of children and families. Women at the top of the economic structure are able to "buy out" of some of these responsibilities by hiring other women for child care. Women at the bottom of the economic structure have no such alternative. The unanticipated consequences of the class limitations of American feminism were to deny how much time and energy those responsibilities take, and to deny the possible satisfaction and joys available to women in the family.

What ended up being minimized turns out to be the emotional, social, and psychological components of motherhood. Left as irreducible reality were the physical phenomena, which were then treated as medical problems from which one can "recover" with "treatment." So rather than expanding the fathering experience, encouraging men to share in these personally and socially meaningful parts of mothering, the mothering experience becomes narrowed to its physical side.

While the implications of a disability model for pregnancy and childbirth on the job are still being hotly debated within feminist circles, the issue of direct medical management of pregnancy and childbirth brings a surprising consensus. The consensus is not only from the various feminist perspectives, but also from the most traditional of women. Critics of the medicalization of childbirth include noted feminists such as Adrienne Rich,[4] the group of traditional 1950s housewives who joined together to form La Leche League, professional women like physician Michelle Harrison,[5] and women like Marilyn Moran,[6] a mother of ten who says "in the conjugal social exchange coitus must be followed by childbirth as a love encounter." All agree that the medicalization of motherhood, the treatment of pregnancy and of birth as medical events, has not served the interests of women.

That is not to say that individual women have not benefited from specific medical services, such as the necessary cesarean section, and the appropriately used antibiotic. These and other procedures have certainly saved lives and health, but the institutionalization of childbirth as a medical event goes far beyond individual treatments. It has meant placing doctors in the active role, and mothers in the passive position of patient, recipients of services rather than controllers of their own birthing.

When childbirth became a medical event, women lost control over their own birth experiences. The medicalization began with the eradication of midwifery as a profession, and continued largely unabated until the home birth and midwifery movement of the 1970s. Observing childbirth in Boston hospitals at the end of this period, in the early 1970s, Nancy Stoller Shaw described the typical American birth. The woman was placed on a delivery table similar to an operating table. The majority were numbed from the waist down, while they lay in the lithotomy position (legs spread apart and up in stirrups), with their hands at their sides, often strapped there, to prevent their contaminating the "sterile field." The women were unable to move their bodies below the chest. Mothers were clearly not the active participants in the birth. That role was reserved for the doctor:

> This does not mean that the woman becomes unimportant, only that her body, or more specifically, the birth canal and its contents, and the almost born baby are the only things the doctor is really interested in. This part of her and, in particular the whole exposed pubic area, visible to those at the foot of the table, is the stage on which the drama is played out. Before it, the doctor sits on a small metal stool to do his work. Unless he stands up, he cannot clearly see the mother's face, nor she his. She is separated, as a person, as effectively as she can be from the part of her that is giving birth.[7]

And in Boston hospitals over a decade later, Michelle Harrison, then an obstetrical resident, made virtually the same observations.[8] Although the situation may be very different in home births and in some midwifery-run birth centers, the pattern in hospitals remains the same: doctors deliver babies from the bodies of women. The women may be more or less awake, more or less aware, more or less "prepared," and more or less humanely and kindly treated, but within the medical model, the baby is the product of the doctor's services.[9]

The alienation of the woman from the birth, and more fundamentally from the *body*, is, I believe, the most important and consistent theme in modern obstetrics. The perception of the fetus as a person separate from the mother draws its roots from patriarchal ideology, and can be documented at least as far back as the early use of the microscope to see the homunculus. But until recently, the effects of this ideology on the management of pregnancy could only be indirect. For all practical purposes, the mother and fetus had to be treated as one unit while the fetus lay hidden inside the mother.

Radical change began with the development of techniques for fetal monitoring. The way that medicine used to "monitor" or, to put it more simply, watch labor was to observe the laboring woman. *Her* heart rate, *her* blood pressure, the frequency and intensity of *her* contractions, and the rate at which *her* cervix was opening up provided the information on how the labor was going. An additional technique, more directly a measure of the fetus, allowed the heartbeat of the fetus to be heard by placing a stethoscope to the mother's abdomen.

Electronic fetal monitoring was first introduced for "high-risk" pregnancies, but as is so often the case, its use rapidly became widespread. Electronic monitoring provides direct information about the status of the fetus in three ways: externally, by ultrasound monitoring of the fetal heart rate and uterine contractions; internally, by fetal electrocardiogram obtained with electrodes passed into the uterus through the cervix; and by sampling of fetal scalp blood, obtained from an electrode screwed into the fetal head. As it turns out, electronic monitoring may not really provide all that much more information than does good nursing care—in controlled studies, monitoring by nurses with stethoscopes staying by the mothers produced just as good fetal outcome (and a lower cesarean section rate) as did electronic fetal monitoring.[10] But the electronic monitoring certainly looks like more information, producing endless strips of printout for the duration of the labor.

But more important than the sheer quantity of the data, impressive though that is, is that the information comes in a new context. Instead of having to approach the woman, rest one's head near her belly, smell her skin, one could now read the information on the fetus from across the room, or from down the hall. While woman and fetus were still one being on the bed, medical personnel came to see them as two separate and different patients. The problem was exacerbated by continued development of a technology which renders the fetus visible, giving obstetricians more and more direct access to the fetus itself, its tissue and blood, and the direct observation of its movements provided by sonography.[11] In a patriarchy, the sense of separation of the fetus and mother was already there as a concept; the new technology allows the separation to be reified. More and more, doctors developed a relationship with the fetus, what they saw as a separate patient within.

As the fetus emerged as a new patient, so too did a new medical specialty, as Monica Casper has described in *The Making of the Unborn Patient: An Anatomy of Fetal Surgery*.[12] Fetal surgery is the most dramatic example of fetal medicine, if also the least successful. Casper estimates that fewer than one hundred fetuses have been operated on for congenital defects, and only about 35 percent have survived.[13] It may not have saved very many fetuses, but it does indeed serve as the "cutting edge" of fetal medicine. Fetal surgery has changed the way that people in general, and medicine in particular, think about the fetus. Most fundamentally, it both figuratively as well as literally removes the fetus from the woman.

> Fetal surgeons are trained as pediatric surgeons and not as obstetricians, illustrating that fetal surgery is viewed as pediatric surgery but "with a difference." (It is also pediatric surgery with an attitude.) Framing fetal surgery as a pediatric issue renders pregnant women barriers to be breached, bodies to be manipulated, and constraints to be managed—if they are made visible at all.[14]

The fetus became a patient at just the time that increasing numbers of pregnant women were rejecting the patient role for themselves, often to the irritation and distress of their doctors. Wherever midwifery services were offered, women flocked to them. Home birth, virtually unheard of in the United States outside of rural poverty areas, reemerged as a respectable alternative. Out-of-hospital birthing centers were opened in cities and towns all over the country. As pregnant women increasingly declared themselves healthy and rejected the labeling of pregnancy as an illness, as a fundamentally medical process needing medical control, the doctors began looking more and more closely at the fetus within, the tiny, helpless, dependent fetus.

Fetal Power[1]

THE SOCIAL RELATIONSHIP that is pregnancy is largely disregarded in the medical and scientific, and therefore in the legal, arenas. The focus has been entirely on the physical relationship between woman and fetus.

Now that new knowledge and new technology have shown us that the mother can no longer be relied on to automatically, biologically, protect her fetus, now that the uterus is no longer seen as a fortress, questions are being asked about who can be trusted and who cannot be trusted to protect that fetus. These questions are being debated within the fields of medicine, ethics, and law.

The debates are generally concerned with rights: the rights of pregnant women, the rights of fetuses, the rights of the state to intervene, the rights of physicians to call in the state and to use the power of the state to enforce their medical judgments. Those arguing for the rights of pregnant women, as I am, are asking that no distinction be made between pregnant women and any other category of citizen. The American legal system permits people a great deal of freedom in what they can do with their own bodies, including the right to refuse any and all medical treatment they do not want. Pregnancy should not be used to change the status of the individual in regard to her own body.

The other side of the argument, the "fetal-rights" claim, argues that fetuses have rights to protection, including protection from their mothers. The attempt is being made to extend child-abuse statutes to the fetus, creating a new legal category of "fetal abuse." If the state will intervene to prevent a parent from harming a child after birth, the argument goes, then why doesn't the state have the right to protect the child from its parent before birth? A variation of this argument is the question of prenatal torts. A born child has the right to sue for harm that was done to it in utero. That is, for example, the basis of the DES suits. DES was a drug prescribed for pregnant women to prevent miscarriages that has since been shown to cause serious problems, including fatal cancers, in the people who were exposed in utero. These men and women who were harmed by this drug their mothers took while pregnant with them can, in adulthood when the damage appears, sue the manufacturer of the drug. Well, some people have asked, why hasn't the child that right to sue its mother for harm she caused while pregnant? One man, for example, has successfully sued his wife on behalf of their child, because the tetracycline antibiotic she took while pregnant discolored the resultant child's teeth. The courts do not always find on the side of "fetal rights." Judges in Illinois, asked to allow a child's lawsuit against his mother for negligent driving while she was pregnant with him, refused, saying such lawsuits would permit "an unprecedented intrusion into women's rights of privacy and autonomy."[2]

Lynn Paltrow is a New York-based attorney who has been involved in many of these cases asserting claims of fetal rights. She says that over two hundred pregnant women and new mothers in approximately thirty states have been arrested. Most of these cases have focused on low-income women of color with untreated drug addictions, but women who drink alcohol and those who fail to get prescribed bed rest during pregnancy have also been arrested. For many years, she says, advocates were able to have most of these cases dismissed or overturned. But by linking fetal rights arguments with the war on drugs, prosecutors have been more successful. In October 1997 the South Carolina Supreme Court held that viable fetuses are persons, and therefore a pregnant woman who uses an illicit drug or engages in any other behavior that might endanger a viable fetus may be prosecuted as a child abuser. These women face sentences of ten years in jail. Paltrow, along with the Women's Law Project, a feminist legal advocacy organization, has formed the National Advocates for Pregnant Women to respond to these kinds of cases.[3]

I don't want to get mired here in the fascinating but seemingly endless legal arguments. Rather, let us step back and look at the assumptions underlying such an argument. This argument typifies the acceptance of the ideology of patriarchy, the child as the product of a seed planted in the woman, and the ideology of technology, mother and fetus as separate beings, like nesting Russian dolls, one inside the other.

Consider in contrast the woman-centered model of pregnancy I have presented: the baby not planted within the mother, but flesh of her flesh, part of her. Maybe, as very early in an unwanted pregnancy, a part of her like the ovum itself was part of her, an expendable or even threatening part, or maybe, as is most often the case by the end of a wanted pregnancy, an essential part of her, a treasured aspect of her being. If one thinks of pregnancy this way, then the rights argument is an absurdity. It is not the rights of one autonomous being set against the rights of another, but the profound alienation of the woman set against part of herself.

What might the implications be? Like the child that was a fetus and part of its mother, our old selves, our aging selves, are part of our young selves, and yet become someone very different. Can I in my old age come to sue myself for behavior I engaged in when younger? What if my coffee drinking in youth turns out to cause disease in my old age: can I sue myself? What if I trip in my youth against a ladder I left leaning against the house. If this old wound begins to trouble me, to incapacitate me, in my old age, can I sue myself under the home-owners policy I had when younger?

The fetus within the woman, this fetus that will become someone else someday, is not yet someone else. It is part of the woman. To have the fetus bring suit against its mother, or against its father for harm he did to his own sperm before conception, seems to me to be equally absurd.

And yet some would move the law in that direction. Pregnancy, as Ruth Hubbard has been pointing out for quite a while now, is increasingly seen as a conflict of rights between a woman and her fetus. And some doctors see themselves as the arbiters between the two parties in presumed conflict.

Consider the following debate, sponsored by the Hastings Center, the ethical think-tank. *Hastings Center Report* publishes case studies, cases that are felt to raise important ethical issues, along with two invited commentaries. For the case study titled "When a Pregnant Woman Endangers Her Fetus" two physicians wrote one commentary; I was invited to do the other.

> Janet M., in her early twenties, is pregnant for the third time. She has been an insulin-dependent diabetic since the age of twelve, but has experienced no major complications of diabetes.
>
> Dr. L. has repeatedly advised her of the risks that uncontrolled diabetes poses to her fetus. Congenital malformations are two to four times more common in infants of mothers whose diabetes is poorly controlled. Furthermore, uncontrolled diabetes can result in the birth of a premature, stillborn fetus.
>
> He admits her at fifteen weeks gestation, as an inpatient to treat her diabetes, but she discharges herself against his advice five days later, before her diabetes has been satisfactorily controlled. Once home, she ignores pleas from Dr. L. and other physicians to obtain chemstrips or a dextrometer for monitoring blood sugar. In response, she tells them she "has no money" or "forgot."

> At twenty-one weeks gestation she is hospitalized for a threatened abortion, but quickly announces her intention to leave. Dr. L. decides that her behavior poses a clear risk to the well-being of her fetus. Unless she changes her mind, he says, he will seek a court order to keep her hospitalized.
>
> Is his response justified?

The two physicians, Thomas B. Mackenzie and Theodore C. Nagel,[4] responded that there were three generic questions to be asked in cases like this. Does the physician have an obligation to the fetus that supersedes the parents' wishes? Is there sufficient certainty of the relationship between the condition or behavior and the risk to the fetus? Can the threatening condition be controlled or reversed without significantly endangering the mother? The physicians concluded that the answer was yes to all three questions, and supported "the decision of Janet M.'s physician to seek enforced hospitalization and treatment to protect and preserve the well-being of the fetus."

I did not agree. More important, I did not think those are the only, or the most appropriate, questions. First, had this discussion been written in the 1960s, it might have read as follows:

> Janet M., a diabetic, refused her DES treatment, prescribed as especially important in the prevention of miscarriage among diabetics. Further, although she was eleven pounds overweight at the time of conception, she refused to limit her weight gain over the course of pregnancy to under thirteen pounds.
>
> She compounded the problem by not taking the diuretics prescribed, and twice refused to show up for X-rays, citing a distrust of medications and radiations. Her irrational refusal to comply with her doctor's advice, plus her unwillingness or inability to limit her weight gain, indicate fetal abuse.
>
> Should Dr. L. seek a court order . . . ?

And a potential scenario for the not too distant future:

> Mrs. M., suspecting pregnancy, engages the services of an attorney who specializes in family law, especially prenatal agreements. On her initial visit to the fetologists, Mrs. M. and her attorney will be informed of the conditions to which she must adhere throughout the pregnancy, and a second attorney will be appointed as fetal guardian. Violations of the prenatal contract will result in the state gaining custody of the fetus: either forcibly removing it to an artificial womb, or putting Mrs. M. in one of the new high-security wings of the maternity hospital for the duration of her pregnancy.

These two scenarios, past and future, illustrate the two major problems I see with an obstetrician calling on the power of the state to control a pregnant woman's behavior in the interests of her fetus. First, obstetrics has too long a history of errors in management for us to be certain that obstetricians always know the best interests of the fetus. Each of the procedures cited above, recommended thirty-five years ago, has since been discarded as dangerous. It is too soon to be certain of the standing today's obstetrical practices will come to have in the future.

But even if one had perfect faith in obstetrical knowledge, a second and more serious problem remains: the costs to the civil liberties of pregnant women are too high. We are in danger of creating of pregnant women a second class of citizen, without basic legal rights of bodily integrity and self-determination. Competent adults in this society have the right to refuse medical treatment, even when it is believed to be life-saving. But as reproductive-rights attorney Janet Gallagher has warned, "The law's concern for human dignity and self-determination can all too readily yield to the recurrent temptations to view and treat pregnant women as vessels."[5] It is wrong to allow obstetrics or the state to subsume the interests and the civil rights of pregnant women to those of the fetus within them.

The basic ethical question in cases like this is: what are the obligations of obstetricians toward their patients? Or, more precisely, who exactly is the patient of an obstetrician? A long-standing definition of obstetrics is the "branch of medicine concerning the care of women during pregnancy, labor and the puerperium."[6] But that definition may no longer seem appropriate, as obstetricians such as Dr. L. increasingly define themselves as physicians to the fetus. The medical model of pregnancy as an essentially parasitic and vaguely pathological relationship encourages the physician to view the fetus and the mother as two separate patients, and to see pregnancy as inherently a conflict of interests between the two. Where the fetus is highly valued, the effect is to reduce the woman to what current obstetrical language calls "the maternal environment."

A more appropriate and ultimately more useful perspective is to see the pregnant woman as a biological and social unit. With a more holistic view, Dr. L. might remember that Mrs. M. has controlled her diabetes for over half her life, and through two pregnancies. It may not be a matter of behaving "as she chooses." As a mother of two young children, Mrs. M. may have a variety of compelling reasons preventing her from staying more than five days in the hospital, from returning for an indefinite period, or even from taking good care of herself at home. As *her* physician, Dr. L. might consider what *her* needs are—social and economic as well as medical—and how he might help her to meet those, rather than calling on the courts to control her.

We do not have to consider the fetus as a separate, alien being, locked in its mother's body, a patient we cannot reach without going through the mother. Nor do we have to consider the mother as a fetus container, a walking environment without social context. Women and their fetuses are bound together, and enmeshed in a social world.

The contrasting medical-legal construct of the fetus as a separate patient has come to a head in the situation of court-ordered cesarean sections. When women in labor or in late pregnancy have disagreed with their physicians (or who they thought were *their* physicians) over how to manage the pregnancy or labor, the doctors here too have turned to the courts.[7] In several bedside juvenile court hearings, with one lawyer appointed to represent the unborn fetus, another to represent the pregnant woman, and yet others representing the hospital, women have been ordered to submit to cesarean sections, the fetus within them claimed by the state as a "dependent and neglected child."[8] In 1981 the professional journal *Obstetrics and Gynecology*[9] reported one such case in which the woman, although found to be psychiatrically competent, was forced to undergo a cesarean section very much against her will. The article quoted the current edition of the classic obstetrics textbook *Williams*, which states that the fetus has "rightfully achieved the status of second patient, a patient who usually faces much greater risk of serious morbidity and mortality than does the mother."[10]

Not all of these forced cesarean sections turn out to have been medically correct decisions. The condition of the baby in the case just described was actually far less serious than the doctors had anticipated. In another, more tragic case, in 1987, a Washington, D.C., woman who was dying of cancer was forced to undergo a cesarean section of her extremely young fetus. Neither she, her husband and family, nor her physician wanted the cesarean to be performed. In that case it was a hospital administrator who called in the courts. A couple of years later a higher court overruled the decision, saying that the choice must be the woman's. The ruling came too late of course: the far-too-young premature fetus died within two hours; the mother died within two days.

In another case, one with a happier ending, a woman in Georgia with a placenta previa (placenta blocking the cervical opening) refused a cesarean section. Doctors testified that there was a 99 percent certainty that the fetus could not survive vaginal delivery and at least a 50 percent chance that the woman herself would die. Two weeks later the placenta had shifted and the woman had a normal vaginal birth of a healthy baby. The Georgia medical society headlined the story: "Georgia Supreme Court Orders Cesarean Section—Mother Nature Reverses on Appeal." But as Janet Gallagher points out, a legal and political precedent had been set.[11]

This has been made very clear to me in recent panels I have shared with obstetricians, where similar stories have been told of doctors who felt a cesarean section was necessary and intended to get a court order, but in the interim the woman gave birth vaginally. As one obstetrician told me, "Mother Nature intervened." When I suggested that perhaps the moral of the story was that the mother was right and the doctor was wrong, he corrected me. The mother was not right, he insisted—she was lucky.

Cesarean section is one of the most common operations performed on women, but it is rarely done to save the life or the health of the mother. Much more commonly it is done in response to fetal indications because obstetricians, rightly or wrongly, believe that the laboring uterus is potentially dangerous to the fetus. Major abdominal surgery is conducted on the body of the woman ostensibly to help her fetus.

The situation becomes even more problematic when surgery is performed on the fetus itself, with the mother opened up only to gain access to the fetus. Several operations of this sort have been done, including placing a shunt in the fetus with hydrocephalus, to prevent fluid from building up in the brain. The procedures are experimental and have had little real success—the only babies to have survived appear to be those that probably would have survived without the surgery. But hopes are high that such procedures will eventually work. Anticipating women's possible objections, some doctors, lawyers, and philosophers are already talking about "fetal advocates," people who can make decisions on behalf of the fetus, represent the fetus's interests, presumably particularly in those cases where the mothers resist dangerous surgery.

But are women enemies of fetuses? Women, in fact, do not refuse such procedures nearly as often as they should: women beg for a chance for new, rare fetal treatments, even when it means putting their own health at risk. Monica Casper says that fetal surgeons themselves refer to the women who participate in fetal surgery as "heroic," implicitly recognizing the dangers they face and the sacrifices they are making.[12] Even without the drama of fetal surgery and other in utero treatments, for most women, in the course of a wanted pregnancy, the fetus becomes real, precious, treasured. The overwhelming majority of women accept gratefully the cesarean sections their doctors offer—believing that it is best for the baby, even when current data show quite clearly that probably three out of four cesarean sections in America are not necessary.

Just as women are not the natural enemy of the fetus, doctors
their natural protectors. It was, after all, obstetricians who fought
"natural" childbirth. Starting in the 1950s there was a movement of mothers who wanted undrugged births and undrugged babies; their doctors wanted compliant patients, and were willing to put fetuses at risk to ensure the compliance of their mothers.

When mothers do refuse treatment, refuse surgery, they do not do so to spite the fetus. They are acting out of their own needs, convictions, beliefs, and values about what is right for themselves and their babies. Being pregnant complicates a woman's medical decision making, but so do all our social and moral obligations. We always balance our felt needs for medical treatment against other needs: we decide whether or not to postpone surgery, for example, if an aged parent or sick child or spouse needs our help. Deciding whether or not to undergo a particular treatment, we ask if we can afford it, in terms of our time, money, energy, and other commitments. We make our own individual medical decisions in the context of our complex lives, enmeshed in our relations with others. The presence of a fetus in her body complicates a woman's decisions—but it makes them no less *her* decisions.

Midwifery as Feminist Praxis[1]

In most of the chapters of this book, as I address issue after issue, I find myself trying to imagine woman-centered alternatives. What if, I wonder, women really controlled contraception and abortion, not in isolated, embattled feminist-run abortion clinics, and not in the ever-uneasy alliance with population-control forces, but in an ongoing, empowered way. What would abortion and contraception look like, what would our models be? It is an even greater leap of imagination to think about a woman-centered approach to infertility: how would feminists recreate the infertility clinics?[2] And what would feminist adoption be?[3] Try to imagine a woman-centered, feminist-run adoption agency.

But when we turn to the care of pregnant and birthing women, no such flights of imagination are required. There is an ancient, and continuing, worldwide tradition of woman-centered care: midwifery. Long before the obstetricians arrived on the scene, there was a practice and a tradition of midwifery. And that tradition continues today: with full professional autonomy (that is, the right to control itself as an occupation) in some states, and underground, even illegally, in other states. I am speaking here of woman-taught and woman-controlled midwifery, and not the medically, obstetrically trained nurse-specialist programs which have incorporated the word "midwife." Some women trained as nurse-midwives are, and some are not, part of the midwifery tradition, but it is that alternative tradition, that non-medical model of procreation, which I address.

Midwifery is, I believe, feminist praxis. Marx used the word *praxis* to mean conscious physical labor directed toward transforming the material world so it will satisfy human needs. Midwifery works with the labor of women to transform, to create, the birth experience to meet the needs of women. It is a social, political activity, dialectically linking biology and society, the physical and the social experience of motherhood. The very word *midwife* means *with the woman*. That is more than a physical location: it is an ideological and political stance. Midwifery represents a rejection of the artificial dualisms of patriarchal and technological ideologies. The midwifery model of pregnancy rejects technological mind-body dualism as it rejects the patriarchal alienation of the woman from her fetus. That of course is too negative, and too self-conscious a way of putting it. Rather than rejecting dualisms, midwifery continues to see unity.

The political agenda for feminism is quite clear: we must empower the midwives, enable them to practice midwifery as a fully autonomous profession, not subject to the control of physicians.

It is very difficult, in this society at this time, to even think of pregnancy, and especially childbirth, in non-medical terms, to imagine that midwives are doing anything other than being maybe "nicer," "kinder," or more "sensitive" than obstetricians. But it is not just warmth or empathy that midwives have to offer: there are some lovely obstetricians around too. And it's not just their gender that distinguishes midwives, especially as more and more women enter obstetrics. What midwives offer us is an alternative ideological base, and consequently the potential for developing an alternative body of knowledge about procreation.

The medical model sees a vulnerable fetus caught in a woman's body (the child of man held by woman) and a woman, although stronger than the fetus, also made vulnerable by its intrusion (weakened by what the man has "done to her," what he has growing in her). The job of the obstetrician is to help effect the separation of the two, so they can "recover," so that the woman can "return to normal," and the baby can be "managed" separately. The ideologies of technology and patriarchy focus the vision and the work of obstetrics.

In such a model, the development of hospitalization for childbirth made sense, and the increasing regionalization of maternity services (locating "high-risk" services in a central large teaching hospital) is perfectly rational, even imperative. One would not expect, after all, to do the best job of auto repair in the driveway, or even in the local gas station; the most well-equipped garage is the place for the best repairs. The workman is only as good as his tools. Birth is best done, as are auto repairs, where the access to tools is best.

But there are inherent problems in limiting our vision of childbirth to its technical, medical dimension. That vision of childbirth enables us to think only in terms of morbidity and mortality rates, and not the often wrenching social and personal implications involved in childbirth management programs and technology.

Compare this situation with a very different example of technological progress, that which has occurred in transportation with the introduction of automobiles. What if we approached the history of transportation with the same narrow focus with which we approach childbirth, defining it entirely in terms of life and limb, morbidity and mortality rates, as they vary with different modes of transportation? It is obvious that the shift over time from a horse-based to an engine-based transportation system has had effects on the morbidity and mortality rates associated with transportation. We might try to figure out the effects in terms of lives lost each year in transportation accidents, or in the more sophisticated comparison of lives lost per mile traveled in each system. It would be an interesting and valuable history of transportation to consider. But would anyone claim it is *the* history of transportation, that this is the most salient, most far-reaching effect of new modes of transportation in our lives?

The introduction of new technology in transportation has had a fundamental impact on American life. It has influenced family organization, our perceptions of time and space, our vision of the world in which we live. There is a context, a social context, in which we see the meaning of technology in transportation. A medical history of transportation is interesting and important, but it is only one (rather narrow) facet of the story. And so it is with childbirth.

The medical monopoly on childbirth, its control by physicians, has meant defining birth in medical terms, and thus narrowing our scope of perception. The other equally salient, humanly meaningful aspects of childbirth are lost to us, outside our narrow range of vision. This narrowed vision has given us detailed knowledge of some of the physiology of pregnancy, childbirth, and newborns, but without context. The woman whose pregnant uterus we think we understand is located three bus fares away from the facility we have designed for her care. The newborn whose blood is so finely analyzed is placed at a distance that must be measured in more than miles from the family on whom she will ultimately depend.

What midwifery offers us is not just tossing in a few social or psychological variables, but a reconceptualization of the "facts" of procreation. A profession controls not only people—as doctors control the nurses who "follow orders," the patients who "comply"—more important, a profession controls the development of knowledge. In regard to birth, the profession of medicine determines not only who may attend a birth, or what birth attendants may do, but it controls also what we know of birth itself.

In its control over practice, the profession of medicine maintains control over research—research in its broadest sense. Data are collected, both formally and informally, to support and develop the medical body of knowledge. But the data are themselves generated by the medical practices. The methods of observation in medicine have often been criticized as not being "scientific" enough, but the more fundamental flaw is in not recognizing the social processes involved in the generation of the data, of that which is there to be observed. So it develops that in our society the obstetrical perspective on pregnancy and birth is not considered just one way of looking at it, but rather the truth, the facts, science; others may have beliefs about pregnancy, but we believe medicine has the facts. However, obstetrical knowledge, like all knowledge, comes from somewhere: it has a social, historical, and political context. Medicine does not exist as something "pure," free of culture or free of ideology. The context in which medical knowledge develops and is used shapes that knowledge. In particular, the setting of practice is an important part of the generation of the data on which the knowledge is based.

To begin to make this point clear, I am going to draw examples from two very different worlds, different "settings of practice." I am going to contrast medical obstetrical knowledge with the knowledge of a lay midwife practicing outside of medical settings. The same physiological event, the birth of a baby, can occur in many places—women labor and babies are born in a variety of settings. But the social definitions, our ideas about what is happening, are vastly different in different settings, and these differences create new social realities. In turn, these new realities, or definitions of the situation, create new physiological reality, as the birth process itself is shaped by the settings in which it occurs. Let us begin with a simple, everyday event.

Situation 1

> A woman comes to the maternity floor of a large hospital. She is upset, almost crying, holding her huge belly and leaning against her husband, who seems nearly as upset as she is. "My wife's in labor," he states, and hands over a scrap of paper with times marked off—the seven- to twelve-minute intervals they have timed between contractions. The woman is ushered into a cubicle and examined. The examination might be repeated an hour later. "No," the doctor tells her, "you're not in labor yet. You have not yet begun to dilate. This is just a false alarm, a false labor. You can go home and come back when you really are in labor."

Here we have a physiological event—the painful contractions of the uterus—defined in two different ways, as labor and as not-labor. The woman and her husband are basing their definition on her feelings, the sensations she is experiencing as she has been taught to measure them—in minutes, for example. The doctor is basing his or her definition on what he or she feels as an examiner, the degree of dilation—how much the cervix has dilated. Each definition of the situation carries with it a way of acting, a set of behavioral expectations, for the people involved. As not-labor, the doctor is finished with the woman and can turn his or her attention elsewhere. The woman is to go home and stay simply pregnant a while longer. Defined as labor, however, the situation is very different. The woman changes from her status of pregnant woman to the new status of laboring woman. She will put on the appropriate costume (change from "maternity clothes" to a "hospital gown") and become a patient. The doctor will be expected to provide examination and treatment, to begin managing her condition. Only in labor will she become the doctor's responsibility.

Situation 2

> Cara (an empirical midwife): I got a call that Roberta was having heavy rushes but wasn't dilating and was having a hard time. I wanted to go see her and help. When I got there, Roberta was writhing with each rush and shaking. She just didn't have any ideas how to handle the energy. Joel was sitting beside her looking worried. The whole scene was a bit grim for a baby-having. I got them kissing, hugging, and had Roberta really grab on to Joel and squeeze him. Joel is a big, strong, heavy-duty man. He and I rubbed Roberta continuously and steered in the direction of relaxed. I let her know that she was having good, strong rushes, and that if she'd relax and experience it and let it happen, her rushes would accomplish a lot and open her up. She gradually accepted the fact that there was no getting out of this except to let it happen and quit fighting it.[4]

Here we have the same physiological event, a woman experiencing the same sensations and the same lack of dilation, defined along yet other lines. First note the difference in the language being used. The empirical midwife describing this situation is not talking about "contractions," the medical word for what the uterine muscle is doing, but "rushes." This midwife lives and works on the Farm, the Tennessee commune that published *Spiritual Midwifery*. The midwives explain their language:

> On the farm we've come to call these contractions of the uterine muscle "rushes" because the main sensation that happens when these muscles contract is exactly the same as the sensations of rushing while coming on to a heavy psychedelic, which feels like a whole lot of

energy flowing up your back and into your head. It leaves you feeling expansive and stoned if you don't fight it.[5]

This language relies on internal or subjective cues, sensations the woman herself experiences. The medical language, in contrast, relies on external or "objective" cues, information available to the examiner—how much the woman has dilated. Thus when the subjective and objective cues are at variance, in the medical situation the subjective cues are discounted. The woman's sensations of labor are "false" and the doctor's examination is "true." In the midwifery situation, the woman's experienced reality of the rushes is acknowledged. The "problem," the variance between subjective and objective measures, is here defined as the woman's inability to cope effectively, to "let it happen." This definition, of course, also carries with it consequences for the people involved: the midwife and the husband are expected to help her cope, relax, let it happen. For the woman, one of the negative consequences of this definition of the situation is that it tells her that it is in some way her own fault that she is having a hard time. In that way the midwives are doing the same thing as the doctors: imposing their definition of the situation on the laboring woman. The doctor's responsibility is very narrowly defined: to manage only "real" labor. The midwife's responsibility, in contrast, is defined more broadly, to include "helping" or "managing"—controlling the emotional as well as the physical situation.

Thus each of these alternative definitions carries with it quite different consequences, consequences that will shape the experience of all those involved, but most dramatically of the pregnant woman. It is one thing to be a pregnant woman, and quite another to be "in labor." And it is one thing to be told that the labor that you are experiencing is "false" and yet another to be told that the rushes are real and you have to learn how to relax and stop fighting them. The meaning given the particular uterine contractions of any particular woman becomes the basis for the way the event, and thus the woman, is treated.

These scenarios, and their implications, explain why it matters, even to those of us who are not midwives, that midwives come to have professional autonomy. With professional autonomy comes the power to control the setting of birth, and ultimately to control the birthing woman. As someone who is not a midwife, I prefer midwifery control to obstetrical control because obstetrical control, the "objective" medical reality if you will, diminishes the birthing woman. It makes her an object upon whom the art and science of obstetrics are practiced. The underlying ideology is that of technology, the body as machine. This depersonalizes the birthing woman, making her a suitable candidate for being hooked up to yet other machines.

The organization of the hospital maternity floor influences this mechanistic vision of the woman. Labor rooms look more like regular nursing-care rooms; delivery rooms more like operating rooms. As the woman is transferred from one to another, there is basis for more and more narrowly defining the relevant parts of her, as she first loses full personhood to become a patient, and then in the delivery room, where all the doctor sees of the woman is the exposed perineum centered in draped linen, becomes simply a pelvis from which a fetus is removed. The alternative birth settings—homes, "birthing rooms," and the like—provide a contrasting image, in which the mother is not lying flat, and is surrounded by friends and family, tied to a full social world. Such a setting may very well encourage the awareness of the social and emotional factors in the birth. Thus "contractions" may be the salient feature when palpating the abdomen of a semiconscious woman, but "rush" may seem more appropriate when talking to a woman who is experiencing one.

Is the woman I described "really" in labor when she experiences contractions with "no progress"? Who defines? Who sets the policy about whether such a woman could or should be admitted to a particular hospital? If midwife and physician disagree, upon whose judgment will the insurance company's decision to pay for the day of hospitalization rely? And so how will we learn which definition of the situation results in the better outcome for mother and baby? Unless and until midwifery achieves professional status, it controls neither the birthing woman nor the development of an alternative body of knowledge.

In sum, for midwifery to develop an alternative body of knowledge, to reach new understandings about what is happening in birth, midwives must have control over the setting of birth. I have come to see that it is not that birth is "managed" the way it is because of what we know about birth. Rather, what we know about birth has been determined by the way it is managed. And the way childbirth has been managed has been based on the underlying assumptions, beliefs, and *ideologies* that inform medicine as a profession.

Will the Circle Be Unbroken?

Childbirth is managed within the guidelines established in accordance with "obstetrical facts," but those facts themselves have grown out of the setting of practice established by medicine. The circle is tight, and usually closed. When it is broken, startling things happen.

I have made a study of the breaking of that circle of knowledge.[6] I have studied nurse-midwives, trained within medical settings, who began doing home births. For a nurse-midwife with standard hospital-based training (that is, someone who began her career as a nurse, and then entered a postgraduate hospital-based program in midwifery), doing home births is a radicalizing experience. It makes her think hard about her work and its meaning. In this new setting, she has to question many of the taken-for-granted assumptions of the medical setting and medical model. And she finds herself constructing a new model, a new way of explaining what she sees. This is the process of reconceptualization, taking something you've confronted maybe a hundred times, and suddenly seeing it as something else entirely.

There is a simple experiment that shows this process at work.[7] People were asked to identify a set of playing cards flashed on a screen. Most were standard playing cards, but some were made anomalous—for example, a red six of spades, a black four of hearts. The subjects were able to identify "normal" cards correctly. However, they not only failed to identify the anomalous cards correctly, but without any apparent hesitation or puzzlement "normalized" them. For example, a black heart would be identified as a regular red heart, or seen as a spade. When they were allowed to look at the cards longer, however, the subject began to hesitate. They displayed more and more hesitation until they switched over and began to perceive the cards correctly, identifying a black heart as a black heart, a red spade as a red spade.

For the nurse-midwife making the transition from the hospital to home births, many anomalies present themselves. The nausea she was taught was part of normal labor may not be there. She may begin to see that in the hospital this discomfort was caused by not letting the woman eat or drink anything during labor. The amount of time something takes, such as expelling the placenta, may begin to look, in this new setting, very different from the way it did in the hospital delivery room. At first she will try to apply the medical knowledge in this new setting, attempt to utilize the knowledge gained in the hospital for what she is seeing in the home. That won't always work for her. When she is faced with an anomaly in the medical model that she cannot ignore or "normalize," she has a radicalizing experience: she rejects at least part of the medical model. She may share that experience with other nurse-midwives, and many such stories are told. Hearing the resolutions achieved by others supports and furthers her own radicalization. What were perceived as facts come to be seen as artifacts: obstetrical constructions, artifacts of the medical setting.

Let me review a small sample of these questioned "facts":

1. *Vomiting and nausea are a common part of labor.*

Working outside of medical control, midwives who have not denied food and drink to laboring women have observed that nausea is uncommon. The question is: is nausea caused by labor, or by lack of food?

2. *Infection is likely to occur if much time passes after the rupture of the membranes and before birth.*

Careful and frequent vaginal examinations were standard practice in the hospital to assess progress of dilation once the membranes ruptured (the "waters broke"). Midwives working outside of medically controlled settings, faced with a natural rupture of membranes at term (when the woman is due) but before labor began, have on occasion avoided the examinations, fearing that they may be a source of infection. The question: how likely is infection, and at what interval after the membranes have ruptured, if hospitalization and vaginal examinations do not take place?

3. *Milk does not come in for three days after birth.*

Working against what had been standard medical practice, women (inside hospitals as well as outside) demanded their babies be brought to them earlier and more often. The new knowledge, now no longer even a question, is that milk comes in more commonly within twenty-four to forty-eight hours after birth when mother and baby have unrestricted access to each other. A corollary of this is that the time required for the infant to regain birthweight has been adjusted downward.

4. *Once full dilation is reached, second stage (pushing the baby out) begins. If it does not, the condition, called second-stage arrest, is a sign of pathology.*

Working outside of medically controlled settings, midwives sometimes observed a woman who, on reaching full dilation, rolled over, exhausted, and fell asleep. That is not something one would often see on a delivery table. After a nap, the labor resumed, with a healthy baby and mother. The question: what is pathological second-stage arrest and what is a naturally occurring rest period?

The examples abound. Some of the more interesting, like most of these examples, have to do with medical timetables, with how long the various stages of pregnancy, labor, and the postpartum period are claimed to take. Other questions have arisen about the distinctions between voluntary and involuntary control—just how much of the birth process can and does the mother control?

Where does midwifery stand amidst these questions? Can we turn to midwives to learn answers? The answer: only to the extent that midwifery emerges as a full profession.

The implications of allowing medicine the monopoly on childbirth management thus go beyond the relatively simple question of the infringement of other occupations' right to practice. What I am arguing is that our usual assumptions need to be turned on their head. As a society we claim that medicine has the monopoly because childbirth is more than anything else a medical event. The truth might more nearly be stated that childbirth is a medical event because medicine holds the monopoly on management.

If birth were moved out of the hands of medicine, if birth were defined in other than medical terms, the implications would be far-reaching indeed. Some of the "facts" about birth, as I have shown, would be seen to be "artifacts" of medical management. But it is not just that a new, more lenient and more individually varied set of timetables would be developed to replace the obstetrical timetables. As important as this would be, the effects of demedicalizing childbirth would go beyond even this evaluation. Demedicalizing childbirth would allow us to perceive the experience in new ways.

Such demedicalization would open up the possibility of new outcome measurements for birth. As a medical/surgical event, birth outcome is measured in standard medical terms: mortality and morbidity rates. The incidence of postpartum infection, for example, is perceived as a relevant outcome measure, useful for comparing alternative childbirth management strategies. This perfectly parallels the measurement of postsurgical infection rates in comparing, for example, vaginal and abdominal hysterectomy, or alternative treatments of various tumors.

If birth were defined in other than medical terms, other outcome measures would be perceived as equally appropriate. As things stand now, if two approaches to childbirth result in equal mortality and morbidity rates, the two approaches are perceived as being roughly equivalent. Thus home birth is demonstrated to be at least as safe as hospital birth because mortality rates are equal and morbidity rates are lower.

But birth is also an event in the lives of families, and if perceived as such, outcome measures based on familial experience would also be considered appropriate, along with infection rates or other measures of physiological morbidity. To take extremes, childbirth management that routinely leaves older siblings with nightmares and separation anxiety as the mother is removed from the household to return days later engulfed in the care of the new infant is not the same as a birth that leaves older siblings strongly attached to the newcomer, unshaken in their own secure position within the family—even if the rate of morbidity is the same. A birth management that leaves wives angry at husbands, and husbands feeling that they have failed their wives, is not the same as a birth that draws the two closer together. A birth experience that leaves the woman unsure of her mothering abilities and unable to comfort a crying new baby is not the same as a birth experience that leaves the woman feeling confident and competent. And a birth experience that excludes the father, or whomever the woman is planning on raising that child with, is not the same as a birth experience that leaves the co-parent intensely attached to the child and feeling his or her own parenting competence grow.

Childbirth is also a learning experience for women. Perceived in those terms, birth outcome can also be measured in terms of the woman's knowledge about her body, her baby, and her birth. With demedicalization, teaching skills, long valued in midwifery and largely ignored in medicine, would be considered important. A pregnancy and childbirth experience, again looking at the extremes, that leaves the woman fearful of her bodily functions, unsure of just what was cut "down there" or why, is not the same as a birth that leaves the woman feeling strong and positive about herself, more rather than less comfortable with her body.

In sum, the medical monopoly on childbirth management has meant defining birth in medical terms, and thus narrowing our scope of perception. A birth management that routinely leaves psychological and social trauma in its wake for the members of families, using this narrow definition, is measured as perfectly successful, unless the trauma is severe enough to be measured in appropriately "medical" terms—that is, infant weight gain or some such crude measure.

Because I challenge the usefulness and the validity of such measures, I thus challenge the medical monopoly on childbirth. The policy implications that follow from this challenge are admittedly radical. If childbirth is redefined in other than strictly medical terms, medicine as a profession loses is long-standing monopoly on childbirth management in the United States. The demand by midwives to practice their profession is not an attempt by a less qualified group to engage in the practice of medicine, as it has most often been seen, but rather the claim of a more qualified group to practice midwifery. The state, as granter of professional licensing, remains in a position to license—or to refuse to license—individual midwives or classes of midwives. But redefining birth in non-medical terms means that it will be midwives and not physicians who determine appropriate midwifery qualifications, who set the standards for midwifery practice, and who advise the state on the licensing of midwives.

If childbirth is not merely a medical event, then physicians are simply one profession with relevant expertise. That expertise will continue to be used, as birthing women and midwives will continue to call on physicians for their skills. But breaking the circle of medical dominance would mean that medical practice would not determine women's experience of birth: women's experience of birth would determine medical practice.

Baby Doe: The Relationship Continues[1]

NEONATAL INTENSIVE CARE has been called the new battleground in the ongoing medical war against death. And perhaps it is.

As in any battle, advances are sometimes made and the enemy sometimes retreats. But the costs in human life and suffering are unspeakable, and sometimes, win or lose, *the battle may not be worth the cost.*

There is a growing consensus in the United States, on every level—from legislation on the living will to the films made for children—that the intensive-care unit may not be a place where anyone wants to live.

I was struck by the scene in *E.T.*, for example, where the lovable "extraterrestrial" lies surrounded by tubes, bottles, wires, and monitors in a form of ICU set up in the home of the boy Elliott.

As he appears to be dying, E.T. has become an object of scientific interest and curiosity, and the viewer empathizes with Elliott in his desire to scoop him up and get him out of there. Audiences everywhere cheered as Elliott and his friends took over from the doctors and scientists and gave E.T. what he really needed. They sent him home.

Parents whose babies are placed in intensive-care units sometimes feel very much like Elliott watching E.T. They see their babies wired, strapped, taped, and bound, and they are sometimes horrified. Some parents believe it is necessary, that this is what will make the baby well. Some parents are less sure, seeing only slim chances of survival. And among those who think it is the baby's only chance as well as those who think it is no chance at all, there is sometimes a strong feeling that this is not a place where a baby ought to be.

Some parents try to "humanize" the environment—an interesting expression. No environment could be more human than that entirely artificial, manmade world in which the baby lies. It is not so much that they wish to humanize the *environment*, I think, but that they need to declare the humanness of their *babies*. Parents, nurses, and doctors, too, share that concern. Teddy bears are placed in the corners of the boxes the babies occupy. Decals of butterflies and balloons grace the walls here and there. It does not change the essence of the unit, though, or what is happening there.

Some of us feel that what is happening in these units is not necessarily in the interests of the babies, but in the interests of the people who run them. Some people feel they are run to make money. I spoke to one mother recently who had removed her baby from a neonatal ICU against medical advice. She said that the child never needed to be there, had been perfectly fine, she believed, and now, three years later, she still had no reason to doubt her judgment. So why had he been placed there? Money, she said. She was well insured, and the hospital had run up thousands of dollars in bills, and was unwilling to release the baby while more money could be made. That is her understanding.

Others feel the motivations are more complex; not money, perhaps, but knowledge. It is in the interests of scientists and doctors to learn more. It is certainly in their interests in terms of career advancement and professional training. It is even in the interests of future sick babies for scientists to learn more, to look at the baby in front of them in terms of not only what they can do for it, but what they can learn to help other babies later on.

Parents, unlike scientists, have vital concerns only with this particular baby right now, and what this particular baby needs. And not all parents feel their baby needs what medical treatment has to offer. Some feel, like Elliott, that they can offer the baby a better chance of survival outside the medical setting. And some feel that survival is not the only value—that it is sometimes better for a baby to die in peace than to live in horror.

When parents make such a decision, there are those who see the choice not as an act of great personal sacrifice and love, but one of selfishness. The parents are accused of behaving not in the child's best interests, but in their own, preferring the death of their baby to the distress and difficulties of raising a child with disabilities, a child who is not now and probably never will be "perfect." Of course, someone has to make decisions in the baby's interests, and some claim that the conflict of rights between parents and child is too great for us to be able to trust parents. Therefore, babies need to be protected against their parents, we are told.

It is from this belief—that parents are not trustworthy advocates for their babies—that the Baby Doe regulations developed. Someone—not the parents, but someone *else*—has to represent the babies. The idea that parents, and particularly that mothers, do not act in the interests of their babies, and most especially their disabled, disfigured, or otherwise needful babies, represents a significant change in the popular American image of motherhood. Our earlier images portrayed mothers as self-sacrificing, all-accepting, all-loving.

Let us turn from 1982's *E.T.* to 1941's *Dumbo*. Dumbo is a baby elephant who is grossly disfigured. His ears trail to the ground so that he trips over them. He is clumsy and foolish, in appearance and in action. Of course, the other elephants laugh, and reject him. Dumbo's is, as they say, a face only a mother could love, and his mother loves him, indeed. When he is humiliated and threatened, she flies into a rage, bringing the circus tent crashing down. Her frilled cap and sweet, maternal smile disappear as she rears up to full elephant size and power.

I do not believe that the shifting image, from mother as protector to mother as potential enemy of her children, represents a change in maternal behavior or protectiveness. I believe it represents, among other things, a response to the feminist movement. If women can look out for our own interests, then, some fear, perhaps we cannot be trusted to look out for the interests of our children.

It is in the context of this lack of trust that the Baby Doe situation must be understood. Neither motherhood nor medicine is an institution society has much faith in these days, although babies are as highly valued as ever, and maybe more so.

And it is the context of the changing ideology that makes me so profoundly distrustful of even the most well-meaning and sincere attempts to protect newborns with disabilities.

In Defense of Mothers: A Rebuttal

Much of the support for Baby Doe legislation—laws requiring physicians to aggressively treat all newborns who have any chance of survival—has come from the "right-to-life" lobby. There has also been strong support for this position from some, though by no means all, disability-rights activists. One such activist is Adrienne Asch. Asch is a feminist, concerned with procreative rights for all women, and a disability-rights activist, concerned with the rights of disabled people. Where the right-to-life groups see the Baby Doe issue as an extension of the abortion issue, Asch sees it as an issue of discrimination against people—newborn people—with disabilities, and a reflection of our society's profoundly negative feelings about disability. She asserts that "newborns with disabilities should be treated, even against the parents' wishes, even if it requires state intervention." That is a clear statement of the position represented in the Baby Doe regulations designed to protect newborns with disabilities. In what follows, I will examine, and challenge, the words and phrases used in her statement.

"NEWBORNS WITH DISABILITIES . . . "

Let us begin at the beginning, Asch's reference to "newborns with disabilities." Is that the population to be protected by the Baby Doe regulations? Sometimes, surely. Some of the Baby Does have been full-term infants, with evidence of disabling conditions. That, of course, was the case with the initial Baby Doe, the 1982 Bloomington, Indiana, baby born with Down's syndrome and a blockage of the esophagus, whose parents decided not to treat the blockage.

But that is not the case for the majority of the patients in neonatal intensive care. The predominant problem is prematurity. Had the pregnancy continued to term, we have no reason to expect that most of those babies would have been other than healthy. The longer the pregnancy continued, the better the condition of the baby; conversely, the shorter the period in utero the greater the chances of death or severe damage. The disabilities are created in the course of continuing what should have been a period of gestation, and the best of neonatal intensive-care units is a very poor substitute for the mother's body.

As the technology of the neonatal intensive-care unit (NICU) becomes more powerful, premature babies are being kept alive at earlier and earlier stages, and at this point, definitions of prematurity are coming to overlap our definitions of miscarriage. The implications of treating a miscarried fetus as a newborn can be devastating: a miscarriage can be prolonged for months or even years as the fetus/baby slowly dies. A poignant, yet Kafkaesque description of this situation can be found in *The Long Dying of Baby Andrew*, Robert and Peggy Stinson's journal of the miscarriage of their baby at twenty-four weeks.[2] As she lay in the recovery room following the miscarriage, Peggy Stinson was shocked to be informed that the "baby" was doing well. The baby, named Andrew, spent six months dying in unremitting agony, as sores ulcerated to the bone and the bones themselves shattered. The miscarriage was finally completed six months later, as even all the tools of the NICU failed to keep Andrew from dying.

Where do such "newborns" or, more accurately, "extrauterine fetuses" come from? Some, like Baby Andrew, appear to be genuine accidents of nature—a poorly placed placenta, a uterine malformation, or some other idiosyncratic tragedy. But something far more systematic, and far more sinister, is happening. Prematurity is race and class linked. Prematurity is in large measure a problem of poverty. When mothers are not adequately cared for and nurtured, when they are not well fed, when they are stressed beyond endurance, then they cannot continue their pregnancies.

If, as a society, we wished to protect babies, we would be wise to begin by protecting mothers. We now spend millions of dollars treating babies whose problems could have been prevented cheaply. Our failure to do so results in the presence among us of ill, weak, and suffering extrauterine fetuses, the newborns with disabilities we only then feel a collective need to protect.

". . . SHOULD BE TREATED . . ."

"Treated" is a seemingly innocuous word that has come to mean medical treatment; in our society, treatment is what doctors say it is.

Many of us are coming to understand that medical treatment is sometimes inappropriate, sometimes unnecessarily harmful, unnecessarily painful, and unnecessarily psychologically distressing—and not always the most effective treatment around. There is some evidence to suggest, for example, that one highly effective treatment for prematurity involves wrapping the baby and mother together, and caring for the mother as she cares for the baby. In continuous, skin-to-skin, breast-to-mouth contact, even quite small babies have been shown to do well. In American hospitals, mothers and fathers are now more often allowed to be with their babies and children than they were just ten years ago, but more as *visitors* than as healers.

In cases involving children of all ages, parents' rights to decide on alternative treatments—treatments the parents could choose for themselves—are being overridden in favor of the medically approved treatment. As long as a single professional group maintains the monopoly on defining treatment, any claim that newborns "should be treated" will be a politically loaded sentiment.

". . . EVEN AGAINST THE PARENTS' WISHES . . ."

To refer to the needs of parents to do what they feel necessary for their babies as "wishes" trivializes the depth of their concern. I perceive the needs of people to prevent their child's death from being prolonged into months or lives of agony to be something more than "wishes." While some would have us think that the refusal of medical treatment is always destructive, others of us believe that it is sometimes protective—even if it means choosing death over continued existence. Parents who are sincerely acting to protect their children, to do what they genuinely believe is the right thing for the children, are not acting out of "wishes."

"... EVEN IF IT REQUIRES STATE INTERVENTION."
It is in this single phrase—in the bringing in of state power—that we come to the heart of the matter. For we are now talking not only about the kinds of decision-rules we should develop—that is, the direction in which we prefer to err when in doubt—but about where the power to make these decision-rules will reside.

I think we are all wise enough to know that whenever there are difficult questions to be decided, mistakes are going to be made. Some babies, who by almost all standards should have been allowed to die quickly and well, will be made to die slowly and in pain. And some babies, who by almost all standards should have received medical treatment, will suffer or die needlessly because such treatment was refused. And we must all be wise enough to realize that we may never know whether the right decision was reached in any given case.

Those who feel the Bloomington Baby Doe should have been treated say the decision made was clearly in error; with surgery on his esophagus, they believe, the baby would have been well. He would always have had Down's syndrome, of course, but his life, they believe, could have been a good one.

In Jeff Lyon's fine and thoughtful work *Playing God in the Nursery*,[3] he describes that case—and he also describes the seemingly similar case of Brian West. Brian, too, had Down's syndrome and a missing esophagus. He was treated, against his parents' decision and judgment, through five surgeries, none of which solved the problem. He suffered through two long years, never well enough to be at home, sometimes bound hand and foot to prevent him from tearing at his surgical wounds in agony. He died at twenty-two months, a lifetime from which his parents may well have been right in trying to protect him. Could that same fate have been in store for the other Baby Doe? Who knows? Who *could* know? Decisions to treat or not to treat are made, and then the babies live—or do not live—with the consequences. And sometimes we will never know what would have been, what could have been.

It is not really a question of whose judgment we trust. We cannot know who will be right, but we do know that, inevitably, anyone making these decisions will sometimes be wrong. To me, it comes down not to whose *judgment* we trust, but whose *mistakes*.

Medicine has a long history of mistakes, especially mistakes in matters of disability. It is ironic that the disability-rights movement seems so trusting of medical decision making regarding necessary treatment; there has been so much *unnecessary* medical treatment to avoid or to repair disability. Medicine has long regarded disability, like death, as a sign of professional failure.

The state, too, has a long and horrible history of mistakes on matters of disability. These systematic mistakes of the state can be seen in the history of eugenics in the United States, dreadful as it was, and, even more tragically, elsewhere.

And what about the mistakes of parents? We know, too well, that parents make mistakes. They demand too much or too little of, and for, their children. They are too fearful or too trusting of authority. They give up too soon or hang on too long. Yes, parents certainly make mistakes.

Why, then, do I trust the idiosyncratic mistakes of parents? Precisely because they are idiosyncratic. The mistakes of medicine and those of the state are systematic, and that alone is reason not to trust. Medicine and (perhaps even more so) the state make their mistakes in their own interests, in calculations of cost-benefit ratios, in definitions of "salvageability," in the very drawing of lines. This is not a society that has acted consistently in the best interests of children, of mothers, or of disabled people.

Parents may not be anywhere near infallible in their judgment, but historically it has been parents—*mothers*—who have made decisions in the best interests of children, who have acted to protect and to nurture children, who have even been relied on to put the interests of their children before their own interests. It is mothers, not doctors—and certainly not the state—who have historically demonstrated their trustworthiness (not perfection, just trustworthiness) as advocates for children.

If the situation were such that every objective observer who fully understood the facts of the matter would come to the same conclusion regarding treatment for any given newborn, this would be a far simpler matter. Our only question would be: "Who is best equipped to understand all of the facts?"

But that is very far from the situation we face. We live in a pluralistic society. People decide such issues—the questions of life and death, the kinds of disabilities and of circumstances that make life no longer worth living, the kinds of treatments that are worth enduring—in very different ways for themselves. There is genuine disagreement among us as to when life is, and is not, worth living.

The increasing acceptance of the "living will," a statement of the kind of medical care one would want to have or to refuse, if one becomes comatose or otherwise incompetent, demonstrates our acceptance of individual differences in values and in needs. With the living will, with the situation of people who have led some part of their lives, we ask the state to allow decisions to be made as the individual would have made them. For the newborn, for the extrauterine fetus, we have no way of life, no history of values on which to draw. The closest we can come are the values and way of life of the people who would have raised that child.

Ultimately, no one wants anyone to have the right to make life-and-death decisions for anyone else. But it is in the nature of parenthood that one accepts responsibility for a new life, and makes decisions as one would have the child make the decisions. Parenthood is always the acceptance of responsibility for a life.

These complex issues of life and its meaning involve much more than a straightforward question of disability rights. This is an economic and social issue, centering on access to prenatal care and nutrition, on poverty and prematurity. This is an issue of the individual's right to say no to the encroachment of medical technology into all areas of our lives and at all costs, and it is an issue of a technology bent on taking over reproduction at earlier and earlier stages. In a system that is cutting back on all the services women need to be good mothers, turning all of this into a disability-rights issue is unforgivably naive.

This is not a moment to judge parents. Our first priority must be to *help* parents, to give them what they need, nurturing mothers so that they can bring forth healthy children, nurturing both mothers and fathers so that they have the resources to give of themselves to their children, giving parents the information we want them to have, including information about the meaning and place of disability in the lives of disabled people.

And then, I believe, we are going to have to trust the subjective decisions and judgments of parents regarding the appropriate medical services for their newborns. Because there *are* no objective answers, and there won't be any in the foreseeable future.

Child Care

THE WOMAN IN front of me on the supermarket line is unloading groceries with one hand, jiggling a baby carriage with the other. The baby is fussing, wants attention. The woman has the same flavors of yogurt I buy, I notice. She also has a cantaloupe. I'd thought about buying one, but they're too expensive this time of year. I put it back, took apples instead. Little-baby noises are coming out of the carriage, getting more and more insistent. Sounds like a real little baby, not a newborn, maybe six months. The woman looks harried. The checkout cashier looks impatient. I'm trying to look friendly and supportive and as if I'm in no kind of rush at all. I've got to be home in fifteen minutes if I'm to be sure of beating the school bus. I'd help her unload the groceries, but the carriage is between us. The baby isn't actually crying—yet. The woman gets most of the groceries out on the conveyor and leans over the cranky baby. She looks really annoyed. Then she smiles, chuckles, talks softly to the baby. I guess either the baby smiled when it saw her or maybe it got its hat pulled over its face—that always got a smile out of me. The kid was unhappy because someone all of a sudden put out the lights. She makes a few adjustments (must be fixing that hat, I figure) and picks the baby up. She holds the baby against her with one hand, puts the grocery bags in the carriage, and takes out her change purse. I see the baby over her shoulder, looking at me. Six months, just as I thought, nose red from the cold, cheeks as pink as her snowsuit, eyes as blue as the winter sky. The woman is black.

The baby isn't hers. I wonder if the cantaloupe is.

What is the difference between her experience mothering this child, and my experience mothering mine? Between her experience with this child and her experience with her own children? This one gets cantaloupe in the winter, I guess. This one has parents, a mother, not her.

But what is the difference between the mothering I saw and any other mothering? Is the annoyance different when you get between minimum wage and maybe $15 an hour for it? Is the smile different?

Virtually every study I can find on child care looks for those differences—as they affect the child. It is the same, it's not the same, the child does less well, the child does better, the child is more dependent, less dependent, more advanced in speech, less advanced in speech. The child is the object of study; the woman—a hired babysitter, working mother, homemaking mother, birth mother, adoptive mother, day-care worker, baby-nurse, foster mother, foster grandmother, teacher—the woman is the independent variable.

What does it mean to raise children? What are the effects of nurturance on the nurturer?

The Managerial Mother

Gloria Steinem once took a good look around her and observed, "We've become the men we wanted to marry."

Nowhere is this truer than in parenthood. A generation of women have grown up to be exactly the kinds of parents we wanted our children's fathers to be. Middle-class, educated American mothers of today are the very model of the too-good-to-be-true, all-we-could-ever-hope-for father of the 1950s. We earn "good money" at secure, responsible, interesting jobs. We take our work seriously—but we balance it against the needs of family. Certainly that sometimes means sacrifices by our family: dinners we miss, business trips that take us away, not getting to every school play. But we are there a *lot*, and our families know we are working for them: our salaries pay the bills, and provide the luxuries. But more important, we are there psychologically. We take our families, our children, very seriously. We spend time with them, real "quality" time. We don't come home from work and bury our heads in the newspaper: we come in from a day's work maybe tired, but also in a way refreshed, ready to enjoy our children. We are prime parents. We may have turned over some of the nitty-gritty, day-to-day stuff but on all the important issues we are there for our kids. We don't have to be reminded about birthdays, best friends, school outings, loose teeth. It is the unimportant things we have turned over: the laundry, maybe, or a lot of cooking or cleaning or housewifely tasks. We may not be much on vacuuming, we may not be the kinds of housekeepers our grandmothers would approve of, but we are very good parents indeed.

I am not building this up to knock it down: I do think we are good parents, and I am describing myself here, too. But something does bother me about this. And it is not what has happened to the professional women who "have it all," and it is not what happens to our kids, who are doing just fine thank you, and it is certainly not what's happening to our husbands, who have either learned to iron their own shirts or left. With a few glorious exceptions, men have not taken up the slack here—while women have added full-time employment to the traditional mother role, men have mostly just added a few hours, at best, of "quality" time to traditional fathering. The people I worry about are the people who *are* taking up the slack, the people who have taken over the "unimportant" motherwork, the drudgery of mothering.

Some of that work has been totally split off from mothering, I think to the benefit of us all. While I, too, can get a nostalgic charge out of a wicker basket of freshly done laundry, it's also perfectly okay with me to drop off a bag of dirty stuff and pick up a bag of clean on the way to and from work. And while the smell of fresh-baked bread brings a song to my heart, rest assured there's always an extra frozen supermarket loaf in the freezer. And there's nothing like a homemade pie coming out of the oven—but filling a prepackaged frozen pie shell is as close as I need to come.

The moving of women's unpaid domestic work into the labor market this way, by dividing up the chores and purchasing goods and services, has had some largely unforeseen effects on the economy. The laundry, bread baking, and pie making are now part of the gross national product, in ways that they did not used to be. The woman who would have spent the day frying chicken and doing laundry a generation ago now works to earn the money to purchase fried chicken and laundry services—from other women who fry chicken, fold laundry, and work cash registers. A lot more money is changing hands without a lot more in the way of services being provided and, some would argue, even with a noticeable drop in the standard of living. I would regard full-time, live-in homemaking help as a luxury too decadent to even consider, not even if I won the lottery. That luxury used to be the birthright of every middle-class man. It was called a wife.

A wife baking your favorite pie, or folding your underwear, is providing a personal, even an intimate service. Dealing with dropoff, same-day laundry services and Mrs. Smith's frozen pie company is not an intimate experience, either for the consumer or for the provider of the service. Wiping a child's behind or nose, settling an after-school squabble between siblings, putting on a new Band-Aid, unsticking the zipper on the toddler's snowsuit—these *are* intimate services.

And these are the services we have also purchased from babysitters, homemakers, housekeepers, au pairs, nannies, and whoever else occupies the maid's room in rich folks' houses or works days in almost-rich folks' houses.

It is very difficult to get accurate data on child-care workers: who they are, where they work, how much money they make, and who hires them. We can know something about those employed in day-care centers and other relatively formal arrangements, but some—maybe a great deal—of paid child care is done at home and "off the books." Workers are paid in cash, without being taxed, but also without receiving social security and other benefits.

Something of a scandal around child-care hiring practices erupted in 1993 when Zoe Baird was the first woman ever nominated for the position of attorney general. Baird and her husband, it was learned, had hired an undocumented Peruvian couple to look after their three-year-old child, knowing they were illegal immigrants and did not pay taxes. Baird's nomination was withdrawn. The controversy brought the issue to public attention, and questions were raised about the child-care arrangements of other political nominees. The IRS reported a 17 percent increase in tax returns for domestic workers that quarter, as many other Americans who had illegal child-care arrangements rushed to legitimate them.[1]

In spite of that, it is still virtually impossible to know who is raising the children. Labor statistics cannot separate the woman who makes the beds, puts away the toys and last night's dishes, and meets the school bus from the woman who does all of the housework without children in the home: whether housekeepers or child-care workers, as has been true historically of mothering work, the tasks are combined.

What we do know is that there is almost inevitably a class difference between those who hire child-care workers and those who perform that task. And many employers prefer it that way. Julia Wrigley, in a study of middle-class parents and their in-home caregivers, found that while some parents seek class peers—primarily American college students, European au pairs, young women from the American midwest, and Irish and British nannies[2]—many "choose difference," "minimizing expense and maximizing their control."[3]

Motherworker

There's a new kind of mother manual out these days. The old ones told us how to mix formula, or how many minutes on a breast, how to be firm, be gentle, protect the baby, toughen the baby, let it cry, never let it cry—how to mother by the current rules of the game. The new how-to tells us all that, and also how to find, use, train, supervise, relate to, (not) compete with our children's caregivers.

I find reading through such books, listening to such conversations, deeply troubling. It is not just the "good help is hard to find" elitism of it all. What troubles me is listening to women talking about the mothering work of other women in a way that sounds to me like Victorian fathers must have talked about their wives. Maybe this is indeed the way rich people have always talked, and I am just new to the world of servants. But whether historically rooted or a new variant, this is not what I thought the women's movement was about.

First of all, as in every other discussion of child care, it is focused entirely on the mother. The slipping in and out of nonsexist language and assumptions is extraordinary. The *Big Apple Parent's Paper* (not mother's, parent's) ran a multipart series on "In Search of Mary Poppins." It was Part III that happened to come my way, on "Training and Supervising Your Caregiver."[4] The article began, "The time has come for you to go back to work—and to turn your baby over to someone else to be the mother all day." So much for nonsexist assumptions. The "parent" reading is a woman, and the caregiver is also a woman. Nothing else is imaginable. The reader is quite specifically told "First get your husband's agreement that only one person—namely you—will be supervising the caregiver. Any suggestions or complaints on his part about her performance should go through you." It is not just being patronizing, saying that caregivers "perform" and employers suggestions or complaints need to come from one person only. It is specifically that that one person is "namely you," the mother. Parents genuinely sharing child care, as they are apparently sharing responsibility for earning money, is not to be considered.

And how are we to treat Mary Poppins? "The general principle here is to relate to your caregiver in the way you want her to relate to your baby." That sentence is in italics. We are to relate to her as we do to the baby, but fortunately, it is a good era for babies: "Give her the feeling that you respect her and have confidence in her. Praise her for the things she does well. Don't attack or criticize her for mishaps or mistakes." Just what is meant by doing well? What are the standards for performance? Apparently, making sure that she is doing things "your way." The reader, presumably not an old hand at raising babies or she would not be reading this looking for direction, will begin the relationship with the caregiver by taking three days off "training her to take care of your baby by letting her see how YOU do it." The caregiver, never quite described here, is actually not Mary Poppins, who would have flown off the job. More likely she is a mother, maybe a grandmother, a woman who has herself raised children, her "own" or others on her previous jobs. But we will not learn from her, not even work with her, not even teach her. We will train her.

As I read this—and it is typical; similar articles are appearing monthly in women's magazines and in books for new parents—I am reminded of the centuries of childrearing advice from male experts to mothers.[5] I think specifically of the control exercised by fathers, who without actually taking care of the children set the boundaries, the moral tone, and the values under which mothers could rear the children of men. Barbara Berg, for example, in *The Crisis of the Working Mother*, tells the reader, "Knowing that you are in control—that your values and standards are being transmitted to the child even in your absence—will reinforce the feeling that YOU are the mother even if you are away at work."[6] Written a century ago, it would have been the father being reassured that he remained the head of the household, in control even in his absence.

Women want good child care, want deeply to have someone the child can feel secure with, feel love for—and yet feel threatened by that love. The pull and tug for the child's affection, as it is described today, reads like the Oedipal drama, stripped bare of sex, and left with the naked power issue. The mother wants the child to identify with her, not the caregiver. The child expresses its attachment to the caregiver. Berg describes her own feelings of distress when her child spoke of the babysitter as his other mother. She describes other women firing a caregiver precisely because the child grew to love her "too much." But as Freud showed us, if the child has access to power, it will turn to power, just as sons turned to fathers.

In the Oedipal situation as described by Freud, sons begin by loving their mothers, their caregivers, more than their fathers—the attachment, the identification is with the nurturant, caring mother. The father, unlike the mother, is a distant and frightening figure, who has power over the child, and over the mother. Once the boy child learns of the physical differences between the sexes, Freud hypothesized, he fears the powerful father will mutilate the son just as the boy believes the mother has been mutilated, by the loss of the treasured penis. Eventually the boy resolves his dilemma and fear by changing his identification to his father. The boy comes to want to grow up to be a man like his father, possessing for himself a woman like his mother.

Freud thought that this was universal. Bronislaw Malinowski, in his study of the Trobriand Islanders, gave one proof that it is not. There the boy fears his uncle, the man with the power over the boy and his mother in that matrilineal society. In the modern American family drama I am describing, both mother and father are sources of power—but it may be that neither is the daily caregiver. The child is asked to switch identification from the nurturant caregiver to the powerful parent, mother or father. And so in this situation, the source of power is not gender, but class.

Berg says she was comforted by someone assuring her, "Just as you can't feel the same way about another person's child as you do about your own, your child can't feel the same way about a caretaker as he or she feels toward you." But what does "own" mean here? Berg is no biological determinist. In a previous book she described her adoption of this child. What makes this mother-child bond so sure, so irreplaceable? It is not biology. It is not gender. It is power. We won't be "vulnerable to our children's declarations that they love their baby sitters more than they love us" because we will remember who is in control: "Remember that they are really our assistants rather than our substitutes."[7] And so might Freud have reassured the Victorian father who left his son in the care of the mother all day: the young child may profess his love of his mother, but he will grow up to walk in his father's footsteps.

If we are the fathers here, setting the tone, controlling the mothers, what are we looking for in these mothers? Compliance, certainly, is always important if we are going to remain in control. But there are other qualities, too, ones that vary with the age of the child. Berg describes Sara's search for a suitable replacement caregiver for three-year-old Gary. It is a discussion I've heard in playgrounds, school lobbies, kitchens, and offices for years. Lucy, the first caregiver, "had been wonderful with Gary when he was a baby. She was warm, nurturing, honest, neat and willing to follow directions. But she was not really interested in engaging Gary in intellectual or creative activities, and Sara felt these to be increasingly important as Gary grew older."[8]

These qualities of Lucy's are distinctively, stereotypically feminine qualities. Sara, and the dozens of women like her I know, are doing what men have long done. Men left the babies and little children to the warm, neat, nurturant, compliant care of women. As their sons outgrew the world of women, the private world, men took them off to schools, apprenticeships, the world of men, the public world. The new mother, the managerial mother, is doing the same thing, only she wants her daughters, too, to leave the world of nurturant women and enter the world of intellect and creativity.

Racism and classism enter into this equation, too. Poor women, women of color, are often valued for their nurturant qualities. I've been told that it is "island women," or "old southern black women," or "Mexican women" who are believed to be so motherly. But by the age of three or four—just the age at which the "Oedipal" drama begins—these aren't the qualities that are being sought, just as these feminine qualities were inappropriate for the Victorian boy. At this point, European, American, middle-class caregivers are wanted, with class and ethnicity replacing the gender in this revised Oedipal story. They're also expensive. While some people can afford the "au pair," or the graduate student live-in, more commonly such care needs to be provided in groups. Preschool and "enriched" day-care programs become the choice for entry into the world of intellect, what used to be the world of men, the public world.

Julia Wrigley has done one of the few studies of these caregivers. She points out, as I have, that as the children get older, "cultural issues acquire more weight."[9] The "quality" of care comes to be defined in more class-specific terms. Middle- and upper-class parents, in firing an immigrant or minority babysitter/housekeeper and moving on to more class-appropriate child care, see themselves as enriching their children's lives. And maybe in a sense they are, but caregivers, Wrigley shares with us, "have their own thoughts and insights into the meaning of their work. While parents seldom mention this, caregivers believe that the deepest lesson many children learn concerns their own entitlement."[10]

What happens to the discarded, outgrown caregiver? Some move from job to job, home to home, child to child. One friend told me about firing the babysitter her child had outgrown. A responsible employer, she found another job for the woman, in a household with a baby, and for more money. The child took it well, the mother told me—didn't seem more than passingly sad to hear the babysitter was leaving. But the babysitter—she cried. She said she'd miss the child. She's cared for her for four years. She'd grown to love her.

In a book called *The Managed Heart: Commercialization of Human Feeling*, Arlie Russell Hochschild describes the work of flight attendants. In the work that they do, "processing people, the product is a state of mind."[11] They are paid for what she calls emotional labor. "This labor requires one to induce or suppress feeling in order to sustain the outward countenance that produces the proper state of mind in others—in this case, the sense of being cared for in a convivial and safe place. This kind of labor calls for a coordination of mind and feeling, and it sometimes draws on a source of self that we honor as deep and integral to our individuality."[12]

The emotional work of mothers done without pay, or the emotional work of hired caregivers done for a salary, is a more intense version of the flight attendant's work, with the similar goal of creating a state of mind in others—just that sense of being safe and cared for. To do such work, Hochschild shows, calls for "deep acting" as Stanislavsky described it: we must call forth the emotion from our very selves. To soothe a child, it must feel cared for, nurtured, loved. To make the child feel that way, the caregiver must act like she indeed loves the child. To act so convincingly—and children are a tough audience—requires calling forth her own feelings of love, of tenderness.

What do caregivers *feel* when they rock an infant to sleep, kiss a boo-boo to make it better, play peekaboo, settle a playground spat? What did slave mammies feel as they nursed these white babies, lullabied them with songs of their own children's suffering, sale, even death? Perhaps it is not so surprising that child caregivers, from Roman slave nurses[13] to the American black slave and on to today's minimum-wage caregivers, are so often remembered with affection by their grown charges. At unknown costs to themselves, they were mothers.

Mid-revolutionary Mores

Is the moral of the story that no one should ever hire anyone to do child care? Maybe, in a better world, it would be. Maybe, in a better world, communities of people, not just mothers, would be responsible for children. I haven't the imagination to envision how such a world would work. The highly imaginative author Ursula K. Le Guin says that she could only make that work in a novel by having the people live in small communities.[14] Small communities of like-minded people have no great appeal for me personally, a resident by choice of one of the largest and probably the most diverse city on the planet. So maybe, in a better world, there would be no need of paid child care—but I don't even know what such a world would, could, or even should look like.

In this world, something has to be done about child care and paying for it is an inevitable part of what needs to be done. Some would like to see all child care institutionalized, with marvelous, state-subsidized or state-run day-care centers for children from birth on up. I'm not so sure. I worry about state-run or, worse yet, corporate-run day care, and the values either might teach children. I wonder about maintaining intimacy, warmth, individuality, nurturance in an institutional setting. I know it has been done in some fine centers, with a committed, excited staff developing wonderful programs. But on a large scale? For all children?

For now, we need to keep our options open. We need a variety of child-care arrangements: co-ops or communes of parents, mothers and fathers, sharing child care; small in-home child-care centers run by individuals; housekeepers; babysitters; lots of parental leave time; day-care centers—all of that, and whatever else our imaginations can conjure up. And it all takes money.

Child care is going to have to be provided either in a fundamental rearrangement of the way we live (for starters, flexible time and households and shared responsibility for children beyond just one or even two harried parents) or with a rearrangement of our money. Or both. We cannot go on calling for "affordable child care," if what is meant by that is one person's salary must be big enough to cover another's. That inevitably sets the salary and benefits to be made in child care as too low for that person in turn to be able to afford good child care. If children are to be something other than a burden, the costs must be a societally shared responsibility. Monetary subsidies for child care could help us break out of the class- and race-based pattern, in which the children of the rich are cared for by the poor, and the children of the poor too often go untended.

But it's not just money. *Someone* has to watch the children. *Someone* has to actually, truly, literally be there with them. Whoever that person is—mother, father, adoptive parent, sibling, housekeeper, teacher, babysitter, day-care worker, grandparent—*whoever* is with that child, that person must never be thought of as being there in place of someone else. The person who is there, is there. The person is not a substitute-someone-else. The person caring for a child is in a first-person, one-on-one, direct relationship with that child.

That relationship deserves respect, just as that work deserves to be valued. And respect, as we know from what has happened to mothers historically, is not adequately taken care of with politeness and a Mother's Day card. It must come with legally recognized rights. Someone who has been raising a child has moral rights invested in that child. At a minimum, we have to protect child-care workers from arbitrary firing, from loss of visitation rights to the children they raise, from having the relationship with the child used as a source of further exploitation.

Otherwise we seem to be caught in a trap of endlessly remaking the world in the same image: some people in the public sphere, the world of power, of importance, and some people in the private sphere, rocking the cradle but never really ruling the world.

Fatherhood

What the Problem Is Not

Every now and again, someone discovers that children are raised by women, and writes a book about it. The point of the book is to blame mothers, or mother rearing, for the evils of the world, most especially for the evil that men do. The basic argument of such books is that boy children, *because* they are reared by mothers, have to separate themselves, consequently rejecting the mother and the womanliness in themselves, and dominate women and the world.

The solutions proposed are various. Freud and those who follow his footsteps most closely have told us to live with it; it's the way things are. Feminists rethinking Freud have told us to fight it; it's not the way things have to be. Fathers can rear, too, and solve the problem.

Dorothy Dinnerstein, in *The Mermaid and the Minotaur: Sexual Arrangements and Human Malaise*, formulated the problem this way:

> Freud's contribution has radically deepened our awareness of certain structural defects in human life, one of which is the immense strain imposed both on male and on female personalities by the fact (a fact whose effects stem from certain cognitive and emotional peculiarities of humans; they do not occur in other animals) that the main adult presence in infancy and early childhood is female. In this sense Freud is revolutionary. What is conservative is his assumption that this structural defect constitutes a fixed condition of our species' existence, and that all we can gain from understanding it better is the grace to accept the inevitable without wasteful fuss.[1]

We are, Dinnerstein tells us, in very deep trouble, and a conservative acceptance of the inevitable is too dangerous to consider. By dividing our species in half, by making male and female worlds, we are each and every one of us less than whole. We have created "a division of responsibility for basic human concerns, a compartmentalization of sensibility, that makes each sex in its own way sub-human. The sub-humanity of women is proverbially obvious. What is now surfacing is a venerable underground intuition: that the sub-humanity of men may in fact be more ominous."[2]

The conclusion that Dinnerstein has come to, what she takes in fact as a *starting* point for analysis of human relations, is that mothering is the problem. It is not so much that it is a problem for mothers. She recognizes "the drain on adult female energy that it involves," but believes that could be fixed, perhaps by reordering ourselves back into smaller communities and sharing the load. What is important is not the effect of mothering on mothers, but "the effect of predominantly female care on the later emotional predilections of the child: the point of crucial consequence is that for virtually every living person it is a woman—usually the mother—who had provided the main initial contact with humanity and with nature."[3]

A couple of years later, Nancy Chodorow, in *The Reproduction of Mothering*, saw much the same problem, and much the same solution. Freud was right: mother-rearing has consequences that are not good. Freud was wrong: it is not women who are so horribly damaged, but men.

> Girls emerge with a stronger basis for experiencing another's needs or feelings as one's own (or for thinking that one is so experiencing another's needs and feelings). . . . From very early, then, because they are parented by a person of the same gender, . . . girls come to experience themselves as less differentiated than boys, as more continuous with and related to the external object-world and as differently oriented to their inner object-world as well.[4]

The loss, the ominous subhumanity, is men's. The solution is to involve men fully in child care, enabling boy children to experience the continuity, connectedness, womanliness in themselves that would make them whole.

I am not writing this year's book making that discovery or argument. There is a trap there, and I do not intend to fall into it. I do not think that mothers rearing children is the source of male dominance any more than I think that black women rearing white children is the source of racism. As Alison Jaggar puts it, summarizing a socialist feminist critique that has been made of Dinnerstein's and Chodorow's point of view, "A male-dominated society is always going to be misogynistic, no matter who rears the children. It may be that women rear children because they have low status, rather than that they have low status because they rear children."[5]

But what bothers me even more about this argument that "we must break the female monopoly over early child care," as Dinnerstein puts it, is the assumption that people are in fact in a pretty bad way, and that the source of that is mothering. What if we think instead that there is an extraordinary capacity for good in people, *including* men, an enormous ability to nurture, to care, to love, to be *good*, and *that* is a result of their mothering. Maybe the evil, especially the large-scale truly terrifying evil men do—war, nuclear bombs, death squads, concentration camps—comes from things like capitalism, racism, and nationalism, comes *in spite of*, not because of, the work that women have done in rearing children.

What I am suggesting—and I all but blush to say such a thing—is that motherhood is a force for good in the world. Taken one at a time, people are not so very bad. I am not prepared to make Will Rogers's statement about never having met a man I didn't like—but in the overwhelming majority of people there is some good, and I think that is generally because their mothers put it there.

It is not mothering by women that is the source of the trouble. Mothers—black mothers, white mothers, "hired" mothers, birth mothers, adoptive mothers, foster mothers—have done a pretty good job, under the circumstances. The problem is not the mothering, it's the circumstances: the limitations imposed on us in our mothering. This is not a world created in the interests of the mothering project.

It is with this understanding that I turn to look at fathering. Fathering is not the solution because mothering is not the problem.

The Capacity to Nurture

Whether we need them to or not, *can* men mother? The sociobiologists might make one think mothering is a matter of genetics, instincts, hormones.[6] And the kind of argument Chodorow and Dinnerstein put forth might make one think women have not raised men whole enough to mother.

Let's begin with the first issue: is it within the genetic, biologic capacity of men to mother? Do men have what it takes?

The answer depends on the question.

Research on the relationship, the attachment, love, bonding—as it has variously been called—of mothers and infants has generally addressed the question: what makes infants love their mothers, and what makes mothers love their infants? The search has been for characteristics and abilities of infants and mothers that make them able to love each other. Both mother and baby must be loved, and in turn lovable by the other.

It is a fascinating world of study: how infants engage their mothers, and mothers their infants. We learn that infants are more attracted to a facelike drawing than to a similar drawing with the features scrambled. It is not just the complexity of the mother's face, but its order that attracts the child. And if we pull in babies with our faces, so too do they capture us. The big round head, the large eyes, the babyness of it all is powerfully attractive. Mothers, we learn, turn to their babies "en face," lining up their faces parallel to the baby's, gazing into the baby's eyes with their own eyes.

Obviously mothers and babies are attracted to each other. Mothers knew this when doctors were still trying to tell us that peaceful fleeting smile was gas, and that searching gaze couldn't see, didn't recognize. It is rather nice that science has caught up with mother-wisdom.

But again, what you get for an answer—scientists and mothers alike—depends on what you asked in the first place. If you ask why mothers love their babies, you observe mothers and learn about them. If you ask what makes babies lovable, you observe non-mothers, too—and you learn that they do all the same things, are attracted in all the same ways. Thus Marshall J. Klaus and John H. Kennell called their initial, highly influential book *Maternal-Infant Bonding*[7] but said that they observed the same kinds of attraction to the babies on the part of researchers. Similarly, if you ask, "Why do babies love their mothers?" you get one kind of answer. If you ask, "*What* do babies love?" you might get a different answer.

Quite some years ago Harry Harlow, in his now-classic experiments with rhesus monkeys, demonstrated this—without particularly noticing it. Harlow was raising rhesus monkeys in sterile environments, isolated from other monkeys.[8] The baby monkeys raised in the empty cages were not psychologically sound. But of particular interest to Harlow was that they grew pathetically attached to the rags that lay in their cages. Not only did they curl up on them to go to sleep on softness, but they clung to them, held them close when frightened, screamed when they were removed. Like little Linus, the monkey babies used their rags as "security blankets."

Harlow asked the question: is this what infant monkeys love about their mothers—this softness, touch, "contact comfort"? He ran some other experiments using real baby monkeys and wire columns topped with vaguely monkey-shaped wooden heads. These he called "surrogate mothers." Half of the mothers he covered with soft cloth, and half were left as bare wire. Each monkey got two such "mothers," one cloth and one wire. In half the cages the milk bottle was placed in the wire mother, and in the other half it was placed in the cloth mother. What Harlow found was that it was the cloth doll to whom the monkey babies became attached, regardless of the source of milk.

They clung to "her" when frightened, clung when nursing, even if that meant stretching to reach from one doll to another, slept against her, seemed reassured by her presence in a frightening situation, and so on. They used this cloth doll much like a mother. The wire doll, on the other hand, meant nothing to the baby monkeys. Even if that was the source of their milk, they displayed no attachment to it, got no security from it, had no need for its presence.

So what Harlow learned is that what monkeys love about their mothers is their contact comfort and not their milk.

But what if I wanted to run a study on the question: do infant monkeys necessarily love their mothers, or could they just as well love their fathers? I might set up each monkey in a cage with two parent dolls. One would give milk, and I would call that the mother doll. The other would give no milk, and that would be the father doll. In half the cages the father would be wire and the mother cloth, and in the other half the mother would be wire and the father cloth. I would learn that monkeys can love whichever parent, mother or father, offers them contact comfort.

It is of course exactly the same study, with different names. Sticking a wooden head on a cloth column does not a mother make. Harlow certainly showed that infant monkeys look for contact comfort and get quite attached to its source. We've learned something about infant monkeys, quite a bit about Harlow, not much at all about mothers, and not a word about fathers.

Rhesus monkeys in the wild are raised by their mothers, and that is indeed their prime source of contact comfort. We know this because most animal research about parenting behavior has asked the question: "What is?" The answer, not universally, but most often, is that mothers and other females do most of the nurturing, as they do among the rhesus monkeys.

There are researchers, however, who have asked not the ordinary "What is?" but the more creative, challenging "What if?" In one such piece of research, in the early 1970s, Gary Mitchell, William K. Redican, and Jody Gomber at the University of California at Davis asked the question: can a male rhesus raise a baby?[9]

The researchers, in essence, gave several mature male rhesus monkeys infants for adoption. One of their pairs was Mellow and Pierre. The researchers were concerned about the possibility of fatal aggression, having heard reports of infanticide by adult males of this genus. So they began by familiarizing the pair. They housed a mother and her newborn baby, Pierre, in one half of a large indoor cage, separated by a clear Plexiglas barrier from Mellow, an unrelated mature male rhesus. For one month Mellow observed Pierre and his mother. Then Pierre was taken from his mother, in an adjacent room so that Mellow could hear but not see the process. His response to the distressed outcries of mother and child was violent, biting himself repeatedly. After a few days, when Pierre had learned to feed from a bottle, he was placed in a small stainless-steel cage within the larger cage that housed Mellow. Mellow spent time near the cage, resting his arms on its top.

> In the final stage of pairing, we took Pierre out of his small protective cage and let Mellow approach. They touched, then independently explored the cage. After a few minutes, Mellow groomed Pierre until the infant turned around and touched him. For the next six minutes Pierre clung to Mellow, climbed on his back and head, and leaned over backwards, holding on to Mellow's ears. Mellow withstood these infantile liberties, albeit with some anxiety. Then he began to threaten Pierre; several times his open mouth hovered over the infant's head. We stood by nervously. When Pierre screeched, Mellow pushed him away. The infant fled up the side of the cage and watched Mellow pacing the floor. Then Pierre climbed down again and huddled in the corner and began sucking his penis, a behavior often seen in animals whose social development has been distorted. Within seconds, Mellow sat down beside Pierre and began grooming him. During the entire seven months of rearing, when Pierre assumed this depressed posture, Mellow would usually begin to groom him. This grooming was an important part of their physical interaction. On occasion, Pierre groomed Mellow.[10]

Mellow successfully raised Pierre. He didn't raise him quite the way a mother would: they played more roughly, and their attachment seemed to grow closer over time, compared to the growing independence of a baby monkey from its female mother. At the end of the seven months of research reported, Pierre was a healthy normal monkey, physically and socially. And he and Mellow remained deeply attached. A two-day separation at seven months had Mellow biting himself so severely he cut several major blood vessels in his leg and required life-saving veterinary treatment. Pierre regressed to penis sucking and distress calls. Reunited, they clung to each other.

Can a rhesus male monkey raise a baby, love it, be loved by it? It would seem so. And it's not just monkeys. So, too, can male rats raise babies. With sufficiently intense exposure to infants they show the same four impulses toward pups as do postpartum females: crouching, retrieving, licking, and nest building.[11] Mellow and Pierre are not unique. Even in species in which males do not usually mother, males *can* raise babies.

Maybe they can, but *do* fathers raise babies? In one species, yes; in another, no. What does it tell us about humans? Not a lot. Which kind of species are we? In one culture fathers do more baby raising and in another less, but no, fathers do not seem to be doing most of the baby care anywhere. There are men in our culture who rear babies—not many, surely, but they are there. In his study of seventeen such men and their families, *The Nurturing Father*, Kyle D. Pruett found they do a good job of it, and more:

> It is good for all of them—not simple and not easy, but most certainly *good*. What is then ultimately allowed and experienced is a *real* masculinity that is nondefensive, creative, feeling and unafraid of being full of care.[12]

The men Kyle Pruett studied came to being full-time parents by a variety of routes: some planned it, and some fell into it as jobs were lost or shifted or schedules adjusted. However they came to it, the bond between parent and child grew. The men fell in love with their babies just as mothers do: they were pulled in by the child. Several described the power of initial eye contact, at or even during the birth:

> Her head came out and she opened her eyes and looked at me, *right at me*—I swear to God! Her shoulder popped out and then the rest of her slid out. Perfect, just perfect. . . . she opened her eyes again when I touched her—like she liked it! A shiver went up my back.[13]

And from another father:

> I held her in close—just pulled her in—kind of like a magnet. . . . She opened her eyes and we just looked at each other. She's the greatest.[14]

A third father, who had already spent years as full-time parent to his firstborn, described the birth of his second child:

> I remember holding him when the doc handed him to me—he was so perfect. I just talked to him—talked, talked, talked. I told him about his sister and his mom and dad, and how handsome he was. He opened and closed his eyes like he was actually listening and interested. Can you believe that? . . . I believe that the delivery room stuff is important. But it's not magic. . . . The stuff that really matters is what happens later on—at home.[15]

That is the thought echoed by all seventeen of these men: the bond with the child grew out of the care, out of the fathering. They raised the children, nurtured them, and made them their own.

Barbara Reisman did a study that involved interviews with fathers and children in a variety of households. Some men were sharing parenting with their wives, but Reisman also interviewed men who were single parenting by necessity, widowers and men whose ex-wives were not sharing child care. She found that not only were men perfectly capable of taking on the household work, what she called "making a house a home," but also did the intimate emotional work of child care and showed the overt affection children needed. She concluded, "I am indeed confident, then, that men can mother and that children are not necessarily better nurtured by women than by men. Even men who did not choose to be single fathers were able to invent mothering that works."[16]

In sum, research asking "Do fathers rear babies?" gives you one answer. Asking "Can fathers rear babies?" is a different question altogether. Clearly they can. We've seen individual fathers who have done it, and we've seen that a rhesus monkey, with no inclination to get involved in social revolutions or changing family life-styles, also can do it.

The biological, genetic capacities are there: I haven't scratched the surface of the data now available that tell us men can provide nurturance for babies, and have even the potential capacity to lactate. But even if it is within the biological or genetic capacity of men to mother, have they been raised to it? Are these nurturing fathers the exception? Are most men so "subhuman," so much less than whole, that they cannot mother?

Turn again to the argument Chodorow makes. Chodorow wrote about the reproduction of mothering, saying that because of the sameness of daughters to their mothers, daughters grow with the capacity to mother, to nurture, more highly developed: that is, mothers reproduce themselves in their daughters.

There is undoubtedly some truth to that: the more mothers see their children as like them, and coming to live lives like theirs, the more they will teach those children their way of thinking. And the more children experience themselves as like their mothers, the less they will be pushed into differentiating themselves, distancing themselves from mothers. But genitalia are not the only source of sameness and difference between mothers and their children. The slight, red-haired child brings forth feelings of self in the slight, red-haired mother that the large, dark-haired child does not. The shy child brings forth feelings of self in the shy mother that the outgoing child does not. We identify with, and distance ourselves from, our children in uncountable ways in the course of our mothering: appearance, temperament, skills, talent, interests, style—characteristics both born and bred. And our children do the same with us: experiencing sameness here, difference there, over and over, throughout our years of mothering.

The difference allows for individuation, a sense of a unique self. The sameness allows for identification, attachment, connectedness, ultimately what we call empathy. The "goodness" that I think is there, far more often than not, in men as well as in women comes from this ability to empathize, to feel for and with others. And maybe it is, indeed, for just the reasons Chodorow and Dinnerstein suggested, a more highly developed capacity in our daughters than in our sons—but it is far from absent in our sons. How much capacity for attachment, how much of this sense of continuity and relatedness is necessary to mother? And is this a fixed capacity, or is it not itself affected by the experience of mothering? Mothers, after all, do grow, learn, and develop as mothers.

Mothering is not just a feeling of identity, a sense or capacity for empathy. Just as we are not empty nests, not passive refuges, most surely we do not experience ourselves as entirely at one with our children. Mothering is also an activity, a project. Sara Ruddick has described "maternal thought," the intellectual work of mothering, the attitudes, the values—in essence, the *discipline* of mothering.[17] That motherhood is a discipline does not mean that all who engage in it achieve its goals—not any more than all scientists live up to the demands of the discipline of science, or achieve its goals. But motherhood, Ruddick reminds us, is not just a physical or emotional relationship—it is *also* an intellectual activity. It is this unity of reflection, judgment, and emotion that she calls "maternal thinking."

Mothers are working in the nexus between the child and society. Children need their lives preserved and their growth fostered. The social group needs that growth shaped in ways appropriate and acceptable to it, for its own continuation, preservation, and growth.

Maternal practice must meet three interests then, those of preservation, growth, and acceptability. These, Ruddick points out, are the demands that shape the discipline. The initial and most powerful demand is preservation: simply keeping the child alive, especially through its vulnerable early months and years, beginning, for birth mothers, with conception. But the mother must do more than keep this heart beating: she must foster the child's physical, emotional, and intellectual growth. And she must do that in such a way that her child becomes an acceptable adult. Both for the sake of the child and for the sake of the society of which the mother, too, is a member, the child must fit in, must grow to meet the needs of the society.

Looking at motherhood this way, as a discipline, a way of thinking, a response to the needs and demands that exist outside of the mother, shifts our focus from who the mother is to what she is doing. Who she *is*, who she feels herself to be, is deeply gender based: she is a woman, a mother. What she is *doing* is not gender based: the similarities in behavior of mothers has more to do with the similarities in their situations, in the demands they face from their children and from their societies, than it has to do with the similarities in the women. And so the person engaged in this discipline of motherhood need not be a mother, need not be a woman, to engage in these activities, this way of thought and practice that is mothering.

Fathering as a Relationship

A personal introduction: My early understanding of what the women's movement was about was that we were going to remove gender as a category where it was not relevant. Which is to say, almost everywhere. In homes, offices, playing fields, laboratories, hospitals, wherever we went, we would not be constrained by gender. There would be no more "men's work" and "women's work," but just work, which men and women would do, according to need, interest, ability, temperament—according to anything but gender.

With some enthusiasm my husband and I tackled the problem at home, in our new marriage. Did I make the dinner parties and he do the electrical work? I'd learn wiring, he'd stuff a goose for ten. We constantly questioned the gender basis of our relationship: were we doing things because we wanted to, because it suited us as individuals, or because we had learned that gender arrangement? And didn't the one flow right into the other, gender shaping our interests? We would circumvent our training by applying the rules of childhood: we would take turns, divide jobs, share.

We were married five years in 1974, and decided to have a child. We figured the same rules would apply. And they did. We shared, divided, took turns. We didn't use "mommy" and "daddy" language—we didn't want to *become* Mommy and Daddy, entrenched in gender-based parenting roles. For a long time the only sure point of communication between us was the diaper box: if we had something urgent to tell each other, that was the place to leave the note. Sometimes it seemed we only saw each other at what we came to call the "changing of the guard," passing the baby back and forth as we ran off to work.

I thought all of this would give my son double the security of mommy-reared children. I learned it also gave him double the vulnerability. Just like any child, he would sometimes cry when I left him. But I also found that I could not always comfort him when Hesch, his father, left. I offered the comfort and security of the breast. And Hesch offered the comfort and security of his shoulder—holding the child's head on his shoulder as month by month, year by year, the legs came to dangle down longer and longer. I've seen my very young children, both the boy and the girls, offer a doll the breast, and I've seen both hold a doll on their shoulder, walking back and forth in sharp imitation of Hesch.

I know nurturing care, the mothering acts, can be separated from gender.

AND NOW I've made two points that some would see as contradictory, developing an argument that seems to go nowhere. In the first place, I've said, children don't need men to mother, because women are doing the job very well. But I've also said that men can mother, will if they have to. Why bother showing men can mother, if children don't need them?

There are powerful reasons why men should mother, and it is not to save the children from their mothers.

Men should mother, should provide intimate, daily, ongoing nurturing care to children, in the interests not only of the children, but of mothers, of the men themselves, and of achieving economic justice and a better world. As in the general issue of child care, children are not the only ones involved, not the only ones affected by how we organize their care. How the children "turn out" is not the only question to be asked.

How the mothers are doing is also a fair question. Women may not need fathers to share the mothering with, but we certainly need someone. We cannot do it all ourselves. The problem of the double day for women, the unending circuit of paid work and then work in the household, not enough sleep, and back to work, takes its toll. We need help. But why the *father*?

It is not because of his sperm. Like mothering, fathering should not be thought of as a genetic connection, but a social relationship. A fair percentage of us, it turns out, are not genetically related to the men we grew up with as fathers anyway. Some physicians doing tissue typing for organ donations estimate that maybe 20 percent of people are not genetically related to the men who claim fatherhood; others say it is less, perhaps as low as 5 percent. In either case, the social relationship is the essential one: unless one is doing organ transplants, it doesn't much matter. Some children look just like their parents, and some do not. On any inheritable characteristic a child may, or may not, resemble the parent. They are not clones.

The social relationship of parenting, of nurturing and of caring, needs a social base, not a genetic one. Through their pregnancies, women begin to establish that base. Through their relationships with women, and then with children, men too can establish that base. Pregnancy is one of the ways that we begin a social relationship with a child, but obviously not the only one. Remember the fathers' descriptions of eye contact with their babies: the child pulled them in.

If women are not to drop from exhaustion and lose all pleasure in life, someone is going to have to help with the kids. If women are sharing their lives, and sharing their children, with someone, then that is the obvious person to share the work of child care. For some women that is a lesbian partner, for some the woman's own mother, but for many of us that is our husband. It is not by virtue of their paternity, their genetic ties to children, that men have an obligation to rear and to nurture them, but by virtue of their social relationship. If someone, man or woman, is going to be the life partner, the mate, of a woman who mothers, then that person must share the child care. And in turn it is by sharing the care and rearing of the children that the partner comes to have a place in the life of the child. We have to move beyond a paternity standard to a standard of nurturance.

Mothers also need men who can mother because we *ourselves* need that mothering—women are tired of mothering the whole world. Mothering, like everything else in life, is best learned by doing. I think that the mothering women have done has taught many of us the skills of listening to what is said and to what is not said. I think in mothering we hone our empathic abilities, learn to understand the vulnerability in others without profiting from it. I think that the experience of mothering teaches people how to be more emotionally and intellectually nurturant, how to take care of each other. It is not the only way we learn that lesson, but it is hard to mother and not learn it.

I *know* that mothering teaches us physical nurturance. Having nurtured the literally unselfconscious child, we are more competent, more confident providing other kinds of intimate, physical care. I remember my own awkwardness providing "nursing" care to my mother during an illness of hers in my adolescence. I compare that with the competence with which I can now provide such care. And I particularly remember my husband's awkwardness providing such care to me before our first child, and the skill and ease with which he does it now. Nursing me through my first labor, he was infinitely well meaning. Nursing me through my second, he knew what he was doing. He had been nurturing for seven years, years of nursing earaches, bellyaches, changing diapers, calming night terrors, holding pans for vomit, taking out splinters, washing bloody wounds. He had grown accustomed to the sheer physicality of the body, the sights and sounds and smells. More essentially, what I showed him in my pain and my fear was not foreign—he saw the baby, the child in me, not the one I was birthing, but the one I myself am, and he nursed it. Now *that* is a man to enter old age with.

If men are not providing this kind of care, learning these skills, with their children, they're not going to be much help with their elderly fathers, or with their own sick wives. When women do all the mothering, it's not just the child care the men are being excused from—it's all of the intimate care women end up providing for children, for men, and for each other.

And finally, men should join women in mothering because it is the only way to avoid recreating the gender and class system and still live together.

We can pool our resources, join together in infinite varieties of social arrangements to rear our children, but we must not recreate endlessly the separate worlds of power and of care. We must not do this in any of its guises: not as separate public and private worlds, not as separate worlds of men and of women. It is morally wrong to have children raised by one group for another group, whether it is Mrs. John Smith raising John Smith Jr. in her husband's image, slave nurses raising their masters, or hired caregivers raising the children of dual-career couples.

Caring people can and do raise whole and healthy children, and they do it across lines of gender, class, and race. It is not that the children are "subhuman," but that we ask them to turn away from humanity, away from care, and toward power. We do that whenever we separate the world into the kinds of people who take care of children and the kinds of people who rule the world.

In this I share a vision with Sara Ruddick. With her, I look forward to a day when

> there will be no more "fathers," no more people of either sex who have power over their children's lives and moral authority in their children's world, though they do not do the work of attentive love. There will be mothers of both sexes who live out a transformed maternal thought in communities that share parental care—practically, emotionally, economically and socially. Such communities will have learned from their mothers how to value children's lives.[18]

And in so doing we will learn to value all of our lives—and that is still what I think the women's movement is about.

On "Surrogacy"[1]

A *Question of Policy*

The first thing to bear in mind is that surrogate motherhood did not come to us as a new procreative technology. The business of "surrogacy" had nothing to do with scientific progress, and everything to do with marketing. The procreative technology used was artificial insemination. Artificial insemination with donor sperm has been used in human beings for over a hundred years. The "techonologies" involved are the technology of masturbation, and of the turkey baster or its equivalent.

It is important to remember that is the case, because we are sometimes overwhelmed with the developments of the new procreative technology, as with our other technologies. Sometimes we think—and sometimes we are encouraged to think—that there is nothing we can do to halt "progress." If science can produce "test tube babies," how can we ever stop it? And if our new knowledge gives us these new powers, should we even want to stop it?

These are important questions. But they are not the questions of surrogate motherhood. Surrogate motherhood was not brought to us by the march of scientific progress. It was brought to us by brokers, by people who saw a new market and went after it. And the market is something we know we *can* control, and often *should* control.

When artificial insemination was introduced, it was used to support the traditional family structure, husbands and wives having and raising babies. In earlier times, when couples were unable to start a pregnancy, it was most often assumed to be the fault of the wife, and in some cultures husbands had the recourse of divorce. With expanding knowledge, infertility was shown to be sometimes a problem in the husband's body. Wives were not given the recourse of divorce under these circumstances, and artificial insemination became a way of maintaining the intact husband-wife unit. Wives were not encouraged to take a "surrogate," a substitute lover, but rather doctors used semen, given anonymously, to impregnate wives.

The process was undertaken with the greatest of secrecy. According to some accounts, the wife herself was not told what was done to her in the first American use of artificial insemination.[2] Certainly, no one outside of the couple and the doctor were told—artificial insemination was shrouded in silence. This enabled men to be the social fathers of the children their wives bore.

Social fatherhood is the key issue here. What makes a woman a mother has always been quite obvious. But what makes a man a father has been subject to some question. The formula our society (along with many others) has arrived at is that fatherhood is determined by the man's relationship to the child's mother. A man married to a woman is the recognized father of her children. This way of reckoning fatherhood builds on two things: the obvious and unquestioned nature of biological motherhood, and the traditional patriarchal relationship of men and their wives. This is a way of acknowledging parenthood that is based on relationships: the relationship of the woman to her baby as it grows within, and the relationship of the man to the woman.

And so it stood for over a hundred years: artificial insemination was a way of managing male infertility that kept the patriarchal family intact, that allowed children to be born to a couple, children who would be truly theirs, to bring into the world together, to raise and to cherish together.

So what changed? For one thing, infertility appears to be more of a social problem: the actual rates of infertility may or may not be rising, but societal concern certainly is. For another, the supply of babies available for adoption has dropped dramatically. Young women, faced with unwanted pregnancies, have been given choices: the choice of abortion and the choice of raising a child without a husband. Infertile couples can no longer benefit, no matter how innocently, from the tragedies of young mothers. Our attitude toward infertility has also changed—and this may indeed be an indirect result of scientific progress. Progress against infertility has become a newspaper and television staple. Remember the excitement that surrounded the first in vitro baby, the first American in vitro baby, the first in vitro twins, and so on. The first in vitro quints were the cover story of *People* magazine in 1988.[3] And the first high-tech septuplets generated a little media flurry a decade later. The idea began to be generated that infertility was curable, if only a couple tried hard enough, saw enough doctors, went through enough procedures. The reality is something quite different. There is a more than 75 percent failure rate with that technology.

What we have done is to create a population of desperate, heartbroken infertile people: people who cannot find babies to adopt who have "tried everything" and cannot get pregnant, people who have devoted years of their lives to trying, one way or another, to get a baby.

The medical technology has enabled the couple to sort out "whose fault" the infertility is. When it is the husband who is infertile, the use of insemination with donor sperm remains a solution, enabling the couple to have a pregnancy and the much-wanted baby. When it is the wife who is infertile, the pressures mount on the woman to feel guilt at not being able to "give her husband" a child. A baby is what they want more than anything. And he could have one, if not for her.

It is in this context that the marketing of "surrogate" motherhood developed. Brokers entered the scene, telling the couple that they can indeed have a baby, and it will be "his" baby. "Surrogate motherhood" was sold as a solution to the tragedy of infertility and a way of resolving women's guilt at their own infertility. For couples who had spent untold thousands of dollars on medical treatments, the thousands more for surrogacy contracts may have seemed a bargain. For people without these many thousands of dollars, infertility remains unsolved.

With this new use of artificial insemination, the relationships of the parties involved changed totally. The relationship of the mother to her baby within her no longer counts. The baby has become a commodity, something a woman can produce and sell. She is encouraged to think of the baby as no more hers than a factory worker thinks of the car he works on as his. The relationship of the father to the mother no longer counts: it will cease to exist as motherhood is made anonymous, handled by brokers and doctors. The relationships that will count are that of the father to his sperm donation and that of the market: the contracts and the fees. What makes a man a father is not his relationship to the mother, we are told, but that it is his sperm and his money.

The brokers tell us that this is not baby selling: how can a man buy his own baby? they ask. And true enough, how can someone buy something which is already his? But what makes the baby his? If the sperm donor in more traditional artificial insemination came up to the couple a year later, said he had had an accident and was now infertile, and would like to have their baby, he would have no right to it. If he offered them money, he would not be buying that which is his but that which is theirs: producing a semen sample does not make a man a social father, does not make that his baby. Is it then his intention that makes the child his? The fathers in the surrogacy cases do not donate their sperm. They are not donating or giving or selling. They are buying. Then how is this different from any other example of baby buying and selling? The answer is it is not.

Under surrogacy arrangements, to buy a baby one needs sperm and money. Couples—or just men—who have both can buy babies. But what of lesbian couples? And what of men without adequate sperm? Many cases of infertility involve both partners. What of a couple desperate to have a baby in which the wife cannot carry a pregnancy and the husband has insufficient sperm, or carries a deadly disease? Sperm, too, is for sale: we literally have sperm banks. Once sperm is purchased, the owners of the sperm can use that sperm as their "own" to make their "own" baby with a surrogate. We sell babies in "kit" form, purchasing the pieces and services separately: sperm here, an egg there, a rented uterus somewhere else. This is of course a "slippery slope" kind of situation—once you permit some people to buy some babies under some conditions, it is very hard to justify any given person not being allowed to purchase a baby under other circumstances.

So surrogacy is baby selling. As Angela Holder has said, "If I order a widget from a widget maker, and I pay cash money for that widget, and a widget is delivered to me, I defy you to tell me I have not bought a widget."[4]

And what would be wrong with simply opening up a market economy in babies? Others have argued eloquently what the problems are with baby selling, and we have as a society accepted those arguments. Some things, we have felt, should simply not be sold—and certainly not people. One of the strongest arguments against baby selling is that we know that if we allowed babies to be sold, some people would be put under great pressure to sell their babies. This is the same reason that we do not allow organs to be sold from living people, even when we know that lives might actually be saved. If we allowed some people to sell, say, a kidney, we know that some might feel forced to do so. And so now and again someone with much money dies for lack of an organ that he or she was willing to buy and someone else was willing to sell because such a sale, such a contract, even if arguably in the best interests of the parties involved, would be against the best interests of the society as a whole. I believe that "surrogacy" presents a situation parallel to organ selling, and that the same arguments apply.

I began by saying that surrogacy was not a result of new procreative technology, but must be understood entirely as a marketing strategy. Let me now amend that slightly. Most of the surrogate motherhood cases that first reached the courts and the media were based on the old technology of artificial insemination. But there are newer technologies. We must consider what these new developments in procreative technology mean for surrogacy contracts.

The new technologies are varied, but share in common the use of genetic material from one woman to create a pregnancy in the body of another woman. There are several ways this can be done. An egg from one woman can be removed, fertilized in vitro (in glass), and put into the body of another woman. Some in vitro fertilization clinics are doing this for women who want to become mothers but cannot produce eggs. Other women, who produce "extra" eggs, donate those eggs for the use of infertile women who cannot produce their own eggs. Sometimes the donors are other women in the program who are ovulating well, sometimes they are hired egg donors, and sometimes they are friends or relatives of the infertile woman. Whether donated or purchased, genetic material from outside of the couple is used to enable a woman and her husband to have a pregnancy and share in the birthing and rearing of a baby. The situation is most closely analogous to artificial insemination with donated or purchased sperm.

Another way that this same thing can be accomplished is by allowing fertilization to take place within the body of the woman who is donating the egg. A fertilized egg, what some call a pre-embryo or pre-implantation embryo, is moved from the donor and placed within the body of the woman who will be the mother. This, too, is much like artificial insemination. Some months later we look at a pregnant woman and her husband expecting their child. In these situations of embryo transfer or egg donation, like the situation of artificial insemination with donor sperm, genetic material from outside the couple is used to create the pregnancy, but social parenthood, from the point of early pregnancy on, is shared within the couple.

That then is the technology. And what of the marketing? Like the marketing of artificial insemination, egg donations can also be turned around and used to create a pregnancy not within the family, but in a hired woman, leading to the ultimate purchase of a baby.

With this technology, it is not necessary for the "surrogate" to be genetically related to the baby she bears. So one marketing strategy is to hire a woman to carry a pregnancy for a woman who can produce eggs but not carry a pregnancy for herself. Now something challenging happens to our thinking: we are forced to confront the question of what makes a woman a mother. Is it the egg, or is it the pregnancy? In the cases mentioned above, where a woman is unable to create an egg, the transfer of the egg or embryo left the pregnant woman the social mother: it was the pregnant woman who intended to be the mother, who not only intended to bear and birth the child, but to raise the child as well. But if we hire a woman to carry the pregnancy, who then is the mother? Is it the egg donor, or the pregnant woman?

The legal situation has resolved itself much as one would expect: "surrogate gestators" are not legal mothers. In the state of California, where the largest of the surrogate businesses operates, the name of the "gestator" does not even appear on the original birth certificate. Sometimes the egg used is that of the woman who is hiring the "surrogate," but sometimes the egg too is purchased. Some individuals or couples do this precisely to lessen any potential tie—legal, social, or psychological—between the "surrogate" and the child; some do it to put together precisely the package they want. They choose the egg (and the sperm) that most represents the "kind of child" they hope to have and then hire a different woman to gestate the pregnancy. As gestational surrogacy has increased, "there has been a commensurate increase in the number of Hispanic American, Asian American and African American surrogates."[5]

Surrogacy is expensive. The Center for Surrogate Parenting[6] estimates $56,525 for "traditional" surrogacy in which artificial insemination is used and in which the surrogate is also the "genetic" mother of the child. With egg donation, using the egg of another woman, they estimate $69,325 assuming that the woman becomes pregnant on the first cycle. Since pregnancy rates are only about one in four, that is quite unlikely, and the costs of "gestational surrogacy" can run quite a bit higher than that.

Only $15,000 of this is paid to the surrogate herself for the "time and sacrifice" of the pregnancy. The disparity is very much what one sees in child care: it costs a great deal of money and only relatively well-off people can afford to buy the service, but one earns so little that only relatively poor people provide it. When surrogacy agreements first surfaced in the 1970s and early 1980s, there was no payment, and it tended to involve middle-class and blue-collar couples. Once payment entered the scene, along with brokering agencies, that changed: "the majority of couples remain largely upper-middle-class people, whereas the majority of surrogates are working-class women."[7]

It is no accident that the Center for Surrogate Parenting, which reported 652 births as of January 1999 and claims to be the largest of the agencies, is located in California. As it explains on its web site: "CSP is located in California because California offers the most politically and judicially 'friendly' climate towards surrogacy. There has never been a court case in California where the surrogate mother was awarded custody of the child resulting from a surrogate birth." While the couples may be anywhere in the world, and they state that 25 percent of their couples live overseas, "all payments are made in California, contracts are drafted and signed in California, medical procedures are performed in California, and the birth occurs in California. In this way we ensure that California laws apply, which is in the best interests of our couples."

Surrogacy has very much evolved into a business in the best interests of the couples. CSP reports that it accepts 95 percent of the contracting couples who apply to the program. Theirs is an "open program," and "some couples cannot cope with the amount of contact between surrogate mothers and couples in our program." That contact is not extensive: the agency says overseas couples need to travel to California on four occasions: once for a four- to six-hour consultation; a second time to meet the surrogate; a third to meet her doctor, see an ultrasound, and visit the hospital; and finally for the birth itself. After the birth they recommend "a card and occasional photographs to help the surrogate mother 'through this transitional time as she returns to her own life.' " Those who find that to be too much contact can go to a "closed program," in which greater anonymity is maintained.

Surrogate mothers, on the other hand, go through three to five months rather than hours of screening, and 95 percent are rejected. The rather casual screening (not at this agency) that took in Mary Beth Whitehead and the other women who "changed their minds" is probably a thing of the past.

That surrogacy is a business does not mean that people don't love their children, that contracting couples (or individuals) don't value and appreciate their surrogate, or that the surrogate doesn't care about the child and the couple. Consider adoption, or even child-care arrangements: money changes hands, but families are formed and love grows. I think surrogacy is an evil system: it diminishes women and discounts pregnancy as a relationship. That doesn't mean that I think that the people who participate in it are evil people or have less than noble motives.

Helena Ragone has done the first ethnographic study of surrogacy, interviewing twenty-eight surrogates and seventeen individual members of couples. She looked at the eight established surrogacy programs operating in the United States, each of which had been in business for ten or more years. She looked at open programs like the CSP in which surrogates and couples are introduced and at closed programs in which they meet only in court to finalize adoption and paternity claims.

Ragone found that the programs are catering to the couples. Couples receive more information about the surrogate than the surrogate does about them, and couples are more able to flout what rules the agency may have. No one stopped a potential adoptive mother, for example, who pretended to be pregnant and planned to tell everyone that she had given birth to the child.[8] Essentially, "the couple is considered the client and the surrogate an employee of the program."[9]

Who are the surrogates? They are traditional, working-class women. Their commitment to surrogacy, Ragone says, "could best be described as unwavering."[10] Given the screening and ongoing counseling, that is certainly to be expected. Ragone reports: "Over time, I developed the idea that surrogacy provides women who are predominantly working class with the opportunity to transcend the limitations of their roles as wives/mothers and homemakers while concomitantly attesting to the satisfaction they derive from these roles."[11] Surrogates are proud of their ability, their skill in pregnancy and in giving birth: the surrogate "uses the act of reproduction as a means of removing herself from the limitations of the role traditionally assigned to women, caretaking or mothering, by simultaneously employing and transcending that reproductive role."[12] Pregnancy and birth are not generally valued; in surrogacy they are.

While the surrogates spoke with one voice, Ragone found that the couples bifurcated into two strategies of relating to their surrogate, either a pragmatic or an egalitarian approach:

> Once the child has been born, pragmatists redefine their relationship to their surrogate as one of acquaintanceship, in accordance with program guidelines that suggest that the relationship between couple and surrogate be terminated except for cards and photographs on the child's birthday and occasional cards and letters during the major holidays. Egalitarians, in contrast, continue to treat their surrogate as a friend, in defiance of the program's guidelines.[13]

Ragone found that the "overriding concern of egalitarians is the perceived immorality of 'using' someone. . . . One of their greatest concerns is that their surrogate not be treated as a means to an end. They believe that the best way to accomplish this is to continue to maintain a relationship with the surrogate after birth. The continued relationship is thus understood by the couples as evidence of or a testament to their integrity."[14]

Pragmatists simply dropped the relationship, taking the child as theirs, and considering the payment as sufficient acknowledgment of the role of the surrogate. Pragmatists are not just following the guidelines of the program: they are very much "swimming with the tide" of the society, following the model offered both by adoption and by hired child-care arrangements, both of which are repeatedly used metaphorically in surrogacy. There is no social support, no social "place" for an ongoing relationship between contracting couples and the surrogate, any more than there is for adoptive parents and birth parents. I can speak to that as an adoptive mother in an open relationship. When people realize that my daughter is in touch with her birth family and spends time visiting with them, some immediately drop into the language of "fostering" with me. One colleague consistently tells me about the lovely relationship between one of her wealthy suburban neighbors and the "fresh air kid" she took in for two weeks each summer, instantly diminishing my authenticity as the mother of my daughter into a temporary caregiver.

Open adoption and egalitarian relationships in surrogacy face tremendous and very similar obstacles. There are obstacles placed by definitions of "family" which permit one and only one mother per child and obstacles of class that make cross-class "egalitarian" relationships profoundly challenging. The problems are not at all dissimilar to those Wrigley found[15] with people hiring caregivers: those who wanted someone with whom they could share some responsibilities and have some kind of egalitarian relationship also found difficulties in the employer-employee relationship which overshadowed any "shared parenting" with caregivers. There is no reason why the problems would be any less with nurturing in pregnancy. When the child outgrows the relatively classless, profoundly gendered nurturing of pregnancy, like that of infancy, and moves on to middle-class childhood, the attributes of middle-class caregivers are sought. Surrogates, birth families, and early caregivers tend to fall by the wayside, no longer capable of providing the kind of care middle-class parents want for their middle-class children.

The egalitarians that Ragone interviewed were all fairly early on in their parenting years, so it is hard to tell what will happen over time. The class differences are obviously there, but Ragone found "it proved extremely difficult to persuade informants, either surrogates or couples, to discuss these differences in a forthright manner. . . . When couples are questioned about class differences, they tend to gloss over them, referring to their surrogate and her husband as 'people,' implying a shared sense of humanity."[16] This is of course a typical and distinctively American stance. Our lives are as much shaped by class as that of any people on earth; we just refuse to see it or to discuss it.

In a consumer culture, it is difficult to speak of the family in any but consumer language. In an early article on the new technologies of procreation, one that's been quoted back to me a lot, I spoke hopefully of a kind of "reproductive communism: from each according to her abilities, to each according to her needs."[17] I saw the potential for a sharing of parenting and family, with eggs and sperm and perhaps pregnancies used as shared resources. What we've got instead is reproductive capitalism, parenting not shared but purchased.

Surrogacy reinforces the very worst of our ideas about mothering and nurturing relationships, even as the individuals involved might strive to rise above it. "I'm strictly the hotel," one surrogate told Ragone.[18] And, as Ragone points out, that was not a gestational surrogate but a woman who is pregnant via artificial insemination, carrying a baby that is in no way less "hers" biologically than any other baby she could conceive. Another traditional surrogate says in language that Ragone tells us is expressive of many: "I feel like a vehicle, just like a cow; it's their baby, it's his sperm."[19]

This is, Ragone points out, no different than the language one would expect of a gestational surrogate, someone not genetically related to the baby. What is more troubling to me is that it is no different than the language of the most traditional of wives in the most patriarchal of systems. That is the language that permits Mrs. John Smith to bear John Smith, Jr. for John Smith, Sr. and have no claim over the child as "hers." She is but the vessel, the vehicle, the cow: it's his sperm and so his child.

I am grateful to Ragone for doing what she did: showing us the nuances of surrogacy, the way that basically decent people try to do right by each other in this troubled and troubling relationship. But that doesn't change the essential nature of the relationship, in which all kinds of nurturance—all the work of the body, the mind, and the being that goes into maintaining a pregnancy and giving birth—are profoundly devalued as "cheap labor," work that can be hired out to "surrogates." A surrogate is a substitute. In some human relations, we can accept no substitutes. Any pregnant woman is the mother of the child she bears. Her gestational relationship establishes her motherhood. We will not accept the idea that we can look at a woman, heavy with child, and say the child is not hers. The fetus is part of the woman's body, regardless of the source of the egg and sperm. Biological motherhood is not a service, not a commodity, but a relationship. Motherhood can remain obvious. If a woman is carrying a baby, then it is her baby and she is its mother. Of course it is true that a mother, any mother, can abdicate her motherhood, can give away a baby. But it is hers to give. And if we were to allow the selling of babies, then it is hers to sell, or refuse to sell.

And what can we do with fatherhood? How can we protect the relationship between a father and his child? What will make a man a father? One possibility is to stay with the model that we had: a father can continue to take his fatherhood from his relationship with the mother of the child. In a married couple, the father can continue to be, as hitherto, the husband of the mother.

That is not a perfect solution to the troubling question of fatherhood. It gives, in some ways, too much power to women over men's procreation. And it gives, in other ways, too much power to men over women's procreation. But this is not a new problem. We are not struggling here with questions of science and new technology. Here we are struggling with age-old questions of relationships, of family, of how we are bound together. We have not found perfect ways of dealing with these issues in all of history. But we have, in this society, been clear in rejecting the use of money in these relationships. We have said that in our society husbands and wives, mothers and fathers, and babies are not for sale. Nothing in the new procreative technology need change that.

Those engaged in surrogacy brokering tell us that if we do not bring surrogacy into the open market, it, like adoption, will continue to exist in "gray"- or black-market forms. And they are probably right. Preventing the open sale of babies has not prevented couples from having to spend much money on getting babies, nor has it prevented brokers from making money out of matching babies to adopters.

I do not disagree with the brokers over acknowledging the problem, but over choosing the solution. There are grave costs to any form of open market in baby selling. If we wish to legalize baby selling, let us acknowledge what we are doing, and offer the appropriate protections to the parties involved. If we choose to allow a woman to sell her baby, so be it. But let us recognize that it is indeed *her* baby that she is selling. And if we do not wish to permit baby selling, then there is nothing in the new procreative technology that forces us to do so. We do not have to give the support of the state and of the courts to a view of babies as purchasable commodities or motherhood as a salable service.

In sum, the legislation I feel we need to develop as national policy in the United States, as is the case in most countries, would recognize that *the gestational mother is the mother*. Any pregnant woman is the mother of the child she bears, regardless of the source of the egg or the sperm. The rights and the responsibilities of motherhood are the same for all gestational mothers, regardless of the source of the egg and the sperm.

Therefore, *purchasing a baby from its mother, regardless of the source of the egg and the sperm, is purchasing a baby*. Until or unless we legalize baby selling, the law cannot acknowledge paid surrogacy contracts. Surrogacy is not to be used as a way around the laws against the sale of babies: it is itself a variation of baby selling.

Further, *accepting a baby as a gift from its mother, regardless of the source of the egg and the sperm, is a form of adoption*. The laws that govern the rights and responsibilities of all parties to an adoption must apply to so-called surrogate arrangements as well.

A Question of Values

People—friends, colleagues, maybe especially family—kept pointing out to me, with a bemused air, how strange it was to find me arguing on the same side as religious leaders in the debate on surrogacy arrangements. And I, too, occasionally found some amusement in the "strange bedfellows" phenomenon. Indeed, with carefully groomed "happy surrogates" and their equally well-groomed brokers placed on a TV or radio show by a professional public relations firm, I often found myself, side-by-side with some priest or rabbi, brought in by a producer to give a "balanced" view. And so we argued about the problems of surrogacy, sandwiched between car commercials, wine cooler ads, and other signs of the times.

The "tag" they used to identify me on television—the white line of print that shows up on the screen but which I never get to see in the studio—sometimes read *author*, rarely read *sociologist*, but most often they seemed to use *feminist*. And so there we were, "feminist" and "priest" or "rabbi" arguing the same, antisurrogacy side.

But it is only on the very surface that I am on the same side as these religious leaders. We may have landed on the same side of this particular fence, but we've taken very different paths to get there, and we are headed in very different directions. The values that I use in my opposition to surrogacy are fundamentally different from those the religious leaders use, and the goals I seek are just as different. And strangely enough, in many ways my values and goals are much the same as those used by those of my feminist colleagues who have come to an opposite conclusion.

The arguments against surrogacy that come out of traditional religious context most often rest on two basic principles: first that surrogacy is "unnatural," because it goes against the nature of women and especially of mothers; second, that it violates the sanctity of the family.

Feminists are a lot less sure about just what is "natural" for women, but on the whole we've concluded that the institution of motherhood as it exists in our society is pretty far from any natural state. Neither I nor my feminist colleagues are about to get caught up in any "maternal instincts" arguments. Women end pregnancies with abortions, or end their motherhood by giving a baby up for adoption, when that is what they feel they need to do. Being pregnant does not necessarily mean a woman is going to mother, to raise the child that might be born of that pregnancy. Nor are we going to claim that only a birth mother can mother, can nurture a baby. We know that loving people, men as well as women, can provide all the warm, caring, loving nurturance a baby needs.

Feminists are also not concerned with maintaining the "sanctity of the family," a pleasant enough phrase that has been used to cover an awful lot of damage. That was the argument used to stop funding day-care centers, the argument offered to allow men to beat their wives and children, the argument most generally used to stop women from controlling their own lives and their own bodies. The "family" whose "sanctity" is being maintained is the patriarchal, male-dominated family. Feminists have a different sense of family—we need to protect the single young mother and her child, the lesbian couple and their children, the gay man's family. As feminists, we are concerned not with the control and ownership and kinship issues of the traditional family, but with the *relationships* people establish with one another? with adults and children.

So why then, as a feminist, do I oppose the surrogacy relationship? The "liberal" wing of feminism does not necessarily oppose those contracts. As long as the women entering into them do so of their own volition, with fully informed consent, and as long as they maintain their control over their own bodies throughout the pregnancies, some feminists have said that surrogacy contracts should be supported by the state. Some go as far as Lori Andrews, for instance, a noted feminist attorney, who says that these contracts should be binding with absolutely no opportunity for the mother to change her mind.

What then are the objections that I, out of my vision of feminism, raise to surrogacy? And more important, on what values am I basing my objections?

My values place relationships as central. Rather than the ownership or kinship ties that appear to epitomize the "traditional" or patriarchal family, I value the interpersonal relations people establish. A man does not own his wife, nor does he have ownership rights over the child she produces of her body. Men may own their sperm, but children are not sperm grown up. Children are not "owned," and they are not available for sale. On the other hand, children do not enter the world from Mars, or out of a black box. Children, as it says in the books for children, come from mothers. They enter the world in a relationship, a physical and social and emotional relationship with the woman in whose body they have been nurtured. The nurturance of pregnancy is a relationship, one that develops as a fetus becomes more and more a baby.

That does not mean that the maternal relationship cannot be ended. Nor does it mean that the relationship is the most overwhelming, all-powerful relationship on earth. In fact, we know it to be a fairly fragile relationship. The intimacy that a mother and her baby experience can be easily lost if they are separated. If a woman chooses to end this relationship, so be it. When a mother chooses to give a baby up to others who want to raise that baby as their own, she is doing what we have all done in our lives—ending a relationship. Sometimes this is done with less and sometimes with more pain, but rarely is it an easy thing for a mother to do.

The relationship that a woman has established by the time she births her baby has more weight, in my value system, than claims of genetic ties, of contracts signed, or of down payments made.

When I make this argument with traditionally oriented people, I am often asked if this doesn't contradict my ideas about a woman's right to abort an unwanted pregnancy. Not at all, I think. When a woman chooses an abortion, she is choosing not to enter into a maternal relationship. Women want access to safe abortions as quickly as possible, before quickening, before a relationship can begin.

In sum, in my value system, I am placing the woman, her experiences and her relationships, at the very heart of my understanding of all pregnancies.

The second value I bring as a feminist to my understanding of surrogacy contracts is the value of women's bodily autonomy, our control over our own bodies. And I see the fetus as part of a woman's body. Traditional patriarchal values would see the fetus as part of its father's body, his "seed" planted in a woman's body. In a patriarchal system, the father—or the state or the church—is held to have special control over a woman's body and life because of that fetus she can bear. As a feminist, I reject that. The fetus is *hers*. Women never bear anybody else's baby: not their husband's, not the state's, and not the purchaser's in a surrogacy contract. Every woman bears her *own* baby. I believe that is true regardless of the source of the sperm, and regardless also of the source of the egg.

As I said earlier, the original surrogacy arrangements were done not with elaborate new technology, but with the very old and very simple technology of artificial insemination. The "surrogate" was in every possible way the mother to the baby she bore. But some newer technologies allow eggs to be transferred from woman to woman, allowing a woman to be pregnant with the fetus grown of another woman's egg.

The Catholic Church and some other religious groups reject that technology. I do not. When that technology is used to enable a woman to enter motherhood with a pregnancy, in just the way that artificial insemination has been used to allow an infertile man to become a social father beginning with pregnancy, I have no problem with it. My concern is when that technology is used in a so-called surrogacy arrangement—when the birth mother, the pregnant woman, is declared to be only a "rented womb," a "surrogate," and the real mother is declared to be the woman who produced the egg.

The church and other conservative forces object to the technology because they value the fertilized egg itself as an object believed to be human. I object when women are "used," when parts of women are put up for sale or hire, when our relationships are discounted in favor of genetic and monetary ties.

Those feminists, like Lori Andrews, who would allow surrogacy contracts still demand rights of bodily autonomy for the pregnant woman. The compromise position they maintain is that it is indeed her body, and she must have all decision-making control over her pregnancy—but it is not her baby in her body, not if she has contracted it away. I feel that kind of "compromise" does a profound disservice to women. I cannot ever believe that a woman is pregnant with someone else's baby. The idea is repugnant—it reduces the woman to a container. Nor do I think that that kind of compromise, saying the pregnancy is indeed hers, but the fetus/baby theirs, the purchasers', can be workable. The "preciousness" of the very wanted, very expensive baby will far outweigh the value given to the "cheap labor" of the surrogate.

This is the inevitable result of thinking of pregnancy not as a relationship between a woman and her fetus but as a service she provides for others, and of thinking of the woman herself not as a person but as the container for another, often more valued, person. In that sense, surrogacy is the reductio ad absurdum of technological, patriarchal capitalism.

The values that I bring to motherhood, the values that I take from my feminism, all the values that I've tried to express in this book, all come together in my opposition to surrogacy.

Reflections on a Decade

IN THE INTRODUCTION to Part I of this book, I said that I wanted to show that we can use motherhood—as an experience, as a set of values, as a discipline—to fight against the forces of alienation, against the things that drive people apart. We were, I suggested when I originally wrote this book in the late 1980s, at a moment of crisis, with two paths before us. On the one hand, we could have focused on nurturance and caring human relationships, with the values and experience of mothering coming to shape the way we live in the world. On the other hand, we could have recreated motherhood to reflect the increasing commodification of children, embedding motherhood ever more firmly in consumer culture.[1]

And where are we now, more than a decade later? Still, I fear and hope, at a point of crisis. I fear it because I can see how much further we have moved down the path of commodifying children, literally putting price tags on every possible aspect of bearing and rearing children. I hope we are at a point of crisis, because I still do have hope: I see the other path still open before us. We have, in the years since I first wrote this book, moved further along both paths. We are, many of us, more accepting of love and nurturance where we can find it. We have, in many ways, become more open as a society to families put together in non-traditional ways. We are, in America today, more comfortable than we were a generation ago, maybe even more than a decade ago, with men doing mothering, men who engage in daily intimate acts of nurturance for their children and families. We are, many of us Americans, more respectful of gay and lesbian families, and of families created out of adoption, out of fostering, out of communities of sharing people across the social divide of race[2] and within the social divide of gender.[3]

And while I am mindful of that—and as an adoptive mother and the mother of a gay son, deeply grateful for what changes there have been—I am more struck by the ways we have moved down the other path. Some of us still are, as some of us have long been, working to recreate family in the image of nurturing motherhood. But more often, what we see in America is the other path taken, recreating motherhood in the image of the market.

The Best Money Can Buy[4]

Brown eggs cost more than white at my supermarket. From large through extra large through jumbo, there's an orderly progression of prices, with a premium for color. The market in human eggs uses different criteria but is no less a market for doing so.

In the last months of the 1990s, several news stories brought public attention to the market in human eggs. An entrepreneur auctioned off the eggs of fashion models on a web site. Using more traditional media, someone advertized in an Ivy League college newspaper for a woman who was at least five feet, ten inches tall and who had scored at least 1400 on her SATs and offered $50,000 for her eggs. It was the height thing that pulled the story forward, oddly enough. The money wasn't out of line: $35,000 to $50,000 had been the going rate for Ivy League eggs for months. Why so tall? people asked. Not, I noted, why so smart?

Applying a market approach to babies and children isn't new of course, and that's the argument I've been making in much of this book. Consider adoption: that market is no less tightly bound by size and color than the eggs in the supermarket. The hierarchy is reversed though: the younger (smaller) and lighter are more expensive; the older and darker decidedly less so. Big enough or dark enough, and you can't give the kids away. Our foster care system is overflowing with unplaced children, too dark or too long on the shelf.

So we can't suddenly act surprised when the market operates for babies being purchased in kit form. We've had banking in sperm for years. According to Mathew Schmidt and Lisa Jean Moore, the first commercial human semen bank opened in 1972 and by 1998 had become a $164 million per year industry in the United States.[5] Semen or sperm banks sell sperm: they advertize a superior product, chosen, screened, tested, and prepared. They "prioritize differences believed to be important to the client through the ordering of the characteristics of donors."[6] Race/ethnic origin is always the first category presented, Schmidt and Moore found in their analysis of sperm bank catalogs, and one bank "even stores its semen in vials that are color-coded according to the race of the donor—white vials for Caucasians, black vials for African

Americans, yellow vials for Asian Americans, and red vials for everyone else."[7] But the banks also give information about the physical and social characteristics of the donors beyond race/ethnicity: not just height and weight, but favorite sport, hobbies, interests, occupations, grade point averages, and years of college. "The 'scientifically disproven' Lamarkian assumption of the inheritance of acquired characteristics is both re-created and sustained in these categories."[8]

Semen banking, Schmidt and Moore conclude, reconstructs the moral terrain of reproduction, defining who should reproduce. And it does this in a clear market context, "What was once a not-for-profit, informal, altruistic service largely available through medical school clinics has been transformed into a for-profit medical industry."[9]

Banking in eggs is much newer: it is only within the past decade that the technology for freezing unfertilized eggs was developed. But in very short order, that too moved from the medical clinic into the market. Semen is obtained by masturbation; egg retrieval requires hormonal drugs to stimulate ovulation and laparoscopic surgical removal, making eggs riskier to get and thus far more expensive. The market responds accordingly, and eggs cost more than sperm. But eggs themselves are ranked in cost, some eggs worth far more than others on the open market.

In a system in which banking provides the dominant metaphor, of course eggs and sperm are sorted by "worth." Increasingly we are being forced to confront, in no subtle way, what makes for worth in human beings. People don't like to use the word any more, but thoughts of eugenics are unavoidable when people are actively seeking the very best genes money can buy.

Class and commerce, I have shown, go hand in hand in procreation. Elites have purchased the reproductive services of poor women from time immemorial: Pharaoh's daughter not only took the baby Moses from the water but hired his mother as a wet nurse. And, at various historical moments, questions have arisen about what "qualities" a child was imbibing along with its milk. The fluids of human life—blood, semen, and milk—are never "just" the proteins of which they are composed. Every culture and every time has invested them with meaning.

All the more so in our own time. Genes, we believe, encode the very essence of the person, who you really are. The sperm and eggs that we now trade in are at one and the same time purchasable commodities and the roots of life, both commercial and mystical in their power. The core of essential identity is now believed to lie in those tangled strands of DNA, is what we call "in our blood." This is arguably the most genetic-determinist belief system the world has ever seen. Even the *Brave New World* of the eugenics era saw the quality of a person as an interplay between genes and environment: Alphas were differentiated from Betas and Gammas by the material in the incubation fluid.[10] And even the Nazis, the work of historian Robert Proctor reminds us,[11] were environmentalists, worried about smoking and health. In our own era, the role of the environment is increasingly pushed to the background, while genes predominate in our thinking.[12] Every part of the environment, from the cytoplasm surrounding the nucleus of the egg to the pregnant body to the child-rearing practices of a culture, is seen as only permitting or failing to permit the child to develop to its full (genetic) potential.

This is the context in which "quality" eggs have come to demand such a high price. But people are not just chromosomes grown big. People who used sperm from the once highly controversial "genius sperm bank," which solicited semen samples from Nobel prize winners and other "geniuses," had to understand that their kid might inherit the genius's nose, not his brain. Tall, smart women do not always have tall, smart kids. But people are willing to try, and some can afford to pay well for the chance to try.

Most countries do not permit the sale of eggs, sperm, embryos, or "gestational services." Such a ban, I am almost ready to concede, may well be beyond doing in America. If someone is willing to sell and someone is willing to buy, then interfering is downright un-American. It is no coincidence that there was more moral outrage in the civil rights movement in America over an African American with a dollar in his hand not being able to buy a slice of pie at a lunch counter than over the fact that most African Americans in the South didn't have the dollar. The right to buy is all but holy in America, and legislation against it hasn't been working.

If we are going to permit these ads and ensuing sales, are there going to be any limits on what characteristics prospective parents can order? What if it turns out that the purchasing couple in the example given earlier isn't all that smart themselves: what if the woman who is going to be pregnant with and give birth to this potential child has SAT scores that were only around 1100? Has she forfeited her right to buy eggs from someone with 1400 scores? What if she's not all that tall, either, but just wanted to be and thought height an asset? Can she justify specifying a tall egg producer? And what if she's not white, but thought being black in America was too much of a burden, and wants to purchase white privilege for her child? If white privilege is for sale—as it appears when "white" eggs and sperm are in the marketplace and so marked and color coded—do only white folks have the right to purchase it? What about a black woman married to a white man: must that couple purchase only "black" eggs? As we turn these questions over to the market, some human characteristics come to be seen as deluxe extras, while race tends to stand as an essential, essentializing genetic characteristic. Much like segregated housing, gene pools come to reside in gated communities.

You cannot very well write on the bottom of an ad in a college newspaper "Whites only." And yet, most assuredly, having an African American—or a schizophrenic—grandparent will disqualify a donor and profoundly limit her market, as will being fat or having a gay brother or an alcoholic aunt—all things for which no gene has been determined, but all things for which genetic determinist sentiment is running high.

One thing that the market is good at is forcing us to confront our values. Translated into dollars, the incomparable becomes comparable. The cost of an Ivy League egg is approximately that of a German sports car, or in very practical terms, two rounds of egg selling equal one college education. An ordinary egg from, say, a woman likely to be one of my students at the City University of New York, a (white) Eastern European immigrant, fetches enough to pay for half of her college education; a Yale or Harvard woman's eggs pay for half of hers. Symmetry, yes, but fairness? And my African American students don't even have that option. Not only you, they are told, but your forebears and your descendents are not worth much on the open market.

Most of the discussion of the implications of the various new technologies or arrangements for procreation focuses on the protection of the children so conceived. Another focus, the point of view I have taken in much of this book, is what this means for potential mothers and fathers and for our shared social understanding of family as we commodify children and parenting. A third focus and the one least often addressed is that of the "third parties," the donors and sellers of genetic material in what is called "third party procreation." In an earlier sweep of the eugenics movement, elite college women were told to go home and breed, that preventing the dying out of the "elite stock" was their responsibility. Eugenics courses are no longer, as they once were, a regular and respectable part of the college curriculum. The course a woman misses for her egg donation clinic appointment is far more likely to be in bioethics than in eugenics.

And so some women college students are becoming egg donor/sellers, as some men college students became sperm donor/sellers. The risks to the women's health come mostly from the hormonal stimulation, but the laparoscopic surgery is itself not without risks. The most elite women take these risks and whatever unknown psychological costs for a high price; the more ordinary women undergo the same procedures for lower prices. And as new research develops, even "non-elite" women's eggs may well be in demand.

The new cutting edge research in reproductive technologies isn't even about making whole babies: it is more about making spare parts. Embryo stem-cell research is the new hot topic. Embryonic stem cells are "undifferentiated"; they have not yet become specific kidney or bone or liver cells but have the potential to become any of these. The new science of embryology is directed toward using embryonic stem cells to grow organs to order.

Ann Pappert has been studying the development of the new technologies of procreation for many years now, and she is particularly concerned about the potential for exploitation presented by stem-cell research. "For the first time since the development of Assisted Reproductive Technologies, women would be used to 'manufacture' a product, their eggs, in a way that was inconceivable in the past."[13] For women already in infertility programs, the need to create embryos for stem cells would create a conflict between good clinical practice and research needs, Pappert points out. For the health of the woman, only enough drugs should be used to produce the few extra eggs needed for fertilization and implantation. But stem-cell research would demand more eggs. The possibility opens up of a market for cheap eggs, the eggs of women who are not highly valued, particularly poor and minority women, who will undergo even greater risks.

And so we move from growing babies to growing kidneys, from infertility research and treatment to the world of biomedical research, treatment, and marketing. It's no longer about women becoming mothers, or helping other women become mothers. Now we are talking about women as resources for valuable genetic material.

A Note on the Intersection of Infertility and Genetics Research[14]

If infertility did not exist as a "medical" condition, it would have to be invented. And some would say it has been.

There is absolutely no question that there are people, enormous numbers of people, who would choose to begin a pregnancy with heterosexual intercourse and are unable to do so. There are men with insufficient viable sperm; there are women with blocked fallopian tubes or failure to ovulate. There are physiological bases for an inability to begin and to maintain a pregnancy to term.

But infertility is no simple thing to define. Fertility is time-bound. How long must a couple be "trying" before infertility can be diagnosed? It is not uncommon now for a woman in her thirties to seek diagnosis after six months; a year is the new standard, down from two years more commonly used at an earlier period. Infertility is also time-bound within the life cycle, for women more dramatically of course than for men. Women experience high rates of infertility at the very beginning of their reproductive years and again at the very end. There have been no sweeping social changes that make infertility among thirteen-year-olds appear to be a tragedy, let alone an epidemic. But there have been changes that make infertility among women in their forties appear to be just that. Is a young woman at the beginning of her menarche experiencing infertility? Is an older woman at the beginning of her menopause experiencing infertility? Up until recently, most people would not have thought of it that way; increasingly we do. As treatments are developed to create and maintain pregnancies in women up to and beyond menopause, the condition known as infertility can be seen in women later in the life cycle.

The relationship between the availability of a treatment and the existence of a condition as socially acknowledged problem has been made starkly clear recently with the introduction of Viagra, a pill treatment for men who have difficulty achieving or maintaining an erection. In a matter of months, occasional impotence in middle-aged and older men went from being a stigmatizing if fairly ordinary part of aging to being a widely discussed and treatable condition. Management of the problem is no longer a personal and private accommodation within any given intimate relationship; it is medically treatable and—with almost astonishing swiftness—covered not only by private insurance but Medicaid as well. (This against a backdrop of unavailability of coverage for birth control pills for women for lo, these many years.)

When infertility treatments began to become available, or more accurately given their low success rates, began to seem possible, infertility too changed from a stigmatizing personal problem to which individuals and couples made private accommodation to a treatable medical condition—although with notably less success on the insurance side of the picture.

Thus we can say that while infertility most assuredly does exist, it is also a product of invention: the conditions we define as infertility are socially constructed and socially legitimated. Involuntary childlessness has been medicalized.

Why do I say that infertility as a medical condition would have to be invented if it did not exist? Infertility provides the opportunity, the occasion, to do the kind of work in reproductive science that would otherwise be unthinkable in human beings. The removal of fertilization outside of the body of a woman, the first IVF attempts, created extraordinary concern. The photos of a joyous Leslie Brown holding newborn Louise Brown were the justification for doing such a thing. With each reproductive technology breakthrough, a new series of "New Hope for the Childless!" headlines was produced. The kind of work that was being done with mice for research purposes, with cattle for breeding purposes, could only be done with human beings for clinical purposes, to treat something. And what could one possibly treat by removing eggs and sperm to petrie dishes, by growing blastocysts and embryos in vitro? If not for infertility, such work would be beyond the moral pale. Infertility justifies research.

Can you replace the nucleus of one woman's egg with that of another? The answer, it turns out, is yes. What would justify such a thing? The claim that the possessor of the nucleus has "aging eggs" and "requires" younger cytoplasmic material to achieve a pregnancy. There is no shortage of similar examples. Name anything that is going on in embryology and genetic research in the laboratory and consider its application to humans. Time and again, what is called upon as moral/ethical justification is the curing of infertility. And with the marvelously expandable concept of "procreative liberty," as John Robertson likes to call it,[15] there are essentially no limits.

There are no inevitably impassable barriers to infertility as the definition comes to center on genetic criteria: to be infertile is to be unable to have one's genes develop into a child "of one's own." Death itself has been overcome as a cause of infertility, as sperm are removed from the bodies of dead men and as brain-dead women are kept alive to continue pregnancies, and as frozen embryos are posthumously implanted in "gestators."

Each new genetic technology accomplishment is quickly framed in terms of infertility treatment. Adult somatic-cell cloning was introduced in animals to achieve an adequate and dependable supply of a rare protein produced in the milk of a sheep. What purpose could it possibly serve in humans? One can almost hear the wheels turn as the story is created: Well, there's this guy, see, and he has no sperm at all, so he is infertile, but he wants a child "of his own." Cloning would be the answer to his infertility.

And so it goes: Infertility makes permissible a variety of technological accomplishments in embryology, genetics, and microbiology that one would be hard put to justify otherwise.

Selling Choice in Procreation[16]

America, I have heard it said, does not have a culture; it has an economy. The democratic ideal with which we approach procreation, as everything else, is that each person should be free to make her or his own choices. The capitalist system puts the limiting clause on that sentence: given what she or he can afford. Anybody with money can buy anything that is for sale, and given the capitalist ideal, it is extremely difficult to argue why any given thing should not be for sale. If there is a market for it, so be it.

That is a very American understanding of choice, an extremely useful starting place for political action, but ultimately limited. Choice may be a useful or even essential political tool and concept, but it has a way of flattening everything out, reducing everything to the same level, all individual choice. This consumerist model of choice is probably best represented by something like ice cream flavors: chocolate, vanilla, or raspberry swirl? Ordinary or exotic, the choices are in a sense equally weighted. Walk into an American ice cream store, and you will have a lot of choice, with all of the flavors costing the same. It is an entirely free choice.

But even consumer choices get complicated fairly quickly. I would, for example, like to choose the safest possible car. But I cannot afford a new car, and among used cars, I am limited to what is available and what is in my price range. Am I sacrificing some safety quality of the brake system to get the lower-mileage car? I choose, and given the limited number of used cars available to me within my price range, I balance the factors that seem to matter most to me. Safety, mileage, size, cost—all get thrown into one pile, and somehow a decision has to emerge, and that decision will be counted as "my choice."

In procreation, the choices became if, when, and how. Women had choices about whether or not to become mothers—to conceive at all, or, having conceived accidentally, to continue the pregnancy or not. The decision about entering motherhood was quickly subsumed into the language of choice, and "choice" ultimately has come to represent primarily that one choice, the one we are "pro" as good feminists. Decisions about the timing of motherhood were similarly framed as choices but mostly in one direction, namely to postpone motherhood, to wait until we had finished school, established ourselves in careers, until we were ready. The choices about how to enter motherhood started with the relatively simple issue of where and with whom in attendance we would give birth but over time have burgeoned into choices about a vast array of technological assists, substitutes, and impediments. The (liberal) feminist response to everything, from home birth to breast feeding in public to egg harvesting to frozen embryos to prenatal diagnosis to surrogacy contracts to donor insemination for lesbian couples to IVF and the whole alphabet soup of infertility treatments, to *everything*, has been "choice."

My first indications of the ways the concept of choice was not working came when I was interviewing women about their decisions to use, or not to use, prenatal diagnosis.[17] Testing was available to them, testing that would tell them if their fetuses had Down's syndrome, neural tube defects, or any of an increasingly large number of identifiable conditions. The women, deeply agonizing over this decision, used a phrase that continues to haunt me: "my only choice." Whatever they chose, to use the testing or not, to continue the pregnancy or to abort, the decision was often framed as an "only choice." What could that mean, that deep contradiction? It was a no-choice choice, a forced choice, a choice a woman makes when she is told she has a choice but sees only one way out.

A woman who lives in a fourth-floor walk-up in a city without curb cuts or services for people with disabilities and who terminates a pregnancy for neural tube defects is not exactly engaging in an exercise in free will, making a choice. A woman who knows what state services will be like for her Down's syndrome child in the years after she has died, and who aborts rather than subject anyone to that treatment, is not experiencing a choice.

Even access to the testing itself is not a matter of choice. I did research in the Netherlands about how the midwives there were using, and not using, prenatal diagnosis in their practices. When I spoke to them about which women chose to use the testing, the differences between our two understandings of choice were all but laughable. In the United States, any woman who can afford the testing and wants it feels she has a right to it. In the Netherlands, the midwives earnestly informed me that they always offer women over the age of thirty-six the choice of amniocentesis. It is absolutely the woman's choice and her right to have that choice. No woman who is over thirty-six and wants the test is denied it; it is available for every eligible woman. But women under thirty-six, I asked, what of their choice? "Oh, they're not eligible." End of discussion. The Netherlands had made a decision, as a society, as a community, and as a state, about what is reasonable in light of risks, of costs, of potential benefits all around. The point of demarcation was established as thirty-six; the test was freely available to every woman over thirty-six who wanted it and unavailable to every woman under thirty-six.

The American in me bristled: You mean a thirty-five-and-a-half-year-old woman who wants the test can be refused it and then give birth to a baby with Down's syndrome and that's the way it goes? Yup. Or more accurately, "Ja." That's the way it goes.

Yet as an American, I recognize the sad inevitability that in this country a thirty-eight-year-old woman who wants the test may not be able to afford it, even though she just as surely cannot afford a disabled child, and that's the way it goes. Just as a young woman who wants an abortion, who wants very much not to have a baby now but to finish school, who wants to grow up first, may not be able to afford the abortion she has a legal right to purchase. And that's the way it goes. Life, even our more morally responsible presidents have informed us, is not fair.

Choice was, all things considered, a good place to start. Choice offered feminists concerned with procreation a point of entry, a wedge into the discussion. But in this, as in the civil rights movement, it was only a start. Seating in the front of a bus matters only if you have the bus fare. Questions of social justice provide the context in which issues of choice can unfold.

Gender, Race, and Class: Situating Procreative Choice[18]

While it is possible to discuss issues of motherhood and procreation in terms of abstract principles like "autonomy" or "procreative liberty," and in gender-neutral terms like "gamete donors" and "infertile couples," it ultimately does a genuine disservice to the women involved. Certainly infertility exists in *couples*; *parents* make decisions about genetic screening; gametes are donated. But in the real world, infertility, whether male or female in origin, most often plays out in the medical treatment of women's bodies; the person who experiences both the screening tests and the abortion if the screen leads to a positive diagnosis is the woman; and sperm and egg donation have about as much in common as, well, masturbation and surgery.

Discussions of the new reproductive technologies, particularly those using third-party participants as gamete donors and "surrogate gestators," frequently refer to experience with adoption. Adoption too has been a world of women's experiences: it is most often birth mothers, most often alone, who place their children for adoption; it is most often women who are the driving force behind adoptive parenting; when adoptees search it is most often women adoptees searching for birth mothers. Women outnumber men searchers three to one, and the majority of searchers, both male and female, do not go on to search for the birth fathers.[19] Gender-neutral language renders the experience of all of these women invisible.

This is not to minimize the impact procreative issues may have on the lives of men. We clearly need more research exploring just that. A 1998 book was able to summarize pretty much all we know about men's procreative experiences in less than two hundred pages of text.[20] Gender-neutral language does a disservice to men as well.

It is the specificity of procreative experience that is lost when the language of third parties and initiating couples and gamete donors takes over. Sex/gender is an obvious category in procreation—women's experiences and men's experiences will necessarily be different—but it is far from the only category. In a society divided by racial categorization, procreation is experienced in race-specific ways. The commodification of procreation affects white people and people of color differently. While the prices for socially desirable white eggs more than doubled, the costs for gestational surrogacy remained stable or even went down in real dollars because the race of the gestator was deemed irrelevant. Women of color experience infertility at one and a half to two times the rate of white women; the costs of infertility treatment are prohibitive for the majority of people of color. Infant mortality rates among black babies are double that of white babies. White babies are a precious commodity and the object of considerable national and international marketing; children of color languish in foster care systems in this country and the world.

Racial categorization has long been an integral part of genetic ideology. In the 1920s, when U.S. immigration laws were passed based on eugenic principles, Southern Italians, the Irish, and Eastern Europeans were considered undesirable races. At this point, our eugenics thinking has taken a different turn. Eastern European immigrants are considered by many a welcome (white) alternative to darker skinned immigrants. This has had two direct consequences for reproductive concerns. One is the importing of Eastern European infants and children for adoption. The other is that it is this particular group of immigrant women who are being used for egg production. While the language of "donation" is routinely used, envelopes of cash just as routinely exchange hands as the fertility clinics pay the women for their services in producing eggs. Just who is it that needs the money badly enough to undergo the physical risks and distress of hormone treatments and surgical procedures, as well as whatever emotional distress may be involved, and yet will be acceptable donors/sellers to purchasing couples? In the New York area, where poverty and skin color are closely and clearly related, Eastern European immigrants are the light-enough, poor-enough women to be useful in this role.

It is this kind of detailed, textured, socially located analysis that has been missing in most bioethical discussions of reproductive technology in the United States. The paradox is that it is precisely in situating the discussion in lived experience that we also place the reproductive technologies in the social structure. The discussion of abstracted individuals stripped of their gender/class/race placement is disingenuous. While it clarifies certain kinds of ethical dilemmas, it obscures other kinds: some issues become highlighted as concerns of reproductive freedom while other issues are shadowed.

Look for example at a premature baby in a neonatal intensive care unit. The baby is there as a result of an IVF procedure in which six fertilized eggs were transferred in order to increase the odds of success, resulting in a triplet pregnancy and this baby's suffering. Another baby, across the aisle, equally premature and equally suffering, is there because of its mother's poverty, maternal zip code still being one of the best predictors of infant outcomes in the United States. The existence of the first baby generates much concern about the ethics of the new reproductive technologies, calls for guidelines, conferences, and books. The second baby is a fact of life.

Or consider a grieving woman sitting by an empty cradle. She is a forty-three-year-old attorney who delayed childbearing while she went through law school, clerked for a state supreme court judge, and established a lucrative practice. She has gone through an early menopause. Attempts at egg donation have failed. She is contemplating using a hired gestator, her younger sister's eggs, and her husband's sperm. We are asked to respect her procreative liberty, to value her empowerment in reproductive decision-making. Across the city another grieving woman sits by an empty cradle. She is a seventeen-year-old whose baby was stillborn. She has had a history of lead poisoning and asthma and spent part of this past winter homeless. What can we say of her procreative liberty and of her empowerment in reproductive decision-making? Her baby's death is a fact of life.

Why do we tend to frame one kind of situation in the language of bioethics and the other as sorry facts of life? Bioethics has tended to focus on situations of choice: the very development of bioethics as an occupation was linked to the needs of medical decision-makers for guidelines. What has evolved in bioethics is thus primarily what one might think of as *microethics*, ethical decision-making as it takes place in clinical or individual circumstances.

What is most striking in the lives of people without power is that there are so few choices. To understand the ethical dilemmas presented by these "fact of life" situations, we need a *macroethics*, an analysis of ethical decision-making at the level of policy formation and practice.

Dorothy Roberts, in *Killing the Black Body: Race, Reproduction and the Meaning of Liberty*, draws a related distinction between liberty and justice as ethical frameworks:

> The dominant view of liberty reserves most of its protection only for the most privileged members of society. This approach superimposes liberty on an already unjust social structure, which it seeks to preserve against unwarranted government interference. Liberty protects all citizens' choices from the most direct and egregious abuses of government power, but it does nothing to dismantle social arrangements that make it impossible for some people to make a choice in the first place. Liberty guards against government intrusion; it does not guarantee social justice.[21]

Those of us who really care about motherhood and mothers must go beyond liberty concerns to address issues of social justice. Reproductive decision-making does not occur in a vacuum, nor does it occur only in the socially sanctioned privacy of the bedroom, doctor's office, or hospital. Reproductive ethics are also played out in the adoption and foster-care policies that shape decisions about infertility, abortion, and the management of drug-using women; in the workplace organizational principles and policies that shape decisions to postpone pregnancy past the years of prime fertility; in the educational and mass-media policies that shape the information and messages made accessible to young people who are making decisions about sexuality and contraception. The more standardly acknowledged areas of reproductive ethics—including contraception and abortion, the uses of the new reproductive technologies, the place of prenatal diagnosis and selective abortion, and what is (mis)conceptualized as maternal/fetal conflict—need to be placed in a larger context while not losing sight of the highly grounded, specific factors which do indeed shape individual decision-making.

This is difficult to do, especially in the American context in which individualism makes the development of coherent social policy difficult. Given the primacy of liberty commitments, "choice" serves as a trump card. If there is a choice to be made, then individuals have to be allowed to make their own choices. In order to make those choices, individuals need information. Every ethical, social, political, moral, religious, and policy question in the area of procreation then becomes translated into the language of consumerism.

The decision to have children at all is couched in terms of one's ability to afford them, the state taking minimal responsibility for the provision of the necessary goods and services; and with the dismantling of "welfare as we know it," the state takes even less responsibility. Americans facing genetic testing for disabling conditions in their potential children, whether in prenatal or pre-embryo diagnosis, need to decide whether they can afford a special-needs child in a society that has no universal health-care coverage, no day-care provisions, and locally funded education which consequently varies widely by class.

As genetic technology gets more sophisticated, the limits of such market-based thinking become more apparent and more dangerous. The dilemma we are about to confront is perhaps best discussed in a recent British novel. *Mendel's Dwarf* has as its protagonist an achondroplastic dwarf who is both a geneticist and a descendant of Gregor Mendel's family. In this passage, he is presenting a lecture on eugenics to "The Mendel Symposium":

> "At least the old eugenics was covered by some kind of theory, how ever dreadful it may have been. The new eugenics, our eugenics, is governed only by the laws of the marketplace. You get what you can pay for. . . . Are we really such intellectual dwarfs"—ah, they shiver at that one—"as to imagine that the laws of supply and demand can be

> elevated to the level of a philosophy? Because that is what we have done. We have within our grasp the future of mankind, and as things are going, the future will be chosen according to the same criteria as people now choose silicone breast implants and liposuction and hair transplants. It will be a eugenics by consumer choice, the eugenics of the marketplace. All masquerading as freedom."[22]

But the problems are not looming off in the future. They are with us now, as the focus in procreation is increasingly on the baby as a product: the product of the reprotech industry, the product of its own genetic programming, the product of unskilled and sometimes untrustworthy workers. The United States stands virtually alone in permitting contract pregnancy, in an openness to marketing a full array of reproductive technologies, and in applying the logic of product-liability regulation to pregnant women. Nancy Hartsock has written about this as a product of late capitalism, but in my reading of international approaches to technologies of procreation, I see it as a specifically American constellation:

> Despite the different ways pregnancy is treated, depending on race and class, a commonality that women face is the increasing commodification of life in late capitalism. One can see this in the treatment of the fetus as a consumer good that needs to be engineered into the best possible product; in the enforcement of contract law over biological relationship in cases such as Baby M; and in the increasing concern over legal obligations to the unborn resulting in charges of fetal abuse. All of these trends represent the logic of late capitalism entering into thinking about pregnant women.[23]

Throughout this book, and throughout this decade, I have argued against these trends. As genetic technologies develop, and as the technologies of procreation become more sophisticated, this argument becomes ever more urgent.

Choice without justice will not make the world a safe place for mothers.

Beyond Choice[24]

The choices we face now in procreation are no longer just about parenthood, about motherhood: they are increasingly about the child itself. People are being asked to think about the kind of baby they are willing to raise. And "kind of baby" has come, more and more, to be understood in terms of genetics, as if genes are the cause and people the result.

When genes become more and more important in our thinking, we start assigning them greater causal power, moving them to more central positions. Sometimes that has meant giving up, metaphorically throwing your hands in the air and saying "it's genetic," meaning "and that's that." Fate. Which is acceptable if the situation is one that we might want people to take their hands off and leave be. So the "gay gene" might be useful as a political tool if invoking that gene becomes another way of saying, "Give it up—you have to accept that some people are inevitably, determinedly, gay." But if the question we are looking at is not "Why are some men gay?" but "Why are more black men in prison than in college?" then saying "It's genetic" is quite dangerous. That of course is the underlying premise of racism: that there are genetic differences between categories of people. In the United States, such racist arguments resurface periodically, with books like *The Bell Curve*[25] making the bestseller lists as they invoke genetic determinist explanations for social problems.

In the context of procreation, from the perspective of would-be parents, what the developing technology of genetics might mean is that "it's genetic" is less a throwing-up-your-hands situation than a rolling-up-your-sleeves kind of problem. "It's genetic" might come to mean "Let's fix it," engineer it, construct it to order. Let us make the determination, let us predetermine: let us *choose*.

Take that highly publicized "gay gene," XQ28, now officially recorded as GAY1. Individual prospective parents of privilege should soon be able to include that—or any other given gene—in their list of things to select for or select against. Many people would be considerably more distressed to learn that their child is gay than to learn that he has some disability. The idea that there is a genetic component to being gay leads quickly to either selecting against that gene or engineering to change it.

Does that kind of selection assure parents that their child will not be gay? Certainly not. A person without the "gay gene" can grow up to be gay, just as a person with it can grow up to be straight. But with the selection, say those who believe this gene has anything to do with sexual orientation anyway, one shifts the odds. People have demonstrated their willingness to pay—in time, money, physical risks, and pain—even to shift those odds for sex selection. Knowing that the technology cannot guarantee a child of chosen sex, or if it is a child of chosen sex, cannot guarantee the "kind of girl" or "kind of boy" the parents seek, still they enter the sex selection clinics. People using prenatal diagnostic technologies know that whatever diseases are screened for and against, they cannot guarantee themselves a healthy, bright, happy child. But they find it worthwhile to do what they can to shift the odds in their favor. They rule out what they can, exercise control where they can. Offer more technology promising yet more control, and people will use it.

Gay is a highly politicized trait. But every day seems to bring some other gene for some other quality, characteristic, trait. Can we control all of it? Can we test and select and read and decode and splice our way to what we really want in our children, for our children?

And have we any right to do that? I'm not talking about our legal rights but rather about our moral rights as parents in our relationship with our children. Do we even want to have them custom made? Would we have wanted our parents to have chosen our traits, predetermined whatever they could and wanted to about us? Whether a trait is what you like best or like least about yourself, you probably would not like thinking about it as something your parents put on an order form.

As if they could. As if the traits and characteristics and parts of our being that we cared about were all separately and distinctively coded in genes that we could choose for our children.

Parenthood does not come with guarantees. Motherhood, I have often said, is one more chance for a speeding truck to ruin your life. The world has plans for our children, and our children have plans for themselves. We will not be able to control this.

The demands of the information age drive us toward getting all the information, taking all the control we can. Perhaps wisdom lies in not always doing so, in making wise judgments about what information we want and what information we do not want, which choices we want to make and which choices are not ours to make.

Choices about if, when, and how to mother are ours to make. In a just and decent world, those choices would be available to all women and all men who want to actively nurture in the way we call mothering. A good and just world, I believe, would provide people with opportunities to nurture if that is what they want to do. A just world would provide women with genuine choices about pregnancy, would support them in their choices about who will attend them, and where, as they labor to bring their children forth into the world. A good and just world would provide us with choices about *our* mothering. But it may go beyond what a good world, beyond what a just world should offer to give us choices about whom we will mother.

Our children are no more our property, subject to our consumerist choices, than we are the property of our parents. The geneticists like to talk about having unlocked the secrets of life, found the bible, the blueprint. The human genome, they tell us, is our book of life. We must not permit it to become a catalog.

Converging Streams[26]

The millennium arrived on the crest of a reproductive revolution that would have been unthinkable just twenty-five years ago, barely imaginable a decade ago. Women in their sixties give birth. Sperm removed from dead men is implanted in their widows. Mice bred to develop cancer are patented. There are freezers filled with human sperm, eggs, and embryos. Sheep are cloned. Technologies move from the laboratory to the clinic almost at once. The human genome is scheduled to be completely mapped shortly after the publication of this book.

How does one begin to make sense of all of this? The changes are coming rapidly, from disparate arenas: medical genetics, infertility, microbiology, animal breeding, from labs and vast computer centers and small sheep farms. Yet they converge and move us along rapidly, forcing us to think about things we have always taken for granted, like why dogs don't have kittens and why babies come from mommies. Every morning's news brings another story, another challenge to conventional wisdom. It is as if we are standing in a valley and can see the ice melting on the mountain tops. Streams begin to trickle down, first one, then another. Two streams converge, pick up strength, come rushing down more quickly. Another stream from another place breaks through.

One thaw took place in infertility. Research directed at resolving infertility, much of it coming from work in animal breeding, broke some of the earlier barriers. Embryos could be created outside of the body. To treat male infertility, micromanipulation of sperm—selecting a particular sperm and injecting it into a particular egg—became possible. Conception moved from a random encounter at an unknown moment some hours after sexual intercourse to the deliberate choice by a white-coated worker of an individual egg and individual sperm, to be implanted with equal deliberation some days later in a woman—either the producer of the egg, the wife of the producer of the sperm, or someone else entirely—chosen by those who foot the bill.

Genetic research is another tributary. Particular stretches of DNA are being decoded, to be read as written. Specific errors or variations in DNA, constituting different alleles of human genes, can be distinguished. The gene for sickle cell anemia, a single misprint, just one letter replaced, can be found and read. The gene for Huntington's disease, a long string of repeats where it should not be, can be spotted. This genetic reading can be done from a scraping of cells from inside the cheek or from a drop of blood. But it can join up with the work in infertility. "Pre-implantation diagnosis is where molecular biology, genetic medicine, and IVF converge."[27] A cell from an extra-uterine product of conception can also be broken off and read. Now a gene can be identified not in a person but in a potential for a person, a few fertilized cells not yet implanted.

As progress is made in breaking the code, reading the human genome, more genes are decoded and more traits read. When it is all reduced to CGAT, the letters of the genetic code, reading sickle cell or Huntington's is no more or no less difficult than reading the gene for red hair or the much debated XQ28, officially designated "GAY1." There is talk of putting the information technologies of genetics and computer analysis together, creating a gene chip that will read an entire embryonic genome.

One of the older streams flowing toward us began trickling almost a hundred years ago, as doctors took over pregnancy. Midwives were displaced; birth moved from the home to the hospital and went from being a family event to a medical/surgical event. In the last twenty-five years it has for many women literally become surgery as the rate of cesarean sections zoomed upwards to near 25 percent. As pregnancy became a medical experience testing began to dominate, diagnosing not only the health of the mother but the potential health of the fetus. Prenatal diagnosis introduced the possibility of abortion into even the most wanted pregnancies.

Another thaw occurred as the fetus itself broke loose of pregnancy and entered the cultural landscape as a force to be reckoned with. Tumbling toward us the fetus acquired rights: rights to be genetically free of defect, rights to be free of "abuse" by pregnant women, rights to medical treatment. The pregnant women in whom these fetuses reside become shadowy, their rights fading. The confrontation between biomedical science and fetus becomes increasingly free of the pregnant woman: she ceases to function as barrier or advocate. Juvenile protection agencies, district attorneys, and court-appointed representatives begin to speak for the fetus.

And over there, the market, long just barely contained by its dam, crashes through. A cash economy, otherwise rejected for body parts, seeps into procreation. Hospital employees turn over envelopes stuffed with hundred-dollar bills to young women for the sale of their eggs. Pregnancy, having faded into the background, becomes unskilled labor, a service to be hired at less than minimum wage. Contract law begins to nudge aside family law, as the logic of the marketplace flows over the world of procreation.

Utopian thinkers look at all this pouring toward us, and see a fine new dawn when every baby will be wanted, healthy, guaranteed free of defect. Dystopian thinkers see a brave new world, with market-driven evolution creating separate species of humans.

There was a time when sensible people could say that they were interested in genetic research and technology *or* interested in the new reproductive technologies *or* interested in the older reproductive rights issues of contraception and abortion *or* interested in adoption and child welfare issues, but not in *all* of them. For those of us concerned with the future of motherhood in America, that time has passed. As these streams join together, it is no longer possible to separate them. They merge and mingle, creating more powerful forces than any of them alone, carving a new motherhood across the landscape.

Recreating Motherhood: Toward Feminst Social Policy

In 1969, THE YEAR that I entered graduate school in sociology, got married, and ordered "Mrs. Herschel Rothman" printed on my stationery, *A Modern Dictionary of Sociology* was published, which defined feminism as:

> A social movement originating in England in the eighteenth century and having as its goal the attainment of certain social, political and economic rights for women, intended to give them equality with men. The feminist movement generally has followed the spread of the Industrial Revolution and the associated breakdown of traditional norms and the attainment of economic independence for women. In the West today, feminism, having achieved its original objectives, has become more of a psychological state—a constellation of certain attitudes held by individual women—than a social movement.[1]

So much for sociology.

The feminism that spread with the industrial revolution and that wanted to give women "equality with men" was *liberal* feminism, the feminist thinking that dominated the first wave of the women's movement and is still the best understood and most successful form of feminism in America.

The simplest and least threatening version of feminism is to ask for what is seen in America as simple *fairness*. Lots of Americans who would never, ever think of themselves as actually being feminists nonetheless expect fairness for women: the "I'm-not-a-feminist-but" arguments one hears. Demands for fairness, the liberal feminist demands, consist largely of the insistence that prevailing liberal ideals be applied to women: things like equal pay for equal work, the same rights for women as for men, and so on. Since in America we are living in a society founded on liberal principles, liberal feminism comes closest to mainstream values, and consequently often sounds like the very voice of reason, especially when juxtaposed with the more "strident" feminist positions.

Liberal feminism has its roots deep in American culture; the feminists we have always had with us, as far back as Abigail Adams's request that the framers of the constitution "remember the ladies." The liberal feminists, in asking that the ladies be remembered, are not so much offering a critique of American life and values as they are seeking full access.

> Liberal philosophy emerged with the growth of capitalism. It raised demands for democracy and political liberties that often expressed deeply held moral convictions about the inherent equality of men. . . . Consistently over the centuries, feminists have demanded that the prevailing liberal ideals should also be applied to women.[2]

On the one hand, that doesn't sound like asking for a whole lot. On the other hand, there is still no equal rights amendment in the United States today.

But would an equal rights amendment solve our problems? We need that, surely, but what will it accomplish for the issues I have been addressing, the concerns of women as mothers?

Liberal feminism works best to defend women's rights to be like men, to enter into men's worlds, to work at men's jobs for men's pay, to have the rights and privileges of men. But what of our rights to be *women*? The liberal argument, the fairness argument, the equal rights argument, these all begin to break down when we look at women who are, or are becoming, mothers.

This is a different aspect of the distinction between "equal pay for equal work" and the much more troubling, much more revolutionary idea of "comparable worth." A woman lawyer is exactly the same as a man lawyer. A woman cop is just the same as a man cop. And a pregnant woman is just the same as . . . well, as, uh, . . . It's like disability, right? Or like serving in the army?

Pregnancy is just exactly like pregnancy.

There is nothing else quite like it. That statement is not glorification or mystification. It is a statement of fact. Having a baby grow in your belly is not like anything else one can do. It is unique.

How can uniqueness be made to fit into an equality model? Strangely enough, albeit for different reasons, both patriarchal ideology and liberal feminist thinking have come to the same conclusion about what to do with the problem of the uniqueness of pregnancy: devalue it. Discount it so deeply that its uniqueness just doesn't matter. In strongly patriarchal systems, as described earlier, the genetic tie for men is the most important parental tie: women grow men's children, what Caroline Whitbeck calls the "flower pot theory of pregnancy."[3] Men have the seeds and women are the flower pots.

Liberal feminists, seeking equality, seeking recognition of women's rationality, women's rights, but discounting the value of our bodies, claim equality of parenthood between men and women: women too have seed, and men too can nurture children. Men cannot nurture with their bodies, not with their blood or their milk as women do—but that is just menial, body work. Both parents have seeds. Children are "half hers, half his." Instead of a flower pot, the woman is seen as an equal contributor of seed—and the baby might just as well have grown in the backyard. It is, after all, only women's bodily experience that is different from men's.

Liberal feminism does not challenge the mind-body dualism posited by and embedded in liberal philosophy, and so falters on the same grounds as discussed earlier—that is has no place for the inherent physicality of gestation and lactation, and no respect for the "menial" work of body maintenance: the *mothering* work of early childhood.

The equality model itself has yet other problems, as Alison Jaggar points out. The liberal belief in "abstract individualism," which she defines as "the assumption that essential human characteristics are properties of individuals and are given independently of any particular social context,"[4] leads to a particular conception of equality. If one thinks of individuals as in some way identical packets, then equality will be focused entirely on "equal rights," ensuring that all the packets, being essentially identical, will be treated identically. It is wrong, *unfair*, to discriminate, to treat black and brown packets differently from white, old packets differently from those that are young (but not so young as to not yet have "rationality" and not be completed packets), female differently from male, physically damaged from those who are physically strong.

Equal rights sounds good, and in many ways it is a fine goal and one that has yet to be achieved for any of these groups: racial minorities, old people, women, disabled people. But a focus on "rights" ignores *needs*. Special attempts to get help based on need get called "reverse discrimination." Women as mothers are especially hard hit by this narrow equal rights approach. For one thing, those individuals who are not yet rational—our babies and children—need an awful lot of care and attention, and that falls to our lot. Liberal thinking, including liberal feminism, is a bit shy on what to do with the children—and the other deeply needy people. Even achieving a liberal goal of including men as child tenders does not solve the problem: it remains individualized, privatized.

The second way that women as mothers are particularly hard hit by the "equality" approach of liberalism is that our specific needs as mothers are not taken into account. The liberal argument for formal equality has simply no place for the special needs of any group, including mothers. The reductio ad absurdum of formal equality for mothers was the 1976 Supreme Court decision in the case of *Gilbert v. General Electric Company*. The case was brought by the women employees, claiming sex discrimination because the disability benefits package at GE excluded pregnancy-related disabilities. The Supreme Court, in what Meredith Gould has called the "pregnant person school of thought,"[5] ruled that it was not sex discrimination. One physical condition had been removed from coverage, that's all. The discrimination, if such it was, was against *pregnant persons*, not against *women*.

Giving women all the rights of men will not accomplish a whole lot for women facing the demands of pregnancy, birth, and lactation. Because of the focus on formal equality, because of the value of mind over body, and because all of this is happening in a patriarchal system, liberal thinking tends to diminish the significance of the physical parts of motherhood. The liberal feminist claim too often boils down to women having the rights to be like men. If some women choose not to assert those rights, choose not to be like men, then largely that's their lookout.

The focus on rationality feeds into this. People, including women of course, are assumed to be acting out of their own self-interest. Liberal feminists take as a key issue convincing other liberals that women are just as rational as are men: if rationality is the very definition of what it is to be a person, this is absolutely crucial. Non-feminist, even misogynist liberals may rule the world: and they may see women as having heads full of fluff, overcontrolled by our bodies, hormones, and instincts. Responding to that audience, liberal feminists sometimes find themselves defending women's rights to act in ways that others may see as coerced—defending therefore women's rights to be pornographic models, prostitutes, surrogate mothers.

That is why liberal feminists like Lori Andrews found Mary Beth Whitehead's "change of mind" so threatening. It could be used—and it was sometimes—by traditionalists, conservatives, to claim that women cannot be trusted or relied on. If the hormones of pregnancy invalidate legal contracts, then where are we? And so liberal feminists often found themselves arguing alongside the baby brokers that our highest moral value is "a deal's a deal."

For those people (and they may be the most traditional of conservatives or the most radical of feminists) who want to see women—our bodies, ourselves, our sexuality, our motherhood—treated with respect, liberal feminism fails. There is a logic to defending women's rights to be demeaned if that is what women want, if that is the deal women rationally made—but it feels like defending the right of blacks to sell themselves back into slavery if that is what they want. The important point gets missed: what is happening in a society that makes such a thing potentially a rational choice—what kinds of unthinkable alternatives do individuals face?

The ideologies of patriarchy, technology, and capitalism support each other, prop each other up, but they are not the same thing. And so fighting one does not destroy the others. Liberal feminists are good and strong critics of patriarchal society, but they do not fight the ideology of technology or capitalism. What do we have if we try to pull out the patriarchy, but not challenge the rest of the hegemony? Distinctions remain between the public and the private worlds, and the class system remains. The public world, without patriarchy, is no longer men's world, but it remains the world of power and privilege. The private world remains disvalued, as poor people become the wives and mothers of the world, cleaning the toilets and raising the children. The devaluing of certain work, of nurturance, of private "domestic" work, remains: rearing children is roughly on a par—certainly in terms of salary—with cleaning the toilet.

New Technologies in Old Bottles

I believe that questions about motherhood are the most troubling, disconcerting, confounding, divisive, and (therefore) interesting ones confronting feminism. By slicing right into the (biological) sex/(social) gender distinction, the issues of procreation raise all the essential—and essentializing—questions of feminism.

Adding new technologies of procreation clarifies some things and further confuses others. And it does not take very new or very fancy technology to raise these questions. If I had a nickel for every student who has pointed out to me that women's role as primary child-care provider is based on the biological given of breasts and breast milk, I would be rich. And if I had a nickel for every student who then answered yes when I asked whether he or she had been breast fed, I'd still be broke. If the baby bottle did not deconstruct social motherhood, what hope has a turkey baster, petrie dish, or freezer?

It's the new reproductive technologies that catch the attention when we talk about motherhood: freezing eggs, making old women pregnant, cloning sheep and mice and maybe someday soon people. Technologies, however, do not make social change. They sometimes force us to confront our values and our beliefs and even our policies, but they do not themselves determine those values, beliefs, and policies. If we do not as a society value the work of nurturance, no technology invented will change that. If we choose to invest (some) seeds with higher worth than the labor that fosters their growth, no technology will change that either. We can separate out the seed from the growth, and all that happens is our values are laid bare before us: a "top rank" egg sells for $50,000, nine months of pregnancy for $15,000. We incorporate the technologies into our value system and move on.

It happened so quickly. "How could these technologies have become naturalized and legitimized in such a relatively short period of time? Fifteen years ago the very idea of conception outside a woman's womb triggered science-fiction fantasies and scary speculations," Jose Van Dyck noted in 1995.[6] In no time at all those technologies, and the court cases they occasionally sparked, were made to serve traditional "family values," to reconstruct the family as we knew it, a "biologically rooted, racially closed, heterosexual, middle-class unit."[7] "Notwithstanding the often destabilizing effects of new reproductive practices," Valerie Hartouni noted, "these new practices have been domesticated over the course of the past twenty-five years."[8] Domesticated indeed.

When we look at the way that the lived experience of motherhood is actually being changed, we might conclude that the technology that is most relevant isn't the technology of procreation—the technology found in infertility clinics and so effectively domesticated—but the technology of communication and travel. The internet changes the face of American motherhood as much as laparoscopy or egg retrieval and freezing. Eggs are auctioned off on web sites; infertility e-businesses spring up, matching egg donors with purchasers, "surrogates" with contracting couples; and adoption moves on line. Transportation technologies turn the most remote Chinese villages into offshore sites for babies in trendy American neighborhoods. Nannies get matched up on line too, and workers from all over the world are to be found in American cities, doing the daily mothering of middle-class and wealthy American children.

That said, I still think the import of the new technologies of procreation is being too readily dismissed. Those who favor their expansion ask us to see them as a simple extension of individual reproductive choice. If people are free to choose abortion, proponents argue, then why not contract pregnancy, preimplantation diagnosis, genetic enhancement to improve the quality of their embryos/children, cloning, or whatever else the technologists can offer?

But many of us who are not supportive of the technologies also tend to dismiss their import, claiming that they are essentially irrelevant—as they may well be, at this moment, for the majority of Americans and the rest of the world. The real problems, critics hasten to remind us, are access to the basic services of contraception, abortion, prenatal care, and child welfare. All of this science-fiction work affects so few.

If all of this—the development of infertility research, the work in molecular biology and genetics—was only about how infertile people of privilege can overcome their infertility, without doing any more damage to the selfhood and happiness of others than the wealthy already do in hiring nannies, caregivers, babysitters, or housekeepers, then perhaps we could handle it with minor extension of existing law and policies.

But this goes much further than even the troubling scenarios of poor women of color housed in dormitories bearing transplanted embryos for wealthy whites. Standing shadowed right behind the vision of *The Handmaid's Tale*[9] is the vision of the *Brave New World*.[10] Genetic research unravels the human genome into 100,000 increasingly patented, soon to be purchasable bits. Who will own the "discrete, randomly assorted, stable, dominant and recessive ancestral alleles," as Pollack defines children,[11] when the assembly is no longer random and pregnancy reduced to unskilled labor?

It is not just that a given technology, like egg donation or embryo transplant, may empower some people at the cost of others, allowing one woman to have a much-wanted child while another faces physical and emotional risks for a fee. It is also that the self-same technology can be used to increase personal control and choice, or to increase state/market/social control. The issue is power, not technology. Of course contraception, sterilization, and abortion in the hands of individual women can be personally liberating and empowering. But contraception, sterilization, and abortion have also served as keystones in state-run eugenics systems.

The current U.S. climate makes state-enforced eugenics programs extremely unlikely, but there are other ways of developing eugenics, other ways of bending motherhood to the societal order. The traditional feminist focus on choice and access, absolutely necessary as they are, sometimes blinds us to other truths: *Individual choice doesn't stop social engineering. It can be a mechanism for achieving it.*

If a woman is offered access to prenatal screening for Down's syndrome, but no access to services for a child with Down's syndrome, what does it mean to speak of the "choice" of selective abortion? If parenthood is defined as essentially a genetic tie, what happens to the "choice" of adoption, weighted against IVF?

Ruth Hubbard has said "As 'choices' become available, they all too rapidly become compulsions to 'choose' the socially endorsed alternative."[12] While we worry, with very good reason, about losing the option of legal abortion and about access to safe and effective contraception, that does not mean that women can afford unlimited fertility. The choice of contraception simultaneously closed down some of the choices for large families.

And so it may be with "quality control." The ability to control the quality of our children may soon cost us the right not to control that quality. Amniocentesis and selective abortion, preimplantation diagnosis and embryo screening, contract pregnancies and the other new reproductive technologies are all being used to give the illusion of choice. On an individual level they certainly solve some very grave troubles. People who have successfully used the new technologies have had their choices expanded, have gained control over their lives. In just the same way, contraception and abortion provide us with the very real and very true experience of controlling fertility. Choices open and choices close. For those whose choices meet the social expectation, for those who choose what the society wants them to want, the experience of choice is very real.

Perhaps we should realize that human beings living in society have precious little choice ever. The social structure creates needs—the need for women to be mothers, the need for delayed childbearing, the need for small families, the need for "perfect children"—and creates the technologies that enable people to make the needed choices. The question is not *whether* those choices are constructed but *how* they are constructed.

Thus we have social policies regarding motherhood woven through the fabric of our society and, whether we see it that way or not, in how we define work and family and people and life itself. When we set out to deliberately create or just imagine policy regarding motherhood, what we are doing is trying to set the limits: what are the points beyond which we will not go? Where will the state step in to regulate the market, to regulate intimate relationships, to regulate the body, and where will the state step back? A social policy cannot change a set of values, but neither must a social policy be allowed to stand that reinforces a set of values we find morally unacceptable.

When I review the policy suggestions I made a decade ago, I see that nothing in the new technologies changes what we must do if we are to value motherhood. I offer them here, never intending them to be the last word on feminist policy for motherhood. This is, rather, a starting point, an attempt to reason our way to social policy and law that incorporate a different vision of motherhood, of children, and of family.

Constructing Feminist Social Policy Regarding Motherhood

RECOGNIZE MATERNITY CLAIMS

Infants belong to their mothers at birth because of the unique nurturant relationship that has existed between them up to that moment. That is, birth mothers have full parental rights, including rights of custody, of the babies they bore. Conversely, we will not recognize genetic claims to parenthood, neither as traditional "paternity" claims nor as genetic maternity in the case of an ovum donor. These genetic relationships exist, as do relations of aunts and uncles to nephews and nieces, siblings to each other, and so on. But genetic ties will not give parental rights.

In this I would be basically following the model offered by the Netherlands, with a significant variation. Paternity there is acknowledged only through marriage to the mother, or through adoption. The variation I would offer is that same-sex marriage and same-sex co-parenting will be equally recognized.

Children "belong to" the mother and the mother's spouse if she has one, at the time of birth. In the immediate postbirth period, presumptive custody would always go to the mother in cases of disagreement between mother and spouse or co-parent. After six weeks, custody would go to the rearing parent in the case of dispute. If parenting is genuinely shared, then joint custody of the child is appropriate.

ADOPTION

Adoption agreements can take place only *after* the birth of a child, with a brief period in which the birth mother can change her mind. I would make that period the same length of time in which I would have us recognize presumptive custody of a birth mother over her co-parent: six weeks. The "shadow" maternal gestation casts on custody arrangements[13] is then limited to six weeks in all cases. After that point, custody decisions would have to be based on an analysis of child-care arrangements as they have existed from the time of birth.

There should be two kinds of adoptions: relinquishing, and co-parenting. In the relinquishing type of adoption, essentially adoption as we know it, the mother gives up her custody and parental rights and turns those rights over to the adoptive parent or parents. I would encourage "open" adoption, the birth mother and the child she bore having the opportunity to know each other if they so wish, and would like to see the birth mother included in an "auntlike" relationship with the child. In American society, that "aunt" relationship is recognized, but without legal claim, and without a fixed sense of obligations or rights. The relationship is essentially what people choose to make of it. We must continue in the direction of unsealing adoption records. As Katarina Wegar has persuasively argued, "Since ours is a society that stresses the paramount significance of the blood relation and since adoption professionals in their everyday practices may implicitly reinforce this assumption, the sealed records policy simply demands the impossible from those it affects."[14]

In the second form of adoption, co-parenting, a mother without a spouse (without a male or *female* spouse) could allow a second parent to join her as a legal co-parent. This would allow people who do not want to marry to legally share a child, with full parental rights. Their legal situation would essentially be the same as that of married parents after a divorce; they are parents of their mutual child, though not married to each other. Such arrangements would allow more flexibility, more permeability in family. Women who want to bear a child without marriage could still have the support of a co-parent. And people, men or women, could become parents without either bearing a child or marrying. As with any co-parents, issues of custody and financial responsibility would be negotiated between the two parents. In cases of dispute, custody decisions would, in this and in all cases, be based on the history of child care. Unless proven clearly unfit, custody goes to the prime nurturing parent, with joint custody if this role is fully shared.

SURROGACY

There is no such thing under this system. Every woman who bears a child is the mother of the child she bears, with full parental rights, regardless of the source of the egg or of the sperm. Genetic claims are not to be recognized for parental rights. No pre-birth or pre-conception adoption agreements will be recognized. Every child has one identifiable parent at the moment of birth: the person from whose body it emerged.

Children are not fit objects of contracts. The state, since the abolition of slavery, is not in the business of enforcing contract disputes over the ownership of people.

Should money ever be allowed for adoption? The sale of children, the sale of people, is morally repugnant. The converse argument that I recognize is that women have a right to do whatever they want with their bodies. But women cannot sell themselves into slavery, and I do not think we have to recognize a right to sell a child. Limitations on the rights to sell the body and its parts exist for men as well: we have not recognized a legal right to sell or to buy organs for transplant.

INFERTILITY

We need to find solutions to infertility, in prevention and cure. This should be part of a comprehensive health program in which all people in this country should have access to needed health services, regardless of financial status.

The treatment of infertility needs to be understood in the context of the meaning of parenthood. If we are not thinking of parenthood as a genetic relationship, but as a nurturant social relationship, then treatment is to enable nurturance, to enable the person to enter parenthood. The focus of the treatment is the parenting relationship, not getting one's gametes to grow.

The use of animal wombs, or artificial wombs, is not appropriate. Every human child has a right to a human mother. Every human who grows a child has rights of parenthood, of motherhood, to the child she bears.

FATHERHOOD

If men want to have children, they will have to either develop the technology that enables them to become pregnant (and so be legal "mothers" of children they gestate themselves) or have children through their relationship with women. If men want children of their "own," they will have to either persuade women to marry them or persuade women to allow them to co-parent, to co-adopt, or to fully adopt their (women's) children.

Paternity should not be the focus of fatherhood. As Dostoyevski said, thinking about his own father's "tender and nurturing capacities, . . . it is a lost secret of our language that the word generation is really a verb, masquerading as a noun."[15] Men can have children of their "own" just as women do—in their caring and in their acts of generation, nurturance, and tenderness.

PREGNANCY

Women have full rights of personal privacy, bodily autonomy, and individual decision making in pregnancy. This is for the whole of pregnancy. The separate personhood or rights of the fetus against its mother are not acknowledged. The fetus is part of its mother's body as long as it is in her body.

NEWBORN MEDICAL CARE

Mothers, and the legally recognized co-parent if there is one, have full medical decision-making rights for the care of their newborns and very young children. As early as possible, the child is to be involved in decision making. We must not confuse the issue of protecting children from abusive parents with the separate issue of values in medical decision making.

CHILD CARE

We must as a society take shared economic responsibility for the care of our children. Children and their mothers must not be dependent on the generosity of a high-earning man.

We need to follow the lead of virtually every other country and provide a long period of fully paid (or almost fully paid) parental leave. That leave should be available either to the mother or to the co-parent, or for them to share as suits them. That is, one person could be subsidized for 25 percent of his or her time and the other for 75 percent of his or her time; both parents could be subsidized for 50 percent; or one parent could be subsidized 100 percent.

To compensate for the extreme income disparity between men and women, parental leave will have to be based on individual earnings: a parent earning $50,000 would get twice as much money as would a parent earning $25,000, for the same length or percentage of leave. Otherwise families cannot afford to have the higher earner (usually the man) take time off for child care.

Following the initial several months of leave, parents need to be subsidized for additional part time off, again paid proportional to their income. And we need subsidies for various child-care arrangements. Calls for "affordable" child care in the past have turned out to mean that one woman's salary must cover another's, that inevitably day-care workers and in-home child-care workers cannot themselves afford for their own children the care they give to others. This perpetuates the gender-class-race system. We need to take public responsibility for early child care, as we do for education after the age of five.

Parents continue to need extra days off throughout parenthood, and these too need to be covered out of pooled tax money. If we assume, say, eight extra days of child-care leave a year, to take care of children's sicknesses, special needs, etc., that too can be divided as the parents choose. But if we determine that half the days go to each of the two co-parents, when there are indeed two parents, we are giving a real economic incentive for sharing child-care responsibilities fully.

CHILD-CARE WORKERS

Subsidies for child care can mean that child-care workers are better paid. I would go further, and acknowledge special rights of child-care workers, based on their responsibility and nurturance. For example, someone who has given prolonged personal care to a child should have continued legal visitation rights to that child, and should not be subject to "firing" without cause by the parents.

BEYOND GENDER

A final note, not on a matter of public policy, but on personal language. The women's movement has sensitized us to the power of language, the implications of saying *girl* when we mean *woman*, *man* when we mean *people*. I would encourage us to think about the meaning of language within the family as well.

I would like us to get rid of our "mommy" and "daddy" language. We are individuals, in individual relationships with our children, and not the embodiment of gender-based parental roles. If I am "mommy" to my child, then other people can be understood to be "substitute mommy." But if I am Barbara, then other people are who they are in relation to the child, not to my role as "mommy," and therefore are not my substitute or stand-in.

In turn, we can treat our children as people in their own right, as individuals, and not as property or extensions of self.

A Last Word to the New Edition

The working title of the new chapter for this book, I jokingly told colleagues, was "I told you so." A lot of what I saw coming in the late 1980s came and looked worse yet by the millennium. But on this very last piece here, the "I told you so!" was best directed at me.

When I wrote this piece about rejecting "mommy" and "daddy" language, my husband and I had two children, both born to us, and we were perfectly happy being called "Barbara" and "Hesch." When we adopted an African American infant, we saw trouble looming. We didn't *look* like a family: we needed every bit of social support we could garner to make ourselves understood as a family. And besides, I worried to my husband, what would happen if he was carrying a tantrum-throwing two-year-old out of a supermarket and she was screaming anything but "Daddy!" at him?

So after a lot of talk and thought, we chose "mama" and "papa" and used that gender-based, role-defining language. Once again, race trumps gender.

One day when Victoria was about six, we were at a birthday party for her birth mother's other daughter. Victoria was racing her sister through tunnels and slides at an indoor park, and her head and arm popped out at me. She pointed over to her birth mother: "I'm going to call *her* mommy." And then she did. About twenty times in ten minutes. Her birth mother and I looked at each other over Victoria's head, and all of what we were trying to do, what we wanted for the child, for each other, all of it lay there between us as we smiled and shook our heads at each other. "Whatever," I said, as her birth mother said, "She's mommy—you can call me mother."

I walked into class the next day, a Sociology of the Family class, and we were just finishing this book. I tossed my copy on the desk, and it opened to this last statement.

Other people tell me they want their children to call them mommy, because there's lots of Barbaras or Debbys or Suzies in this world, but only one mommy to their children. Well, no. There's only one me, but lots of people can and do mother my children. Bless them all.

Notes

Part I: Introduction

1. Parts of this chapter have appeared in 1987, "Comments on Harrison: The Commodification of Motherhood," *Gender & Society*, Vol. l, No. 3, pp. 312–316.
2. See Lillian Rubin, 1985, *Just Friends: The Role of Friendship in Our Lives* (New York: Harper and Row).
3. The customary phrase is "reproductive technology," and it was a phrase I used until Ruth Hubbard and Caroline Whitbeck pointed out to me how inappropriate it is. Human beings are not the result of a "production" process. And, as Ruth Hubbard points out, we do not reproduce ourselves: two of us come together and make a third one of us. I now use the word "procreation" rather than "reproduction."
4. I wish to thank Rosalyn Weinman for her insight and wording on this issue.
5. Lynn Davidman, 2000, *Motherloss* (Berkeley, California: University of California Press), pp. 219–220.
6. Betty Friedan, 1963, *The Feminine Mystique* (New York: W.W. Norton and Company).
7. For a discussion of this, see Emily Martin, 1987, *The Woman in the Body* (Boston: Beacon Press), p. 23.
8. For a fuller discussion of the changing economic value of children, see Viviana A. Zelizar, 1985, *Pricing the Priceless Child* (New York: Basic Books).
9. My appreciation to Judith Lorber for her help in organizing and in wording this summary.
10. My vision of motherhood "as experience and as institution" owes a debt to the work of Adrienne Rich, 1976, *Of Woman Born: Motherhood as Experience and as Institution* (New York: W.W. Norton and Company).

Motherhood under Patriarchy

1. Glenn Petersen, 1982, "Ponepean Matriliny: Production, Exchange and the Ties that Bind," *American Ethnologist*, Vol. 9, No. 1, p. 141.
2. Annette Weiner, 1976, *Women of Value, Men of Renown: New Perspectives on Trobriand Exchange* (Austin: University of Texas Press); also Weiner, personal communication.
3. Shirley Lindenbaum, 1979, *Kuru Sorcery: Disease and Danger in the New Guinea Highlands* (Palo Alto, California: Mayfield Publishing Company), p. 15.
4. Kathleen Gough, 1961, "Nayar: Central Kerala," in David M. Schneider and

Kathleen Gough, editors, *Matrilineal Kinship* (Berkeley, California: University of California Press), p. 365.

5. W. D. Hamilton, 1978, "The Genetic Evolution of Social Behavior," in Arthur L. Caplan, editor, *The Sociobiology Debate: Readings on Ethical and Scientific Issues* (New York: Harper and Row), p. 191.

Motherhood in a Technological Society

1. Paul T. Durbin, 1980, *A Guide to the Culture of Science, Technology and Medicine* (New York: Free Press), p. xxxi.
2. Carl Mitcham, 1980, "A Philosophy of Technology," in Durbin, p. 283.
3. Caroline Whitbeck, 1987, "Ethical Issues Relevant to Women's Health and Medical Technology," unpublished paper.
4. Paul M. Barrett, 1986, "A Movement Called 'Law and Economics' Sways Legal Circles," *Wall Street Journal*, August 4, p. 1.
5. Charles Anderson, 1971, *Toward a New Sociology: A Critical View* (Homewood, Illinois: Dorsey Press).
6. John Kenneth Galbraith, 1968, *The New Industrial State* (New York: Signet Books).
7. Talcott Parsons, 1964, *Essays in Sociological Theory* (New York: Free Press).
8. Eliot Krause, 1977, *Power and Illness: The Political Sociology of Health and Medical Care* (New York: Elsevier North-Holland), p. 11.
9. Paul J. Tillich, 1963, "The Person in Technical Society: The Revolt Against Depersonalization in the Modern Era," in Hendrik M. Reuitenbeck, editor, *Varieties of Modern Social Theory* (New York: E. P. Dutton), p. 294.
10. Mitcham, "Philosophy of Technology," p. 311.
11. Durbin, *Culture of Science*, p. xxii.
12. Erving Goffman, 1961, *Asylums: Essays on the Social Situation of Mental Patients and Other Inmates* (New York: Anchor).
13. Barbara Katz Rothman, 1982, *In Labor: Women and Power in the Birthplace* (New York: W. W. Norton and Company), pp. 34–35.
14. Emily Martin, 1987, *The Woman in the Body: A Cultural Analysis of Reproduction* (Boston: Beacon Press), p. 83.
15. Arthur C. Guyton, 1986, *A Textbook of Medical Physiology*, 7th edition (Philadelphia: W. B. Saunders), p. 979.
16. Martin, *Woman in the Body*, p. 50.
17. Ibid., p. 48.
18. Sheila Kitzinger, 1978, *Women as Mothers: How They See Themselves in Different Cultures* (New York: Vintage Books), p. 74.
19. Gena Corea credits Pauline Bart with choosing the phrase "the mother machine" as the title of her book: Gena Corea, 1985, *The Mother Machine: Reproductive Technologies from Artificial Insemination to Artificial Wombs* (New York: Harper and Row).
20. Caroline Merchant, 1980, *The Death of Nature: Women, Ecology and the Scientific Revolution* (San Francisco: Harper and Row), p. 28.
21. Ibid., p. 185.
22. Ibid., p. 214.
23. Robert N. Bellah, Richard Madsen, William M. Sullivan, Ann Swidler, and Steven M. Tipton, 1985, *Habits of the Heart: Individualism and Commitment in American Life* (Berkeley, California: University of California Press), p. 277.
24. Ibid., p. 276.

25. Alison M. Jaggar, 1983, *Feminist Politics and Human Nature* (Totowa, New Jersey: Rowman and Allenheld), p. 186.
26. Ibid., p. 174.
27. John Robertson, 1986, "Embryos, Families and Procreative Liberty: The Legal Structure of the New Reproduction," *Southern California Law Review*, Vol. 59, July, No. 5, p. 1022.

Motherhood under Capitalism

1. Barbara Katz Rothman, 1982, *In Labor: Women and Power in the Birthplace* (New York: W. W. Norton and Company), pp. 35–36.
2. I want to express my appreciation to the Texas midwife who found it so hard to understand how babies could be valued and mothers not—reminding me yet again why I so deeply value midwives; and to the other Texas midwife in the audience who explained it by giving us the example of the South African diamond miners.
3. Margaret Stacey, 1985, "Commentary," *Journal of Medical Ethics*, Vol. 11, No. 4, p. 193.
4. Janet Farrell Smith, 1984, "Parenting and Property," in Joyce Treblicot, editor, *Mothering: Essays in Feminist Theory* (Totowa, New Jersey: Rowman and Allenheld), p. 202.
5. Ibid., p. 201.
6. Cited in Clifton Fadiman, general editor, 1985, *The Little, Brown Book of Anecdotes* (Boston: Little, Brown and Company), p. 6.
7. Smith, "Parenting and Property," p. 202.
8. Ibid., p. 201.
9. This is a point made clear in the work of Carol Gilligan, 1982, *In a Different Voice: Psychological Theory and Women's Development* (Cambridge, Massachusetts: Harvard University Press), and brought home repeatedly to me by Caroline Whitbeck.

Part II: Introduction

1. I wish to express my deepest appreciation to Eileen Moran for once again pointing out to me what it is I am doing.
2. Janet Gallagher has made this point repeatedly at gatherings of people concerned with the new technology of procreation.
3. Lawrence S. Nelson, 1987, conference sponsored by the Hastings Center, San Francisco and Los Angeles, September 9 and 11, 1987.
4. Alison Jaggar, 1983, *Feminist Politics and Human Nature* (Totowa, New Jersey: Rowman and Allenheld), p. 308.

Pregnancy as a Relationship

1. Ann Oakley, 1984, *The Captured Womb: A History of the Medical Care of Pregnant Women* (Oxford: Basil and Blackwell Publisher Ltd.), p. 11.
2. Jack A. Pritchard and Paul C. Macdonald, 1980, *Williams Obstetrics*, 16th edition (New York: Appleton Century Crofts), p. 679.
3. Cited in Gail Sforza Brewer, 1977, *What Every Pregnant Woman Should Know: The Truth about Diets and Drugs in Pregnancy* (New York: Random House), p. 54.
4. This apt phrase comes from the work of Caroline Whitbeck, 1973, "Theories of Sex Difference," *The Philosophical Forum*, Vol. 5, pp. 1–2.

5. Mary O'Brien, 1981, *The Politics of Reproduction* (London and Boston: Routledge and Kegan Paul, Ltd.).
6. Sheila Kitzinger makes many of these points in her chapter "Getting in Touch with Your Baby," in 1987, *Your Baby, Your Way: Making Pregnancy Decisions and Birth Plans* (New York: Pantheon Books), pp. 181–203.
7. Kyle D. Pruett, 1987, *The Nurturing Father: Journey Toward the Complete Man* (New York: Warner Books), pp. 124–125.
8. Caroline Whitbeck, 1981, "Introductory Remarks," in Helen B. Holmes, Betty B. Hoskins, and Michael Gross, editors, *The Custom Made Child?* (Clifton, New Jersey: Humana Press), pp. 119–121.

Redefining Abortion

1. A brief history of abortion can be found in Hyman Rodman, Betty Sarvis, and Joy Bonar, 1987, *The Abortion Question* (New York: Columbia University Press).
2. Kristen Luker, 1984, *Abortion and the Politics of Motherhood* (Berkeley, California: University of California Press).
3. Margaret Sanger, 1920, *Women and the New Race* (New York: Blue Ribbon Books), p. 124.
4. Ibid.
5. Ibid., p. 125.
6. Ibid., pp. 128–129.
7. Ibid., p. 5.
8. This is the contrast Luker focuses on in her analysis of the abortion controversy.
9. Janet Gallagher, personal communication.
10. For a fuller discussion on the link between the abortion-rights movement and the eugenics movement, see Barbara Katz Rothman, 1993, *The Tentative Pregnancy: How Amniocentesis is Changing the Experience of Motherhood* (New York: W. W. Norton and Company).
11. Jonathan B. Imber, 1986, *Abortion and the Private Practice of Medicine* (New Haven: Yale University Press), p. xiv.
12. Ibid., p. 93.
13. Ibid., p. 68.
14. Ibid., pp. 49, 52.
15. Ibid., p. 120.
16. Carole Joffee, 1987, *The Regulation of Sexuality: Experiences of Family Planning Workers* (Philadelphia: Temple University Press).
17. Melinda Detlefs, 1986, unpublished masters thesis, Graduate School and University Center of the City University of New York.
18. Wendy Simonds, 1991, "At an Impasse: Inside an Abortion Clinic," in Helena Z. Lopata and Judith Lorber, editors, *Current Research on Occupations and Professions*. Vol. 6. (Greenwich, Connecticut: JAI Press).
19. Wendy Simonds, 1996, *Abortion at Work: Ideology and Practice in a Feminist Clinic* (New Brunswick, New Jersey: Rutgers University Press).
20. Lennart Nilson, 1965, "Miracle in the Womb," *Life*, April 30.
21. Daniel Callahan, presentation at Hastings Center, September 9, 1987.

The Give and Take of Adoption

1. Chris Probst, 1983, "Our Child," in *Perspectives on a Crafted Tree: Thoughts for Those Touched by Adoption*, compiled by Patricia Irwin Johnston (Fort Wayne, Indiana: Perspectives Press), p. 93.

2. Anonymous, 1983, "Stifled Love," in Johnston, p. 99.
3. Helen Garcia, 1983, "Doin Time," in Johnston, p. 98.
4. B. R. Mandell, 1973, *Where Are the Children: A Class Analysis of Foster Care and Adoption* (Lexington: Lexington Books), p. 16.
5. Alvin Schorr, 1975, *Children and Decent People* (London: Allen and Unwin).
6. Lynne McTaggart, 1980, *The Baby Brokers: The Marketing of White Babies in America* (New York: Dial Press).
7. Dorothy W. Smith and Laurie Nehls Sherwin, 1983, *Mothers and Their Adopted Children* (New York: Tiresias Press Inc.), p. 50.
8. McTaggart, *Baby Brokers*, p. 339.
9. Ibid., p. 338.
10. For an early discussion of this issue, see Joyce Ladner, 1978, *Mixed Families: Adopting across Racial Boundaries* (Garden City, New York: Anchor Books). For a more recent discussion of the politics of transracial adoption, see Elizabeth Bartholet, 1993, *Family Bonds: Adoption and the Politics of Parenting* (New York: Houghton Mifflin). For a report of a twenty-year study of transracial adoption, including interviews with adoptive white parents, their children by birth, and their adopted children of color, see Rita S. Simon, Howard Altstein, and Marygold S. Meli, 1994, *The Case for Transracial Adoption* (Lanham, Maryland: American University Press).
11. Jeff Katz, 1997, "Finally, Hope for Adoption," *Providence Journal*, December 17, p. B6.
12. Jeff Katz, personal communication.
13. Eileen Simpson, 1987, *Orphans: Real and Imaginary* (New York: Weidenfeld and Nicolson). Parts of the following section are drawn from my review of that book in *Vogue*, July 1987, p. 112.
14. Simpson, *Orphans*, p. 22.
15. Meetings of the Advisory Panel for the Study of Infertility Prevention and Treatment, Office of Technology Assessment of the U.S. Congress, April 28, 1987.
16. Simpson, *Orphans*, p. 68.

Infertility

1. Joan Leibmann-Smith, 1988, "Delayed Childbearing and Infertility: Social Antecedents and Consequences," dissertation in progress, City University of New York.
2. Office of Technology Assessment (OTA) of the U.S. Congress, 1982, *Technology and Handicapped People*, p. 19.
3. Ibid.
4. Ibid., p. 20.
5. Ibid.
6. OTA, 1988, *Infertility: Medical and Social Choices*, p. 51.
7. Judith Lorber and Lakshmi Bandlamudi, 1993, "Dynamics of Marital Bargaining in Male Infertility," *Gender & Society*, Vol. 7, No. 1, pp. 32–49.
8. Ibid.
9. Ibid.
10. Arthur L. Greil, Thomas A. Leitko, and Karen L. Porter, 1988, "Infertility: His and Hers," *Gender & Society*, Vol. 2, No. 2, in press.

Medicalizing Motherhood

1. Portions of this chapter appeared in 1987, "Reproduction," in Beth B. Hess and Myra Marx Ferree, editors, *Analyzing Gender: A Handbook of Social Science Research* (Beverly Hills, California: Sage Publications).

2. For a history of American midwifery, see Jane B. Donegan, 1978, *Women and Men Midwives: Medicine, Morality and Misogyny in Early America* (Westport, Connecticut: Greenwood Press).
3. Women and the Law Conference, 1983, *Source Book*, 14th National Conference, Washington, D.C., April 7–10.
4. Adrienne Rich, 1977, *Of Woman Born: Motherhood as Experience and as Institution* (New York: W. W. Norton and Company).
5. Michelle Harrison, 1982, *A Woman in Residence* (New York: Penguin Books).
6. Marilyn Moran, 1981, *Birth and the Dialogue of Love* (Leawood, Kansas: New Nativity Press), p. 100.
7. Nancy Stoller Shaw, 1974, *Forced Labor: Maternity Care in the United States* (New York: Pergamon Press), p. 84.
8. Harrison, *Woman in Residence*.
9. See Barbara Katz Rothman, 1982, *In Labor: Women and Power in the Birthplace* (New York: W. W. Norton and Company), for a fuller discussion of this issue.
10. See, for example, David A. Luthy, Morton A. Stenchever et al., 1987, "A Randomized Trial of Electronic Fetal Monitoring in Preterm Labor," *Obstetrics and Gynecology*, and Albert D. Haverkamp, 1976, "Evaluation of Continuous Fetal Heart Rate in High Risk Pregnancy," *American Journal of Obstetrics and Gynecology*, Vol. 125, pp. 310–321.
11. See Ann Oakley, 1984, *The Captured Womb: A History of the Medical Care of Pregnant Women* (Oxford: Basil Blackwell Publishers Ltd.), and Rosaline Pollack Petchesky, 1987, "Foetal Images: The Power of Visual Culture in the Politics of Reproduction," in Michelle Stanworth, editor, *Reproductive Technologies: Gender, Motherhood and Medicine* (Minneapolis, Minnesota: University of Minnesota Press).
12. Monica Casper, 1998, *The Making of the Unborn Patient: A Social Anatomy of Fetal Surgery* (New Brunswick, New Jersey: Rutgers University Press).
13. Ibid., p. 5–6.
14. Ibid., p. 202.

Fetal Power

1. Parts of this chapter appear in "Reproduction," in Beth B. Hess and Myra Marx Ferree, editors, 1987, *Analyzing Gender: A Handbook of Social Science Research* (Beverly Hills, California: Sage Publishing Company), pp. 154–170, and in "Commentary: When a Pregnant Woman Endangers Her Fetus," 1986, *Hastings Center Report*, Vol. 16, No. 1, pp. 24–25.
2. Stallman v. Youngquist, 125 Ill. 2d 267, 531 N.E.2d 355, 359–61 (1988). I wish to express my appreciation to Janet Gallagher for pointing out this and other cases to me. For a further discussion of the issue of fetal abuse cases, see Janet Gallagher, 1994, "Collective Bad Faith and Protecting the Fetus," in Joan C. Callahan, editor, *Reproduction, Ethics and the Law* (Bloomington, Indiana: Indiana University Press).
3. Lynn Paltrow, personal communication.
4. Thomas B. McKenzie and Theodore C. Nagel, 1986, "Commentary: When a Pregnant Woman Endangers Her Fetus," *Hastings Center Report* Vol. 16, No. 1, pp. 23–24.
5. Janet Gallagher, 1985, "Fetal Personhood and Women's Policy," in Virginia Sapiro, editor, *Women, Biology and Public Policy* (Beverly Hills, California: Sage Publishing Company), p. 112.

6. Blackiston's *Gould Medical Dictionary*, 1972, 3rd edition (New York: McGraw-Hill).
7. Ruth Hubbard, 1982, "Legal and Policy Implications of Recent Advances in Prenatal Diagnosis and Fetal Therapy," *Women's Rights Law Reporter*, Vol. 7, pp. 201–208.
8. Janet Gallagher, 1984, "The Fetus and the Law: Whose Life Is It, Anyway?" Ms., September.
9. Cited in Gallagher, "Fetus and the Law."
10. Ibid.
11. Gallagher, "Fetal Personhood."
12. Monica Casper, 1998, *The Making of the Unborn Patient: A Social Anatomy of Fetal Surgery* (New Brunswick, New Jersey: Rutgers University Press), p. 180.

Midwifery as Feminist Praxis

1. Portions of this chapter appeared in 1984, "Beyond Risks and Rates: Issues of Autonomy in Perinatal Care," *Birth*, Summer, and in 1985, "Childbirth Management and Medical Monopoly," in Virginia Sapiro, editor, *Women, Biology and Public Policy* (Beverly Hills, California: Sage Publishing Company), pp. 117–136.
2. The work in progress of Judith Lorber on in vitro fertilization is addressing this question.
3. For a vision of what a woman-centered adoption relationship might look like, see Suzanne Arms, 1983, *To Love and Let Go* (New York: Alfred A. Knopf).
4. Ina May Gaskin and the Farm Midwives, 1975, *Spiritual Midwifery* (Summertown, Tennessee: Book Publishing Company).
5. Ibid., p. 346.
6. Barbara Katz Rothman, 1982, *In Labor: Women and Power in the Birthplace* (New York: W. W. Norton and Company).
7. The experiment by Bruner and Postman is discussed in Thomas S. Kuhn, 1970, *The Structure of Scientific Revolutions*, 2nd edition (Chicago: University of Chicago Press).

Baby Doe

1. This paper originally appeared in the 1986 *Health/PAC Bulletin*, Vol. 16, No. 6, pp. 7–13.
2. Robert and Peggy Stinson, 1983, *The Long Dying of Baby Andrew* (Boston: Atlantic Monthly Press).
3. Jeff Lyon, 1985, *Playing God in the Nursery* (New York: W. W. Norton and Company).

Child Care

1. Julia Wrigley, 1995, *Other People's Children* (New York: Basic Books), pp. 2–3.
2. Ibid., p. 51.
3. Ibid., p. 20.
4. Eleanor Morin and Harold Davis, 1987, "In Search of Mary Poppins. Part III: Training and Supervising Your Caregiver," *Big Apple Parent's Paper*, Vol. 2, No. 4, pp. 10–11.
5. Barbara Ehrenreich and Deirdre English, 1979, *For Her Own Good: 150 Years of the Experts' Advice to Women* (Garden City, New York: Anchor Press).
6. Barbara Berg, 1986, *The Crisis of the Working Mother: Resolving the Conflicts between Family and Work* (New York: Summit Books), p. 74.

7. Ibid., p. 73.
8. Ibid., p. 75.
9. Wrigley, *Other People's Children*, p. 131.
10. Ibid.
11. Arlie Russell Hochschild, 1983, *The Managed Heart: Commercialization of Human Feeling* (Berkeley, California: University of California Press), p. 6.
12. Ibid., p. 7.
13. Sandra Joshel, 1986, "Nurturing the Master's Child: Slavery and the Roman Child-Nurse," *Signs: Journal of Women in Culture and Society*, Vol. 12, No. 1, pp. 3–22.
14. Ursula K. Le Guin, 1988, Anthropology Department Colloquia, University of Rochester, January 12.

Fatherhood

1. Dorothy Dinnerstein, 1977, *The Mermaid and the Minotaur: Sexual Arrangements and Human Malaise* (New York: Harper Colophon Books), p. xiii.
2. Ibid., p. 15.
3. Ibid., p. 26.
4. Nancy Chodorow, 1978, *The Reproduction of Mothering* (Berkeley, California: University of California Press), p. 67.
5. See Alison M. Jaggar, 1983, *Feminist Politics and Human Nature* (Totowa, New Jersey: Rowman and Allenheld), p. 321, and Pauline Bart, 1983, "Review of Chodorow's *Reproduction of Mothering*," in Joyce Treblicot, editor, *Mothering: Essays in Feminist Theory* (Totowa, New Jersey: Rowman and Allenheld), pp. 147–152.
6. See, for example, Jane B. Lancaster, Jeanne Altmann, Alice S. Rossi, and Lonnie R. Sherrod, editors, 1987, *Parenting across the Lifespan: Biosocial Dimensions* (New York: Aldine de Guyter).
7. Marshall J. Klaus and John H. Kennell, 1976, *Maternal-Infant Bonding* (St. Louis: C.V. Mosby).
8. Harry F. Harlow, 1973, "Love in Infant Monkeys," in William T. Greenough, editor, *The Nature and Nurture of Behavior: Readings from Scientific American* (San Francisco: Freeman).
9. Gary Mitchell, William K. Redican, and Jody Gomber, 1974, "Lessons from a Primate: Males Can Raise Babies," *Psychology Today*, April, pp. 64–68.
10. Ibid., p. 66.
11. Cited in Dinnerstein, *Mermaid and Minotaur*, p. 81.
12. Kyle D. Pruett, 1987, *The Nurturing Father: Journey toward the Complete Man* (New York: Warner Books), p. 236.
13. Ibid., p. 29.
14. Ibid., p. 286.
15. Ibid., pp. 112–113.
16. Barbara J. Reisman, 1998, *Gender Vertigo: American Families in Transition* (New Haven, Connecticut: Yale University Press), p. 70.
17. Sara Ruddick, 1983, "Maternal Thinking," in Treblicot, pp. 213–230.
18. Ibid., p. 227.

On "Surrogacy"

1. Portions of this chapter were presented as testimony to the Judiciary Committee of the New York State Senate hearings on "Surrogate Parenthood and New Repro-

ductive Technology," October 16, 1986, and portions appeared in *Conscience*, May 1987, pp. 1–4.

2. Gena Corea, 1985, *The Mother Machine: Reproductive Technologies from Artificial Insemination to Artificial Wombs* (New York: Harper and Row).
3. *People*, February 15, 1988.
4. Angela Holder, 1984, presentation to the American Society of Law and Medicine conference, "What About the Children? An International Conference on the Legal, Social and Ethical Implications of New Reproductive and Prenatal Technologies," Boston, Massachusetts, October 29, 1984.
5. Helena Ragone, 1994, *Surrogate Motherhood: Conception in the Heart* (Boulder, Colorado: Westview Press), p. 194.
6. Center For Surrogate Parenting web site: http://www.creatingfamilies.com
7. Ragone, *Surrogate Motherhood*, p. 194.
8. Ibid., p. 45.
9. Ibid., p. 46.
10. Ibid., p. 71.
11. Ibid., p. 63.
12. Ibid., p. 72.
13. Ibid., p. 91.
14. Ibid., p. 106.
15. Julia Wrigley, 1995, *Other People's Children* (New York: Basic Books).
16. Ragone, *Surrogate Motherhood*, p. 91.
17. Barbara Katz Rothman, 1982, "How Science is Redefining Parenthood." Ms., July–August.
18. Ragone, *Surrogate Motherhood*, p. 17.
19. Ibid.

Reflections on a Decade

1. For a variety of thoughtful perspectives on the implications of consumer culture for mothering, see Linda L. Layne, editor, 1999, *Transformative Motherhood: On Giving and Getting in a Consumer Culture* (New York: New York University Press).
2. Heather M. Dalmage, 2001, *Tripping on the Color Line: Black-White Families in a Racially Divided World* (New Brunswick, New Jersey: Rutgers University Press).
3. See for example the work of Renate Reimann, 1998, "Shared Parenting in a Changing World of Work: Insights from Lesbian Couples' Transition to Parenthood and their Division of Labor," Ph.D. dissertation, City University of New York.
4. Portions of this section appeared in Barbara Katz Rothman, 1999, "The Potential Cost of the Best Genes Money Can Buy," *The Chronicle of Higher Education*, June 11, p. A52.
5. Mathew Schmidt and Lisa Jean Moore, 1998, "Constructing 'Good Catch,' Picking a Winner: The Development of Technosemen and the Deconstruction of the Monolithic Male," in Robbie Davis-Floyd and Joseph Dumit, editors, *Cyborg Babies: From Techno-Sex to Techno-Tots* (New York: Routledge Press), p. 23.
6. Ibid., p. 31.
7. Ibid.
8. Ibid.
9. Ibid., p. 35.
10. Aldous Huxley, 1932, *Brave New World* (New York: Harper and Row).
11. Robert Proctor, 1999, *The Nazi War on Cancer* (Princeton, New Jersey: Princeton University Press).
12. For a fuller discussion of the ways genes are coming to dominate American

thought, see Barbara Katz Rothman, 1998, *Genetic Maps and Human Imaginations: The Limits of Science in Understanding Who We Are* (New York: W. W. Norton and Company).

13. Ann Pappert, forthcoming, "The Baby Bazaar," Ms. and personal communication.
14. Portions of this section appeared in Barbara Katz Rothman, 1999, "Beyond Choice: Toward Procreative Ethics for the Millennium," a report prepared for the Ford Foundation, Human Development and Reproductive Health Program.
15. John A. Robertson, 1998, "Liberty, Identity and Human Cloning," *Texas Law Review*, Vol. 76, No. 6, pp. 1371–1456.
16. Portions of this section appeared in Barbara Katz Rothman, 1999, "Now You Can Choose!" in Myra Marx Ferree, Judith Lorber, and Beth Hess, editors, *Revisioning Gender* (Thousand Oaks, California: Sage Publications).
17. Barbara Katz Rothman, 1993, *The Tentative Pregnancy: How Amniocentesis is Changing the Experience of Motherhood* (New York: W. W. Norton and Company).
18. Portions of this section appeared in Barbara Katz Rothman, 1999, "Beyond Choice."
19. Karen March, 1995, *The Stranger Who Bore Me: Adoptive-Birth Mother Relationships* (Toronto: University of Toronto Press).
20. William Marsiglio, 1998, *Procreative Man* (New York: New York University Press).
21. Dorothy Roberts, 1997, *Killing the Black Body: Race, Reproduction and the Meaning of Liberty* (New York: Pantheon), p. 294.
22. Simon Mawer, 1998, *Mendel's Dwarf: A Novel* (New York: Harmony Books), p. 273.
23. Nancy Hartsock, 1995, "Introduction" in Patricia Boling, editor, *Expecting Trouble: Surrogacy, Fetal Abuse and the New Reproductive Technologies* (Boulder, Colorado: Westview Press).
24. Portions of this section appeared in Barbara Katz Rothman, 1999, "Now You Can Choose!"
25. Richard J. Herrnstein and Charles Murray, 1994, *The Bell Curve: Intelligence and Class Structure in American Life* (New York: Free Press).
26. Portions of this section appeared in Barbara Katz Rothman, 1999, "Beyond Choice."
27. Gina Maranto, 1996, *Quest for Perfection: The Drive to Breed Better Human Beings* (New York: Scribner), p. 267.

Recreating Motherhood

1. George A. Theodorson and Achilles G. Theodorson, 1969, *A Modern Dictionary of Sociology* (New York: Barnes and Noble Books), p. 154.
2. Alison M. Jaggar, 1983, *Feminist Politics and Human Nature* (Totowa, New Jersey: Rowman and Allenheld), p. 27.
3. Caroline Whitbeck, 1973, "Theories of Sex Difference," *The Philosophical Forum*, Vol. 5, pp. 1–2.
4. Jaggar, *Feminist Politics*, p. 42.
5. Meredith Gould, 1980, "Reproducing Gender: The Sociology of Constitutional Adjudication," unpublished doctoral dissertation, New York University.
6. Jose Van Dyck, 1995, *Manufacturing Babies and Public Consent: Debating the New Reproductive Technologies* (New York: New York University Press), p. 2.
7. Valerie Hartouni, 1997, *Cultural Conceptions: On Reproductive Technologies and the Making of Life* (Minneapolis, Minnesota: University of Minnesota Press), p. 98.
8. Ibid., p. 116.

9. Margaret Atwood, 1985, *The Handmaid's Tale* (New York: Fawcett Crest).
10. Aldous Huxley, 1932, *Brave New World* (New York: Harper and Row).
11. Robert Pollack, 1994, *Signs of Life: The Language and Meaning of DNA* (Boston: Houghton Mifflin), p. 44.
12. Barbara Katz Rothman, 1993, *The Tentative Pregnancy: How Amniocentesis is Changing the Experience of Motherhood* (New York: W.W. Norton and Company), p. 12.
13. Ruth Hubbard, unpublished position paper on surrogacy, untitled.
14. Katarina Wegar, 1997, *Adoption, Identity and Kinship: The Debate over Sealed Birth Records* (New Haven, Connecticut: Yale University Press), p. 137.
15. Cited in Kyle D. Pruett, 1987, *The Nurturing Father: Journey toward the Complete Man* (New York: Warner Books).

Index